THE
CHANGING FICTIONS
OF
MASCULINITY

THE
CHANGING FICTIONS
OF
MASCULINITY

DAVID ROSEN

UNIVERSITY OF ILLINOIS PRESS
Urbana and Chicago

Library of Congress Cataloging-in-Publication Data

Rosen, David, 1948–
    The changing fictions of masculinity / David Rosen.
        p.   cm.
    Includes bibliographical references and index.
    ISBN 0-252-02004-9. — ISBN 0-252-06309-0 (pbk.)
        1. English literature—Men authors—History and criticism.   2. Men
in literature.   3. Masculinity (Psychology) in literature.   4. Men
authors, English—Psychology.   5. Sex role in literature.
    I. Title.
PR151.M46R67   1993
820'.99286—dc20   92–35300
                                                                          CIP

FOR
Randall

Contents

Acknowledgments

I appreciate the support of those who encouraged me: Stanley Fish, David Bergman, Dan Borus, Richard D'Abate, Susan Okin, Ellen Graham, Joanne Ferguson, Fred Reynolds, Jack Armstrong, Geneva Frost, Alvin Bowker, Paul Goodman; and those who have read and commented on parts of this manuscript: Myrna Bouchey, Barbara Hope, James Lehman, Andrea Lowenstein and my many anonymous readers. In particular, Randall Kindleberger not only encouraged me in many tangible and intangible ways, but she read and commented on the manuscript many times. I also thank all the men who have shared their lives with me and whose feelings and ideas I have tried to consider in writing this, in particular Dave Edwards, Walter Spear, John Evrard, V. J. Kumar, Jack Heyrman, and Sam Walker. I need to acknowledge the unstinting support of my immediate and extended families: the three Sarahs, three Charleses, Judy, Alan, Dick, Joan, Sam, Wardie, and my parents, Lois and Norman Rosen. Finally, I want to thank Richard Martin, who believed in the book, and whose patience and kindness over a very long haul made heavy work lighter.

Preface:
Reading Like a Man

A man would never set out
to write a book on the peculiar
situation of the human male.
  —Simone de Beauvoir

FEMINIST SCHOLARSHIP, inspired and fueled by the women's movement, produced the insight that made this book possible: what not so
long ago was called the "human" experience, whether analyzed by
history, literature, psychology or whatever, was actually the "male"
experience, one that ignored women and took men for the norm.
From this feminist perspective one can dismiss male fiction that purports to be the supremely human story. At the same time, one can
show the tyranny of masculine rule and the apparent need men have
had to exercise such tyranny. This book will not dispute those readings, nor does it seek to repeat them. Instead, it will ask, what does a
work like *Beowulf* tell about men?

At first glance, answering this question would seem to be what we
have always done, although we were not aware of it. If these books
have always been about men, then we need merely write "male"
where critics have written "man" and we will have the story of men.
Yet such a simple transposition will not work. First, notions of the
"human" are likely to obscure notions of the "masculine." Second,
when we speak of masculinity, our notions will undoubtedly be
grounded in the present, yet we will appear to make universal claims

about sex and gender. Finally, critics interested in reading as men, like those whom Elaine Showalter has called "feminist critics," must also assume that notions of gender obscure the concerns and behaviors of those so gendered, that concepts of masculinity occlude the shape of manhood and of men.[1]

What has dazzled us about feminist criticism, after all, has been its breathtaking revision of the way we read gender, the way we read generally. Feminism claimed as its project an understanding of women's construction, a deconstruction of their difference, an affirmation of their *jouissance,* a renovation of their world. The male view, defined as a difference, has to a great extent remained trapped in its past, its relationship to the difference of feminist construction and deconstruction—the hero, the constructor, the victimizer, the killer. But it is time for men also to begin decentering old gender ideas about themselves.

This project will inevitably work against the totalized and totalizing notions of "male," "masculine," and "men." While sex-difference categories operate in all societies and while the categories of male and female are nearly universal, the collective known as "men" is not singular or simple. The forces constructing manhood are too diverse to allow singularity—from differences in biology within the group called men, to differences in sexuality, ethnicity, and class, to differences in the way men may be viewed by women and other men of likewise varying differences. Any notion of masculinity faces challenges from forces in society that are beyond its control. Today socially, women compete for shares of public goods once possessed more exclusively by men; technologically, men and women share skills requisite to operate high-tech weapons systems; economically, information-driven enterprises reward the assiduous and imaginative over the hyperphysical, while an expanding service job market makes emotional openness and verbal flexibility valuable. Such events place varying pressures on varying masculine stereotypes to accommodate change.

Nevertheless, notions of gender remain fairly rigid: the pathways for inclusion in a family, class, and social group involve being gendered, which means inheriting rules that grant inclusion into that group and forgoing other satisfying interactions, such as improving education, class status, or job qualifications. Categories for gender inclusion can be flexible enough to accommodate the changes forced by social and cultural change. But they can also be rigid enough to cause powerful pain for those whose rules do not allow adaptation, and to cause residual pain even among the most adaptive. Such pains are usually experienced by men as what social psychologists call sex-role stress. The idea of masculine role stress—a conflict between inherited masculine values and the patterns of actual behavior—was explored by Mirra Komarovsky in *Dilemmas of Masculinity* and more fully developed by Joseph Pleck in *The Myth of Masculinity*.[2] In analyzing the distance between masculinity and behavior, Pleck arrived at this series of propositions:

—Sex roles are contradictory and inconsistent.

—The proportion of individuals who violate sex roles is high.

—Violating sex roles leads to social condemnation.

—Violating sex roles leads to negative psychological consequences.

—Certain characteristics prescribed by sex roles are psychologically dysfunctional.

—Each sex experiences sex role stress in its paid work and family roles.

—Men experience more sex role stress than women.[3]

The studies of masculinity show that no definitive masculine ideal exists and that none is embodied in actual practice. Instead, a loosely related set of shared stereotypes and norms exist. Rather than producing conformity, these produce stress in those expected to observe them.

But the studies also suggest that when men experience abrasion between the masculine ideal and the surrounding world, between a shifting sense of self and world and a restrictive or dysfunctional sense of role, they often try to create a new definition of masculinity. In each epoch groups of men try to pass on a stable "masculinity" that can encompass traditional roles, accommodate new experiences, ensure a meaningful contribution to society, and insulate from the shock of change. But in each new creation, the concept of "masculinity" multiplies and one concept contests another. Moreover, within this contestation, accommodations take place, so that older masculine ideals inhabit spaces in new ones, although they are transmuted by their new residence. In every age, men experience an abrasion between the concepts of privileged manhood that they inherit and try to satisfy and other experiences to which they try to fit their masculine ideals. In this book I discuss men as doubled, and doubled-over, by this abrasion. Again, to borrow the language of sociology, role stress occurs because masculine roles are often contradictory and because the constraint of any role creates abrasions.

Still, while masculine ideals seem unstable as well as variable culturally, subculturally, and personally, some will here object that "man" is not a conceptual category but a marker of a biological reality. While early Anglo-American feminists accepted that biology shaped sex (male/female) and society constructed gender (feminine/masculine),[4] French feminists, from Beauvoir on, have argued against such a binary opposition of male/female that implicitly assumes an "essentialist" notion of sex. For the essentialist, differences in sex are not simply gradations along a continuum but absolute distinctions that imply the existence of "perfect" or "complete" males and females.[5] Essentialists stress that biological sex is fixed, natural, and absolute. They believe that from this universal biology flow the sex roles that societies prescribe to their members, what we call "gender."

Essentialist notions are flawed. First, humans are elastic biologically, as they are culturally. If predispositions exist—whether cultural or biological—they are not destiny, only limits on destiny. Being capable of insemination does not dictate any specific behavior any more than being tall makes one a basketball player.[6] In fact, monozygotic twin studies reveal that common genetic property does not inevitably lead to sameness, although this may be the ideology that sells on television shows and in newspapers.[7]

This behavior-biology connection is made even more tenuous by the elasticity of biology itself. As markers, biological masculinity and femininity are themselves defined by other markers: Barre cells, hormones, genital formations. It has become possible, using Barre tests and gonadal and nongonadal hormonal tests, to show that the grouping of human sexual characteristics, as well as the placement of thresholds within and between groups, is arbitrary. Nor are differences binary or clear, as intersexual studies and sex-testing in athletics show.[8] If primary sex characteristics were clear, I suspect that gender might be. The illusion of binarism exists because we need to regularize information. While we operate in a world rich with information contrary to our assumptions of binary oppositions, this information is heard but not received, in part because it is considered odd, titillating, or non-normative. If the markers of primary sex are useful, they show that, like gender, biological binarism is only a tendency—a dangerous tendency from the viewpoint of contemporary consequences.

So at its best "gender" offers a series of binary reconstructions of multiplicity; the markers deployed to construct that opposition are also developed as a result of a search for oppositions. This is not to argue that sexual characteristics and groups do not exist, but rather that the groupings humans make are "semiotic" rather than "natural." That is, we know biological sex as a series of significant and valuable traits. Since biology cannot in itself determine either significance or value, those features must be constructed by society. What we know as biological sex is, like gender, constructed.

It should be clear by now that when I use the ideas of "sex" or "gender," I am using them as "signs" that, like all signs, have more power to provide meaning than to denote fixed realities and that are slippery and shifting. While I do accept as givens certain ideas about "sex"—some basic differences in reproductive roles—other apparent differences may or may not exist. Regardless of the existence of these other differences, the designations of maleness and femaleness are extremely malleable. Thus, it is also my view that "gender" controls "biology," not in the biosociological sense of environment shaping growth, but in the sense that what counts for biological difference is controlled by what is significant for gender difference.[9]

The above explanations may suggest that this book concerns a multiplicity of masculinities. My focus is, in fact, rather narrow. I examine representations of my cohort, a thin slice of the human pie. What I write about here is the English male heterosexual of fiction in a tightly limited time-culture span, from Beowulf to Paul Morel. Moreover, my dialogue remains one, for the moment, among men—a dialogue that looks about itself at the world but which seeks to share and explore the experiences of other men in just the way that women of the sixties and seventies sought to redefine the feminine by sharing experiences.

In this book, I will first examine the expectations that are formulated for males—"masculinity." Second, I will examine what they experience, regardless of those gender expectations. I will be looking at the ways in which these categories interact—the fluidity, through time, of each of these categories. I will be trying to locate a repetition of themes and concerns that could be marked as the concerns of men. I will also be tracing changes in the cultural prescriptions of gender as they appear in the works discussed and the abrasions of masculine experience within those prescriptions, abrasions that form an important strand in developing gender stereotypes. Given both the range of literature that I hope to examine and the limitation of examples, the conclusions I reach will necessarily be tentative, but I think their suggestions about continuities and instabilities in the assignment of gender, within even a limited group like the one I study, can be powerful.

In part, I will also be trying to answer questions like those of the earlier feminisms: What do I see when I read as a man? The problem alleged against such readings in which women have asked similar questions, that they construct a woman to read as, may be raised against me. Such construction, however, takes place in the tension and relations with works against which one reads. Although a fuller portrait of the man I read as can only be painted at the end of my readings, I can tease out some implications for a strategy that in part repeats the theme of this book. First, the man I construct is both oppositional and antagonistic. Feeling different from Beowulf, Hamlet, or Paul Morel, protagonists in the works I read, I view their masculinities as different from mine. As the inheritor of their masculinities, I resist their defining me. Yet I appreciate the benefits of that inheritance, its enabling power. Finally, while different from those protagonists, I suspect an underlying sameness. Since I too am called "man," I suspect that not only am I like them, but they may be like me. From all these tensions between them and me, I assume that my constructed reader and my protagonists are both sympathetic and resistant to defining notions of "masculinity."

A question may also arise about why I have selected these particular works from the introductory literary survey—*Beowulf, Sir Gawain and the Green Knight, The Tragedy of Hamlet, Paradise Lost, Hard Times, Sons and Lovers*. Perhaps the most powerful place to observe the sorrowful shadow play of masculinity and experience lies in those "great" fictions which men have penned as bulwarks against instability, in order to constitute or perfect themselves.[10]

These works have seemed in their times (to me and to others) exemplary "male" texts, texts by and about men, the particular men of my focus. They marked themselves as male-focused either by title (*Sons and Lovers*) or by chapter headings ("Men and Brothers," in *Hard Times*) or by iconography (the Green Knight in *Sir Gawain and the Green Knight* or Adam in *Paradise Lost*) or by tradition (Hamlet and the oedipal conflict).

But, despite their obvious interest in masculinity, each book purports to be about universal humanity, world, society, spirit. This for me is a strength. The works of the "received" male canon of literature seem most likely to encode the masculine ideals just because they are promulgated as truths about humanity. These "great works" often insist on a fixed, universal or essentialist view of the world that the very necessity of their writing seems to argue against. We are likely to find the themes of masculinity in those works troubled and questioned by the actions, thoughts, and feelings of the main characters. As a refuge, the outworks of male literature are places of both hiding and disclosure. Thus one may expect to see more of those characters and the character of maleness by peeping down the fissures in their fictions. This presentation of universals aids me in performing the delicate operation of peeling men from their universalizing masculinity.

Each writing identifies a different aspect of masculinity. Had I selected a common theme or aspect of the masculine repertoire I might have found more unity. Partially I wished to examine different roles, but I also kept in mind that I wanted continuities. However, even the apparent differences among the works arose in part from their intimate proximities and affinities, because each book was an icon of human and masculine idealism in its period. Each writer (from Shakespeare on, at least) worked consciously with the literature of the previous writers, rehandling their themes. *Hamlet* reappears significantly in both *Paradise Lost* and *Sons and Lovers*. Lawrence had *Hamlet* in mind as he wrote, as testify his letters, the name of Paul Morel's mother (Gertrude), and the book's title. Milton, fully allusive to Shakespeare throughout *Paradise Lost*, reworks Hamlet's "to be" soliloquy as Adam's soliloquy after his fall. *Hard Times* alludes not infrequently to a *Beowulf*-like motif: the women are Grendels and Grendel dams, while the men live in homes that are their castles and which remind the reader of Heorot. Finally *Hamlet* is preoccupied with issues of knighthood, chastity, and masculinity that were constructed in a previous age and expressed in a work like *Gawain*. Similar threads of connection can be found between *Gawain* and *Beowulf*.

The idea that emerges, then, is that this changing shape of literature suggests the changing roles, needs, values, behaviors, problems of

men of a certain class. Moreover, this in turn suggests that these productions, part of a continuous effort to recount the male story, shift
ground to preserve men from betrayals of masculinity and at the same
time to preserve the enabling concept of masculinity for men. The
works form, in other words, a continual treatment of the same subject. The point is that the domestic/social novel of Dickens is the *Beowulf* of its time—at least retrospectively, for a certain group of people.
What it *really* was is not a question I am going to argue for or answer.

The method I adopt in this book is, like that of many Anglo-American feminists, strongly influenced by close reading, informed by ideas
and techniques from semiotics and poststructuralism; my purpose,
like theirs, is other than aesthetic appreciation.[11] In examining these
works, I look for gaps, silences, and contradictions in each work, the
spaces between experience as it is implied or depicted and the order
that the author and his characters attempt to impose on experience.
The words and works are urns which the contents overflow: I examine the spilled, the leftover, the discarded, the unsuitable. In other
words, I will examine the differences between what each artist asserts
that "male experience" consists of and what each artist implies that
men experience.

Because the writings examined in this book come from a particular
culture within a rather short time span, resemblances among notions
of masculinity and among the experiences of men are to be expected.
The many threads of continuity do not constitute transhistorical
unity. The overall import and details of the transcendental or essential
men, maleness, or masculinity that find temporary lodging in each of
these texts vary. Yet men of each age carry some form of the previous
ideals that continue in their new shapes to determine the masculinity
that men imitate and, thus, the ways men experience themselves.
One element, however, does appear constant throughout the works:
in all ages under the burden of the fictions of manhood, men are restless, confused, and grieved. Having been trained, as part of the various roles of manhood, to inhibit parts of their experience that they
have also valued, men, even the most heroic exemplars, have found
that acting like a man means suspecting one is not a man. Thus the
joys of being have been laced with the poisons of masculine self-
mutilations and the killing of enemies one often suspects are one's self.

We perceive such contradictory and destructive strands winding deep
into the fabric of these fictions when we ask, "What do these stories
reveal as stories of men?"

By my choice of subject I do not mean to imply that other males
are not subjects. Nor is such an admission meant to insulate me from
criticism. It suggests instead that such criticism is expected, justified,
and welcome. My selection of the pieces to work on and the approach
to follow rests on my own position. Writers bring to their creations
attributes, preoccupations, structures of thought and language that
they have made their own but which they have partially inherited,
partially created from material available to them. In writing this
work, I try to find the men, but I also embrace the fact that the act of
interpretation is also an act of self-revelation, a statement about ourselves, both what we are and what we would like or not like to be.[12]

Notes

1. Elaine Showalter, "Toward a Feminist Poetics," *The New Feminist
Criticism* (New York: Pantheon, 1985), 125–43.
2. Mirra Komarovsky, *Dilemmas of Masculinity* (New York: W. W.
Norton, 1976); Joseph Pleck, *The Myth of Masculinity* (Cambridge,
Mass.: MIT Press, 1981).
3. Pleck, *The Myth of Masculinity*, 135–52
4. See Ann Oakley, *Sex, Gender, and Society* (London: Maurice
Temple Smith, 1972). Differential psychologists and biologists have long
used this distinction. Catherine Stimpson calls it one of the clichés of
feminism: see "Women's Studies: The Ideas and The Ideas," *Liberal Education* 73, no. 4 (1987): 34–35.
5. I am, of course, referring to Simone de Beauvoir's *The Second Sex*,
ed. and trans. H. M. Parshley (Harmondsworth, U.K.: Penguin, 1972).
Beauvoir did not regard herself as a feminist until the mid-seventies, and
as an existentialist, she places responsibility for the condition of women
on the women who are complicitous in it. Nonetheless, her analysis of
the feminine was crucial for continental feminists and seems to be receiving more attention in the United States of late. Her point about what a
woman is, however, follows Merleau-Ponty more closely than Sartre. As
she states in the "Data of Biology," "Whenever the physiological fact
takes on meaning, this meaning is at once seen as dependent on a whole
context; the 'weakness' is revealed as such only in the light of the ends
man proposes, the instruments he has available, and the law he estab-

lishes" (67). In other words, certain physical data become meaningful only in a social context. Yet if perception and cognition are tied to the social, then the so-called data are themselves selected and constructed because of their meaningfulness to the social discourse. This implication makes Beauvoir's work particularly important on the issue of sex-gender.

6. See, among others, Karl Peter and Nicholas Petryszak, "Sociobiology versus Biosociology," *Sociobiology Examined*, ed. Ashley Montagu (Oxford: Oxford University Press, 1980), 39–81; David Abrahamson, "Tamarins in the Amazon," *Science* 6 (Sept. 1985): 59–63; Susan Blaffer Hrdy, "Heat Loss," *Science* 4 (Oct. 1983): 73–78.

7. The power of extrabiological forces on biology is very forcefully suggested when we look at a comparison of schizophrenics who have been raised separately from their monozygotic twin (genetically identical). In such cases, when one twin suffered schizophrenia, the other did not invariably also suffer from that disorder. Moreover, the percentage of concordance between twins varies from country to country, from a high of 69 percent in the United States to a low of 25 percent in Norway: see Sam Singer and Henry R. Hilgard, *The Biology of People* (San Francisco: W. H. Freeman and Company, 1978), 518–19.

8. Dorcas Susan Butt, *Psychology of Sport: The Behavior, Motivation and Performance of Athletes* (New York: van Nostrand Reinhold, 1987), 148. On the treatment of intersexuals, see John Money and Anke A. Ehrhardt, *Man & Woman, Boy & Girl* (Baltimore: Johns Hopkins University Press, 1972); and John Money and Patricia Tucker, *Sexual Signatures: On Being a Man or a Woman* (Boston: Little, Brown and Company, 1975).

9. See Peter and Petryszak, "Sociobiology"; Julia A. Sherman, *Sex-Related Cognitive Differences* (Springfield, Ill.: Charles C. Thomas, 1978).

10. Works may be written to "explore," but the ideas about language outlined above suggest that explorations inevitably become acts of constitution. By the same token, those very ideas suggest that acts of constitution inevitably remain acts of exploration.

11. In their "Introduction" to *The Woman's Part: Feminist Criticism of Shakespeare* (Urbana: University of Illinois Press, 1980), 3–16, Carolyn Ruth Swift Lenz, Gayle Greene, and Carol Thomas Neely remark that "all the writers [in this book] . . . owe a substantial debt to New Criticism. . . . All use close textual analysis . . . in service of a goal other than, larger than, the discovery of unity of the text" (10). Terry Eagleton has criticized the New Criticism for giving the illusion of "hard" science to what is, in every regard, "soft" and elitist. He has expanded this, as have other Marxist and Marxist-feminists, to attack close reading as "lib-

eral humanism": see *Literary Theory: An Introduction* (Minneapolis: University of Minnesota Press, 1983), 17ff.; "Liberality and Order: The Critics of John Bayley," *Against the Grain: Essays 1975–1986* (London: Verso, 1986), 33–48. However, in *Critical Practice* (London: Methuen, 1980), Catherine Belsey sees the practice of feminist close reading as having affinities to deconstruction.

   12. I subscribe to a notion of "self" constructed differently from that which would make an author either a "genius" or a conduit of social or psychological information. In his paean "The Death of the Author" in *Image, Music, Text* (London: Fontana, 1977), Roland Barthes assumes that those who invoke the author are invoking him or her as singular or knowable. The death of God the Author or of Author, the God, may not mean the death of the author. The author's attempt to communicate with readers by deforming language is part of Barthes's arguments in *Mythologies* (New York: Hill and Wang, 1972), for instance. Although critics such as Stanley Fish, themselves authors, have questioned the notion of authorial presence, none of this seems surprising in an age when a popular bumpersticker "Question Authority" leaves its own authority unquestioned by suppressing the author. Steven Knapp and Walter Benn Michaels have offered an important, if flawed, corrective in "Against Theory," *Critical Inquiry* 9 (1983): 790–800; and "Against Theory 2: Hermeneutics and Deconstruction," *Critical Inquiry* 19 (1987): 49–68. They argue that in reading (defined broadly) one always posits intention. In being interested in what the words mean, we never can be interested in what they mean in themselves, for that is an absurdist (and impossible) position. On the other hand, their notion of the "author" is clearly a poststructural rather than a "local" one: an "author" that is not an "individual," an "agent" always acting with others.

1

The Armor of the Man-Monster in *Beowulf*

[Beowulf] is a man,
and that for him and many
is sufficient tragedy.
—J. R. R. Tolkien

BEOWULF APPEARS to be an archetypal story of masculine heroism. Heorot, the court of King Hrothgar, is repeatedly breached by a loathsome monster, Grendel. None of Hrothgar's men can rid the court of this devourer of human flesh, until Beowulf arrives. Beowulf slays Grendel and Grendel's dam, who has also destroyed one of Hrothgar's men. Years later, Beowulf goes forth to battle a new monster—a dragon—and is killed. Beowulf's nephew Wiglaf, however, quells the monster, claims his uncle's armor, and prepares to assume his position as leader of the people. As J. R. R. Tolkien viewed it, *Beowulf* tells of men who courageously battle to protect the small comforting circle of civilization's light from the barbaric and bestial forces of darkness that everywhere encompass and inevitably defeat man.[1] For many readers *Beowulf* has been the exemplary story of male heroism, whether at Ilium or at Khe Sahn. And it moved others to pity the condition of those heroes who, after all, go down to their death against the darkness that covers all.

Whether this heroic reading is immanent in the story can be questioned. Historically Tolkien's version seems connected to the specter of recurrent worldwide war. His was a sentiment of English heroism that persisted in histories of England, such as this one recounting

Bede's tale of the sparrow: "His speech is our speech, and his thoughts are the thoughts common to Englishmen for over a thousand years, the thoughts of England and eternal life, his two homes."[2] For men of a particular generation, the present became a stage in which to reenact Dunkirks of previous ages.

But if *Beowulf* is a document about masculine heroism, then one must also deal with disturbing presences in the story. As new readings began to show, Beowulf and the monsters resembled each other:[3] each killed thirty at once;[4] each was "swollen with rage"; each was *anhagu*, solitary.[5] The "monster" critics offered reason to believe that Beowulf was not an exemplary hero, neither the perfect Christian knight nor the perfect king.[6] "[I]t is not Beowulf's modesty that impresses, but his pride, the sort of pride that is magnificently evident in his retort to Unferth. Nor is it Beowulf's caution that comes to mind."[7] It is questionable whether Beowulf adequately displays any of the four virtues traditional to the Christian king—fortitude, sapience, humility, charity—virtues once associated with the best of humanity and masculinity. In other words, the hero did not display any exemplary virtue,[8] nor did darkness lie exclusively outside of him.[9]

Tolkien's vision of an essentially heroic story of men fighting the forces of evil, securing something called civilization by their actions, seems to embed a second tale of deep disturbances in the hero and in the heroic code, disturbances in an uncomfortable relationship to heroic action.

From this new perspective Beowulf's story may seem that of a man who is not fully likeable or understandable, living out a particular ethic that is not fully likeable or understandable, in a particular time, place, society, culture which has never been identified, much less understood.[10] Yet when one reads about this alien world, one invariably finds some kinship. Beowulf's bravery against the monsters may disgust one, but one can find this bravery disturbingly familiar. One may not be satisfied by Beowulf's mighty deed of bearing armor or spears or whatever it is across the sea after his king dies: we would probably find Beowulf's exhibitions of strength or valor inadequate to compensate for his failure to save his king. Today we may identify with a Beowulf who needed to do something stupendous to mute his, his folk's, and our appreciation of his failure. This type of compensation may seem familiar. Whereas in the past, male heroics—like those we viewed in Beowulf—seemed transparently good, right and just, one now asks how do those idealized actions become heroic? What is the cost of such heroism? The limits of Beowulf's heroism now seem exposed throughout, and probably most movingly in the final scenes, where for the first time Beowulf appears vulnerable and confused:

> Firm-hearted he stood with his shield high, the lord of friends, while quickly the worm coiled itself; he waited in his armor. Then, coiling in flames, he came gliding on, hastening to his fate. The good shield protected the life and body of the famous prince, but for a shorter while than his wish was. There for the first time, the first day in his life, he might not prevail, since fate did not assign him such glory in battle. The lord of the Geats raised his hand, struck the shining horror so with his forged blade that the edge failed, bright on the bone, bit less surely than its folk-king had need, hard-pressed in perils. Then because of the battle the barrow-ward's heart was savage, he exhaled death-fire—the warrior sprang wide. The gold-friend of the Geats boasted of no great victories: the war blade had failed naked at need, as it ought not to have done, iron good from old times. That was no pleasant journey, not one on which the famous son of Ecgtheow would wish to leave his land; against his will he must take up a dwelling-place elsewhere—as every man must give up the days that are leant him. (2535–91)[11]

In this moment Beowulf, who is emphatically described as having friends, power, gold, who has boundless regard for his own ability and a sense that the task of defending his land rests solely on himself, may be seen as suffering the failures of his role, his society, his culture. He is shocked and confused. With confidence he wields the sword, stands up in his armor and craftily-made iron shield, and he fails.

The failures of Beowulf's arms and strength may be seen to mark metonymically the failures of the protective structures of attitudes, behaviors, skills that society has helped him fashion, failures further emphasized when Beowulf's thanes do not rush to his rescue. "In only one of them the heart surged with sorrows: nothing can ever set aside kinship in him who means well" (2599–2601). Young Wiglaf's solitary sympathy suggests that consanguinity, rather than a specific code of valor, moves otherwise indifferent armor. The poem, in fact, expresses the sadness of Beowulf's failure as the sadness of being driven from one's dwelling: Beowulf's implicit desire to remain in his *burh*, in his home, among his kin.

In this passage one can glimpse the complex relationships between self-destructive arms and moving affections.[12] In this scene the story seems to keep reaching out and touching all aspects of society—its founding, its events, its politics, its kinship and belief systems. From this perspective, *Beowulf* concerns the components of Beowulf's society and its stability. Deeply interwoven with this is a story about how certain forms of masculine behavior produced this society and how this society produced certain forms of masculine behavior. The term "arming" has been found broadly descriptive of male behavior for two thousand years of Western culture and society. Perhaps in glimpsing this bit of our alien past we can find out some of the sources of arming, why arming does and does not work.

The relationship between nature and culture—which has important bearings on the relationship between sex and gender—is never a transparent one. But in *Beowulf* it is particularly troublesome because of the work's apparent insistence on dichotomy: the half-lines, the contrasts of light and dark, the shifts of song and silence.[13] The apparent fixity of the nature/civilization dichotomy within the work has forced some critics to describe whatever lies outside civilization, whether woods, swamps, monsters, or gods, as "natural." As one consequence of looking through the lens of this binary opposition, certain distinctions collapse: the supernatural becomes monstrous and Beowulf appears to resemble the monsters. So too the natural becomes unnatural: because Beowulf's enemies lie outside of the society they threaten, they are part of nature; however, because they are unequivocally monstrous, defective, distorted, and destructive, they are unnatural.[14] The problems with the dichotomy are many and manifest.

The ambiguous relationship among these various categories exerts a crucial force in moving the hero through the narrative, for the hero's job is to clear the ambit of civilization. The impossibility of establishing a nature/civilization dichotomy has devastating consequences for the hero. This emerges, for instance, in the confrontation between Grendel and Beowulf. In extinguishing the threat of Grendel, who represents bestial forces of nature, the good and heroic Beowulf exhibits similar bestial qualities—such as solitude and passion—by virtue of which Beowulf conquers. If Grendel represents a force *outside* society but *inside* the hero, then this force must not be evil. Rather it is valued according to the social usefulness of the form in which it is expressed.[15] Beowulf incorporates the characteristics of Grendel in a socially acceptable and useful way: the warrior creating and protecting borders.[16]

Yet in a way that Beowulf's society never openly acknowledges, Beowulf represents a threat to that society from within, similar to the one that Grendel poses from without. The danger for Beowulf's society is the ever-present possibility that Grendel-like aspects will reemerge in socially and personally destructive forms, as the histories of jealousy and massacre in which the story is embedded show.

For such a delicate balance to be struck and maintained, an exemplar of masculine virtue like Beowulf has been prepared to apprehend aspects of himself as threatening, to project those aspects upon the world, where he is able to recognize and subdue these versions of what he would consider his own "monstrosity." At the same time, his monstrosity in its new form has been revalued as the supernatural. The moment of conquest both calls forth and quells the monstrous in himself and in his victim. Every victory for Beowulf is also partially a defeat, for every death quells an aspect of his self, a self that must be killed repeatedly to create himself, killings that take place without dying.

Once we see that Beowulf and Grendel represent similar qualities that have been differentially valued and thus differently defined by society, we can also see that the function of dichotomy is to suppress similarities.[17] The story of Beowulf's defeat of Grendel might at first seem to be a tale about exterminating passions, but it appears instead to concern channeling and redirecting passion. Whereas Beowulf apparently rids Heorot of its monster, the monstrous has only been transformed in ways that go unacknowledged until it reemerges in its destructive guise, shocking the people who had thought it all settled long ago.

The ideal male in Beowulf's world, then, is a drawer of boundaries—boundaries that must be defended. That is his work too. Boundary drawing can only take place in a world conceived spatially. Yet Beowulf seems situated in a world in which no space exists, in which one thing seems to press into another. Representing this through-pressing universe in spatial terms prepares for crucial masculine virtue—securing a space in a spaceless world: "Many a man said . . . that, south nor north, between the seas, over the wide earth, no other man under the sky's expanse was better of those who bear shields, more worthy ruling" (ll. 857b–61). Over earth, under skies, between seas, the universe impinges. In this ecology men have no separate niche that is separated from earth, air, or water. But although they fabricate the idea of one, the niche is constantly threatened by the forces that occupy—and represent—those other spaces from which their colonial outpost is made.[18] In this description of Beowulf, defining a space ("ruling") requires arms (*rond*). Because of his ability with a shield Beowulf is worthy of a realm. In the last battle his shield fails, his realm collapses.[19]

One could easily find different ways to conceptualize the realms that seem to threaten society: the supernatural from above and the monstrous from below form a vertical axis. The masculine position in the middle of this hierarchy is typical enough—with some adjustments for different periods. The water represents the horizontal axis of temporal existence between birth and death, a significance represented by the story of the tribe's father-founder, Scyld Scefing, who came from and returned to the sea. Or one could see these various spaces carrying the significance of the monsters that inhabit them: the water, Grendel and his mother; the earth and air, the Dragon. It would be difficult to use both structures simultaneously, however, since the Dragon, with its barrow, is certainly associated with death. Regardless of how these various spaces might be thought of, it seems imperative to spatialize the antispatial, to draw boundaries and bulwarks against intruding spaces.

Beowulf abounds in boundaries which are adhered to with an insistence made ironic by the failure of most boundaries to divide clearly. The Warden of the shore guards the territorial boundary of the Shield-Danes and must judge whether those who seek admittance are friend or enemy, belong inside or outside the boundary. The shields, helmets, mail, swords protect the boundary of each male. The hall Heorot, where the men live, is a beacon that distinguishes good from bad and thus serves as a definition for the warrior band, a boundary of the society set down in the midst of nature. So too are various types of activity denoted by the verb *metan*, "to measure," so that Beowulf measures the water with his arms when he conquers it, the steeds of the warriors and the retinue of the king measure the roads and pathways when the intrusion of Grendel has passed. Even the creator may be considered a measurer, as *Metod* seems to imply. So too "mete out" is to measure and in its archaic sense to fix a boundary. Finally, it is Grendel's evil that he is without boundary. He is a *mearc-stapa* (103), one who crosses borders. He is associated with fens and moors, which are neither land nor water. He is, as is his environment, a *deorc deap-scua* (160), dark death-shadow. In this configuration brightness is associated with the clearly bounded, whereas darkness is that which destroys distinctions: "*nipende niht ofer ealle*" (649). It draws under a uniform cover every creature without distinction. It is little wonder, then, that the armor of Beowulf and his thanes is repeatedly referred to as "shining," shedding light. Light here is not simply moral good but morally good because it draws a boundary around things. The battle of light and dark is not simply the battle of order and chaos but a battle of a particularly defined and bounded order against everything that is viewed as chaotic because such a boundary has been established.

Grendel's attacks pose both a real and symbolic threat to the spatial arrangements that the masculine codes of Beowulf's society seek to impose. Grendel, who had apparently roamed freely and harmlessly at one time, only begins to harry Hrothgar's realm after the construction of the hall, the rearing of a new boundary from which he is excluded. If the hall has been built in part to exclude him, why is he excluded? Why does Heorot's boundary turn Grendel into something evil? Perhaps the answer lies in the contrasting spatial senses of Grendel and Hrothgar. Grendel's underwater hall resembles Heorot; however, in Grendel's hall, Grendel, an adult male, lives with his mother. This is not the case among the Shield-Danes. The adult male Shield-Danes sleep, eat, and take counsel in a public building, not a private domicile, Heorot, from which adult females are more or less excluded.[20] It would seem, moreover, that the construction of Heorot marks the fact that the public buildings had recently displaced the public-private households as the center of social-political activity among the Shield-Danes. Thus the men who flee the hall during Grendel's attacks find refuge in the *bur,* those chambers where women reside. With the women, in these private chambers, they are safe.[21]

That the Shield-Danes' concept of kinship has discarded or diminished a previous notion of consanguinity is evident in a number of ways. First, the story of the founder-father of the tribe, Scyld Scefing, gives him no parents. His father-founder relationship to the people comes exclusively from his ability to wage war. So too Beowulf is made a son of Hrothgar and becomes kin partly through his feats of arms. The term *cyn* refers simply to the warriors who are in the hall.[22] Adult males able to render service became kin. In fact, many of the tales that are considered digressions show the dire consequences of following blood lines in political considerations. Although marriage might be thought a good strategy for ameliorating belligerent nations, given that the society only barely acknowledges blood ties and that, partially because of this, ruling more than one tribe is practically impossible, the alliances through marriage are doomed to failure. The boundaries of this society, then, would seem in part laid across connections of blood that the masculine codes seek to displace.

Beowulf records Beowulf's victory to show that ties of duty (Beowulf) defeat ties of blood (Grendel). And yet, having noticed the similarity of Beowulf and Grendel, we might suggest that the hero must also accommodate the values and ideas privileged by the previous order. Duty, in other words, must encompass blood. Nor is this idea unusual, for kinship is often seen as a method to channel what might be called in *Beowulf* "blood energy" into a socially useful form. The allusion to Cain in the Grendel episode resonates with the theme of difference and similarity between Beowulf and Grendel. Cain and Abel share the same blood; moreover, their activities make them almost indistinguishable from one another. The difference between them is simple: one's activities are acceptable, the other's are not. The point is not so much what constitutes acceptability as that acceptable activity, not blood, assures inheritance. In the story, Cain and Seth, Abel's replacement, beget the same line: Enoch, Methuselah, Lammach. In an important way, Cain and Seth are the same, even as they are different. So are Grendel and Beowulf. The boundaries in *Beowulf,* then, seem to represent the need to repress ties of blood—ties that *Beowulf* associates with ties of affection, encroachments of the erotic, enchantments of the household. As the exemplary establisher, protector, and embodiment of boundaries, Beowulf is, of course, childless.

In *Beowulf* males set boundaries across what they imagine to be external nature, but they simultaneously set these boundaries upon themselves to exclude certain aspects of what they take to be nature in general and their nature in particular. Because common boundaries establish the notion of a common good by binding certain aspects together and excluding others, disclosure—unbinding one's self or one's society—is unacceptable. In *Beowulf* to open up the binding is to throw open the gates of Troy, to make oneself vulnerable, to do a foolish, rash, and damaging action to oneself and to one's society. This is exemplified by the images and diction of binding and unbinding that weave through this work. The good building is bound together, both within and without, by iron bands: "It was so firmly made fast with iron bands, both inside and outside, joined by the skillful smith-craft" (773b–75a, also 998). The armor of the building saves it from the fight between Beowulf and Grendel.

Grendel's entrance into Heorot illustrates both the vulnerability of society to intrusions and the qualities that society deems intrusive. Grendel is described as violating the body of the building: "Driven by evil desire, swollen [*gebolgen*] with rage, he tore open the hall's mouth" (723–24a). The hall is conceived as a person who is entered, forcibly, through the mouth, and Grendel as bulging with passion, straining his own limits. Grendel seems to embody emotions that strain the boundaries of society. Grendel's entrance is described as a rape in which the men are the unwilling victims. Although the whole scene seems to be a picture of displaced and inverted sexual relations replayed in their most violent and monstrous guise, the concentration on the mouth as the site of vulnerability also connects with other images of oral binding and unbinding, in particular feasting and talking, which also have potentially monstrous aspects and become sites of violence and instability. The violation images loaded on Grendel's invasion make one aware of the destructive power of unbinding generally, and particularly of blood energy or the erotic as thought of in this society. This destructive passionate-erotic element colors subsequent iterations of the word *gebolgen,* which means not only "stretching" the boundaries but also "aroused."

The violation of Heorot by Grendel is viewed as a violation of masculine society by erotic passions that diffuse their meanings through a wide range of emotions and what are conceived of as blood energies that masculine virtue is focused on repressing in men. Water, which is associated with Grendel and also threatens the kingdom's safety, is suffused with a similar range of meaning: "There the water was boiling with blood, the horrid surge of waves swirling, all mixed with hot gore, sword-blood. Doomed to die he had hidden, then, bereft of joys, had laid down his life in his fen-refuge, his heathen soul: there hell took him" (847–52). In this description of the mere where Grendel has gone to die, we find not only a moral, but an image of passion and death. The water is agitated, heated, filled with blood. The word *weallende,* "welling, boiling," recurs in *Beowulf* in passages of emotion. Here the waves in their direst state, surging and welling, suggest that an internal emotional state has been externalized, made deadly, and moralized. The contortions of passion are "mirthless," "heathenish," "hell-clutched," and generally leading to death. Throughout, blood swirls and disgusts.

What the boundaries bind out, then, are the strong, intrusive, affective connections presumed to arise from the monstrous relationships of blood—the erotic and the domestic. Masculine idealism is engaged in imagining, establishing and protecting a space safe from the forces of blood that seem to move through space unimpeded. The tale also suggests these forces which create the relationships of men to women, mothers to fathers, parents to children tie one to a temporal process of life and death. Were it to surmount the fragile ties of blood relationship, society could free itself from these forces which mean destruction.

In building Heorot, in segregating women and in banishing Grendel, Hrothgar intends that potentially destructive aspects of the men's experience will have been put outside. But with the building of the walls, those aspects of experience reemerge, but this time as fearful enemies. Once one has staked all on boundaries, to open the gates, to taken off one's armor, to unbind one's heart is to risk the destruction of an orderly society.

In this context, one might compare the passion represented by Grendel and the mere with the masculine expression of passion aroused by the death of Grendel. Here, the men express their joy racing their horses up and down the sand.[23] For whatever reason, the transference of emotion to the riding of horses creates a haunting passage, filled with disturbing activity. That the horse was an important appendage of the warrior seems to suggest the channeling of passion into a socially acceptable form. The horse between the men's legs has all the sexual energy of the penis, enlarged and aggrandized, but transformed into a commodity for public display, a sign of masculine strength and bellicosity. The warriors can play with their horses, race them up and down, do tricks with them without any disgrace.[24] And in *Beowulf* this image will reemerge in another haunting evocation—the young warrior "riding" the gallows, society having killed him, putting the definitive circle of hemp around his neck, so that he rides to eternity while his father weeps the loss of his son. It is an image made beautiful by the earlier picture of the youth expending their life energies in the heedless game of riding.

Masculinity as defined in *Beowulf* seems to cut men off from women, from other men, from passion, from the household. This masculinity supports and creates an environment in which those things outside the armor are bad. But in confronting a world of birth, death, and the erotic, men such as Beowulf experience their space in the world as dubious, fraught with anxiety. Such a constructed world that elicits such a response is liable to make men's need for armor all the greater. Moreover, these men's place in this world appears so insecure, so tied to how they perform and what they produce, so limited as to whom they can disclose, that they find it better to stay bound up, armored, and aggressively ready to use their passion against all intruders. Otherwise their physical, material, social, and spiritual integrity may be violated, as the image of the rape of Heorot by Grendel illustrates.

To understand how deeply Beowulf's masculinity is embedded in the project of binding, one must notice how binding produces, reproduces, and sustains the masculinity of Beowulf's world. How these several projects can be brought together in a single undertaking can be grasped if we understand society to synthesize several interrelated variables: (1) the cultural, the domain of the symbolic; (2) the social, the institutions that integrate the other variables; (3) the personal, the collective endeavors that define one's social station—kin, class; (4) the behavioral, the adaptations to the environment that individuals make from the acquisition of language to the making of complex machines; and (5) the biological, the satisfaction of basic needs, such as food, sleep, shelter.[25] These various aspects are both distinct and overlapping. They interact with each other, responding to and modifying each other. In this interactivity, the meaning of activities, things, and events comes from and returns to the cultural which confers values on those meanings. These meanings/values shape the structure of all the other activities, so that in each area and every place, humans are "suspended in webs of significance."[26] In this process, cultural meanings constrain even the satisfaction of biological needs, while the biological side presses, constrains, and directs the cultural side. The biological supplies an energy that shapes culture and that culture shapes.

In *Beowulf,* for instance, the biological is represented as a type of threatening chaos—a mixture of passions and desires that encompass activities from sexual union to nurture, a force conceived as being antithetical to boundedness. We find, as in Beowulf's use of monstrous force to quell the monsters, that culture redirects that chaotic force into the social activity of drawing boundaries, which draws a distinction between what society sees as valuable for itself and a nature defined as destructive and valued negatively. As the biological tries to break out or in it is met by the cultural that defines the perception of reality and channels those conditions into social forms. That is, at every step, even in the definition of what is "biological," meaning is present, predisposing the various forms of social activities and accommodations.

Of course, all these areas in which human actions operate are situated within an environment that includes the contingent and the physical, everything from other animals, vegetables, and minerals to floods, eclipses, storms, or droughts. Therefore, both within and without the integrating semiotics of society, the forces of change are at work. However, the act of perceiving various aspects of the environment brings even that environment, insofar as it is perceived, within the cultural semiosis. The physical environment becomes *something* because of the act of naming, and naming turns something into that which society can manipulate. For instance, once "sea" has a certain meaning, then such activities as boat building and swimming may become relevant to that meaning and in turn dictate various roles and *techne.* Through these activities, which themselves are signifying, "sea" has its meaning recreated. Thus, "sea" becomes involved in a semiosis that allows it to be understood and manipulated.

In this sense, human beings, existing within societies, never can know nature directly, in an unconstructed way, in a way that is not already an extension of the society in which they are situated. In this sense, passion, which in the world of *Beowulf* is an aspect of the biological, physical-organic environment, is neither in its natural or unnatural aspects outside society. That nothing in Beowulf's world exists outside society can be demonstrated in the metaphors for exclusion from society, for rather than consigning those excluded to an existence outside known nature or to nonbeing, exclusion is considered exile or a voyage to another home. The sky is a vault, the sun a beacon, Grendel and his mother live in a hall, Beowulf's death is a journey to another dwelling, hell is a dwelling, and so on. Nature— even its seemingly inexplicable parts—is part of society.

Clearly such structures are not immanent. Humans enact these systems of significance and thus, in a sense, reproduce the world of social existence. The abilities of different humans to reproduce the particular world into which they are born is not innate. They must be trained in the system of significance and given social roles that embody this system. Given such a perspective, warriors are not simply courageous men fighting in a hostile world. That is certainly what they *think* they are most of the time and what everyone inhabiting the same locale and sharing the same social and cultural values and norms are invited to believe as the simple and self-evident truth. But the role makes that a self-evident truth because it posits that meaning as the condition of heroic action. The *techne* and role of the warrior define courage in a certain way and nature in a certain way, so that putting on armor makes part of the world hostile and creates the conditions for a certain type of behavior, attitude, and attribute. Warriors are constructs of the society, resting at one end on a series of cultural values and social norms and at the other on the need of the behavioral organism to adapt to its environment—an environment that has been shaped in important ways by those cultural values and social norms. The role authenticates the reality in such a way as to make that reality and that role inseparable and seemingly inescapable. At the same time, however, the role itself calls up its own challenges in the form of repressed, neglected, or unknown aspects of the self. The warrior, thus, who is the protector of himself and his society, is also an enemy to himself and his society. And although it is plausible from this structure to argue that he is no more an enemy to himself and his society than any other role filler, the warrior's particular kind of enmity is at the heart of the masculine dilemma in *Beowulf*.

We can see how the insidious tautology of behavior is enacted in *Beowulf* through the accoutrements of masculinity, through the *techne* of fighting back a brutal world, through rewards of food, shelter, kinship, and rings. As upholders of their social and cultural order, Beowulf's men fight in response to an environment that their social and cultural order has created, as the transformation of Grendel into a foe when Heorot is built suggests. The world is hostile because the men are armed and the men are armed because the world is hostile: Beowulf's story seems to concern the difficulty in escaping the seemingly apparent truth of this tautology. In the often repeated epithet for God, *mihtig God manna cynnes weold*, God is a mighty warrior who has for his weapon man: He is the wielder of men. The warrior wielding a sword is himself the sword of God. Moreover, the gifts of armor, the elaborate descriptions, the comparison of leaders of men to helmets and shields, all suggest that the *techne* of the armorer, his weaving, binding, welding, contains preeminent meaning, and that armor possesses symbolic value.[27]

Hardly surprising, arming as role and *techne* becomes the definitive feature of masculinity; yet it is remarkable how this extends into many fine features of male activity. We can gain a clearer notion of the cultural importance of armor by observing, as we already have somewhat, the way armor binds and sets bounds. One illustrative case occurs in the feat of swimming. Water, the sea specifically, in the world of Beowulf undoubtedly represents a source of anxiety, a border to be watched, an entity to be walled out. From the sea comes invasion, on the sea men trust their fortunes. We have also noted the sea's associations with life processes, with home, blood ties, the erotic, and the passionate. Because the sea is a cultural construct with a central symbolic significance, human activity that involves the sea will acquire levels of symbolic meaning that will have practical implications for the society. The tamer of the sea is qualified as a leader in many respects. Even as Beowulf sets out on his journey he is called *lagu-cræftig*, the water-crafty man, one who has the skill to cope with water. That Beowulf swims in armor seems appropriate, since armor represents the power that tames nature and allows one to adapt. It makes little difference whether the armor is worn on the body directly or is simply another bodily extension, like a boat.

In this context, Unferth's description of the craft of swimming that Beowulf and Brecca exhibit reports male *techne,* the ideal actions of men approaching the world that lies outside of society: one covers or enfolds the element or territory over which conquest is intended

(513); one measures it (514); one brandishes one's arms or sword [*brugdon* means both "brandished" and "bound"] (514); finally one glides over it (515). The increments of conquest thus involve seizing territory, measuring the boundary, subduing everything within the boundary, enjoying or using that which is in the boundary for one's own pleasure and purpose. In small that covers the craft of swimming and also the situation of the swimmers who float for nine days, subdue sea monsters, whales, and other beasts, and then glide to shore. It also echoes Beowulf's descent to Grendel's household. But it also describes the mentality of the warrior, of the male in mail.

The *techne* of the Geat warrior, with or without his armor, in machines or outside them, moves from experience (contact of men and world) to pleasure (constituted simultaneously as use and enjoyment) via seizing, ordering, and subduing: the approach posits a hostile world which the actions necessarily replicate. This approach leaks into the approach to other areas of human activity, which water symbolizes—passion, the erotic, birth, death, women. Nor is armoring simply a device; it is, as in the case of Beowulf, an internalized approach to relating to one's environment. Beowulf needs no armor to remain armed, as is disclosed by the Warden of the shore's description of him: "I have never seen a mightier warrior on earth than is one of you, a man in battle-dress. That is no retainer made to seem good by his weapons—unless his appearance belies him, his unequalled form" (247b–51a). While the Warden's words emphasize the technical aspect of arming, *searwum* pointing to the clever craft of arming, they also note that without armor Beowulf would still appear one *waepnum geweorðad,* worthy to wield or to be given weapons: he is a warrior through and through, as his bare-handed grappling with Grendel shows, as does his swimming. Just as arming is simply the masculine ideal, water is simply whatever impinges upon man's armor; it is whatever has been ruled out by the arming.

In *Beowulf* the horizontal axis of water crosses the vertical axis of sky and land, cultural hierarchy crosses human history, the temporal and the spiritual world meet at the site of the worm. In the geography of Beowulf's world the air-striding Dragon lives at the sea's edge under the ground. Even more than Grendel, the Dragon defies the borders of human society. Fixing the worm in the vertical and horizontal planes, at the crux, reminds us that questions of where we come from and where we go to have two different answers, one biological, the other spiritual. These two answers do not need to be the same; often they operate side by side without conflict. Sometimes, as in Christianity, they may be partially conflated.

In *Beowulf* the worm is connected with death and desire.[28] The *wyrm* appears an avenging penis that emphasizes not only that procreation is the covenant of mortality, but also that every desire creates similar covenants: acquiring, hoarding, controlling. In all aspects, regardless of how they channel their blood energies, the works of men in *Beowulf* conjure death. By drawing a line between oneself and death one does not wall death out but includes death more surely. Beowulf's society can channel men's vision of themselves and the world, but certain parts repressed in the vision reemerge. Unlike Grendel and his mother, who could be repressed and subdued, the Dragon is inextricable from Beowulf himself. When Beowulf dies, the Dragon dies; when the Dragon's barrow is destroyed, Beowulf's barrow replaces it. In this encounter, Beowulf's underlying vulnerability is revealed—his paternal longings, his desire for home, his expectations of death.

In fact, the last hours of Beowulf's life demonstrate the inadequacy of the role and *techne* that the warrior ethic provided him. The failure of arming is depicted in the clash between the posited security of the warrior society and the unsettling effects of private life, emotions, and affection. Beowulf's last adventure begins after a history of the Dragon's hoard, which recounts the end of societies and blood lines, and after the Dragon has destroyed Beowulf's own home: "Then the terror was made known to Beowulf, quickly in its truth, that his own home, best of buildings, had been melted in surging flames, the throne-seat of the Geats" (2324–26). The loss of his house and his reaction to it reveal Beowulf's vulnerability, his own monster side: "His breast within boiled with dark thoughts—not for him customary" (2331–32). The images of dark boiling within link Beowulf with Grendel, as his protestation against God's judgment links him briefly with Cain.

This sense of vulnerability and its connection with consanguinity, affection, and personal home accumulates in the lines that precede the death struggle itself. In that accumulation, Beowulf is the primary speaker. He allows us a glimpse of his private world, in what for him seems uncharacteristic disclosure. His final talk balances social allegiance and the warrior role against feelings and affections that seem to lie beneath or beyond that role. After having forged a special shield all of iron, made more secure and better arms for himself, and after having declared that he alone, without other men, would confront the Dragon, Beowulf, described as old and full of inner sorrow, makes a last speech to the retainers whom he had selected to accompany him to the Dragon's barrow. Within the warrior's role stir other thoughts. Near the entrance he sits and tells them of his affection for his maternal uncle, Hygelac, and the sorrows of kinship and consanguinity. First he describes how one of Hrethel's sons had accidently killed the other and how that had blighted the father's life, both in the loss of his son and in the guilt of the other. Here is the Cain and Abel theme again—from Adam's perspective, not God's. Moreover, in this new version the brother who lives is not legally or morally responsible for the death. The father can claim no vengeance against his son, nor even if he could would it ease his heart. This society is powerless to help men deal with accidents of the human condition, with affection and ties of blood.

This theme has been expressed elsewhere, both in the Finn episode and in the allusion to the fate of the Shield-Danes. In both these cases the affection and grief of a sister-mother-wife, Hildeburh and Wealhtheow, stands outside a brutally indifferent society. What is conceived as womanly care becomes in Beowulf's heart-disclosing tale the infrequently admitted experience of men—a shadow presence that has stood undisclosed behind the tale. In trying to portray adequately the sorrow of the father and the inadequacy of social systems to deal with it, *Beowulf* produces one of the most moving and highly poetic moments in the work, an elegy on the death of a son hanged. We are given the perspective of a father who loses his son to society in such a way that no recompense is possible. In consequence all social skills, roles, and activities become useless and joyless. The law of society falling athwart affection leaves the father to sing alone in the privacy of his sorrow:

So it is sad for an old man to endure that his son should ride young on the gallows. Then he may speak a story, a sorrowful song, when his son hangs for the joy of the raven, and, old in years and knowing, he can find no help for him. Always with every morning he is reminded of his son's journey elsewhere. . . .

> Sorrowful he sees in his son's dwelling the empty wine-hall, the
> windy resting place without joy—the riders sleep, the warriors
> in the grave. There is no sound of the harp, no joy in the dwell-
> ing, as there was of old. Then he goes to his couch, sings a song
> of sorrow, one alone for one gone. To him all too wide has
> seemed the land and the dwelling. (2444–62)

The pathos of this small poem bleeds into the tale of Hrethel, who
from the death of his son becomes *weallende* with sorrow. Peculiarly
touching is that Beowulf in presenting these pictures of the powerlessness of society, of arming, to help men bear the loneliness of their
experience (which in part society has created or exacerbated) is himself a sad, lonely old man.[29] He feels the power of his own presentation not from the perspective of father contemplating child—he has
no children of his own body, no heirs, only thanes; instead, he views
the picture as a child mourning the loss of his parents, the passing of
his grandfather Hrethel and of his maternal uncle and surrogate father
Hygelac.

There is a special moving quality in the admission of vulnerability
by Beowulf. Although he is primarily telling tales of other people's
sorrows, he is also speaking of himself in the only way possible for
him as a man, at a distance, under the armor of a surrogate story. Yet
we may sense that every word touches himself, his feelings, a revelation of the truth of his passion that has been suppressed by society
and armor. In fact, part of the pathos of the scene grows from the
ways in which Beowulf's familial love is directed by society. How can
he express the strength of his love for Hygelac? By being such a great
warrior that Hygelac never needs to have foreign household members
to fight for him. His bragging here is shot through with the pathos of
his inexpressible longing: "I would always go before him in the troop,
alone in the front" (2497–98). This is the pathetic offering of child to
father, made more pathetic by the limitations that armor imposes on
the form it takes. In his love, Beowulf eternally armed and facing
away from the source of his affection, moves forward—alone.

Now, as he faces the Dragon, all Beowulf's most satisfying relationships are behind him. He is like the father bereft of son. He has cared
so deeply and in such silence and now he emphatically has no one
after himself to care about, so that after he is hurt, his words about
his son who never lived move one. Fittingly he would have liked to

pass along his armor to that son: a son made nonexistent by the armor that put fealty above blood, duty above passion, a son who, had he been born, would have reproduced his father's fate because of the armor.

It is within this con-texture of vulnerability glimpsed beneath the armor, suppressed by it, and partially and perversely expressed by it, that the passage to which I have pointed earlier occurs—the man armed inside ("firm-hearted") and out ("shield high") approaches the monster who is indeterminately death, lust, passion, past—the deep, disturbing reassertion of what has been repressed: "Then the brave warrior arose by his shield; hardy under helmet he went in his mailshirt beneath the stone-cliffs, had trust in his strength—that of one man" (2538–41). Alone, his shield fails, his sword fails, his strength fails, the loyalty of his thanes fails. It would seem too that because he is alone and puts his trust in his role and skill and in the order of society, having repressed his own natural fecundity and affections, the society fails, his people die. He can never fully lay to rest the part of life that has been dormant except by paying for it with the death of himself and his society, a stalemate, not a victory.

Yet Beowulf does find one follower whom, because of the preceding stories and feelings, we perceive to be a follower of affection, not simply of duty. Colored as they are by the tales of Hrethel, Hygelac, and the gallows-robbed father, Wiglaf's actions seem those of filial, rather than social, devotion. For Wiglaf, as he explains to his associates, helping Beowulf is not simply a matter of repaying the war-equipment, helms, and hand swords that Beowulf has given them; it is a response to the misery of someone who has cared for them and whom they should care for: "in only one of them the heart surged with sorrows" (2599b–2600a). And there is also the beautiful moment when Wiglaf comes under the shield of Beowulf with the words "Beloved Beowulf, . . . I shall help you" (2668). The intimacy of that gesture of being let inside the armor makes one wonder if the large shield wasn't needed just so Wiglaf could climb under it with Beowulf, into the space of intimacy. Moreover, the intimacy of their relationship continues when after the battle Wiglaf washes Beowulf's wounds with his own hands and hears the dying hero's last words about the son he had wished for, who would have washed his body and taken his armor.

The moment of moving intimacy and vulnerability, however, swiftly fades in Wiglaf's trip into the Dragon's barrow and the exultant mood of triumph that, understandably, Wiglaf indulges. Yet the weight of what has just happened, of what Wiglaf and the reader have shared, impresses the ending of the poem. The poem creates the sense that an array of tender and terrible desires lie within the brittle shell of masculine roles and ideals and the armor has never fully sheltered the Shield-Dane or Geat males from the press of these desires. If anything, the repression has made them both more dreadful and more beautiful, more to be feared and more to be longed for. Wiglaf is sorrowful for the passing of a man whom he had loved, the last of his blood line, and he is bitter for society's betrayal of Beowulf. He also knows that Beowulf too has betrayed them, that his society is on the threshold of extinction. While Wiglaf glimpses salvation in the nature that Beowulf repressed, Wiglaf knows only how to reproduce the old order. He directs the construction of a new barrow on the site of the old as a memorial to repression, leading us to expect that years later, the cicatrix of earth will reopen and Beowulf's dragon will destroy society and another barrow will be piled high.

Stories are, as the poet in Beowulf instructs us, old legends and new histories "*soðe gebunden*" (867–72), bound with truth. In other words, the song or story itself is a kind of armor or binding. Within this boundary all elements that contain truth—whether myth, fable, legend, or history—have a common ontological status. Truth makes them real. In fact, this is all realism ever was and ever will be: the arming or authorizing of literary elements—regardless of their ultimate mimetic value—by what each society calls its truth. And yet we might say that stories, like people, have a way of binding in more than any body, single or corporate, intends. For whatever reason, the poet could not leave aside tender obligations that men of his time felt for their children and their fathers; he could not leave aside their longing for home, their passion, their experience in its more positive guise. The poet could not reject that truth. The poem unbinds the experiences which the social roles and *techne* of the male in armor hide, the experiences which Beowulf and his men have been trained to bound out, channel, and eradicate.

While the longing for family, home, passion can be acknowledged intermittently as that which imparts life to the society that denies it, neither Geats nor Shield-Danes can conceive how to bring these aspects into their institutions, except as a destructive heroic or monstrous force. For Beowulf this constitutes a personal, social, and historical tragedy. But it also appears an inescapable one that Beowulf is forced to abet. Beowulf, like the monsters, finds his bounded powers reemerge to destroy himself and his society. He is caught in a cruel trap: his armor no longer protects him, in part because his armor has protected him too long, he has trusted it too thoroughly. His story seems to warn: my society cannot survive without a male warrior ethic, but men cannot survive as warriors, and society cannot survive without men.

Even during the events the story recounts, Beowulf's society is passing away, and the particular roles in which men find themselves trapped have become dysfunctional—they are unable to assure the survival of the society.[30] And yet those roles and cultural values did not completely disappear, for the Christianity that *Beowulf* adumbrates seems to accommodate itself to the semiotics of its host culture: the binary oppositions of natural and unnatural forces that are found in Christianity will fit bizarrely, but neatly, into the Anglo-Saxon traditions, as the parable of the sparrow shows, as do the hagiographies that are produced from amalgams of Germanic violence and heroism and Christian suffering and martyrdom. Moreover, the relationships among people on the basis of service, rather than blood, is already prepared for in the protofeudal world of the *comitatus* and Heorot hall. In the end, *Beowulf* suggests that Geat society did not survive because the loyalty of thanes was not enough as it was constituted, nor were the cultural and social systems able to maintain, restrain, or integrate the conditions of life.

Beowulf does not recognize how society had turned him against himself and made him the monster that must die. That we have only recently recognized this ourselves testifies to the power of Beowulf's armor, to the residual power of the male warrior role to define a view of the world that for many still seems natural, and even self-evidently so. This is not to argue that the boundaries that men today fight for are the same as those the Geats gave life for, nor that the fighting takes place in armor against dragons. Beowulf's men were trained to find pleasure, rewards, and motivation in subduing pieces of the environment that signified pieces of themselves, of their experience. This man in armor is transformed but not dead. The significance of each category has shifted, as has the overall structure, but much is still intact, as we will see as we examine the shifting male roles in successive tales of masculinity.

Notes

1. J. R. R. Tolkien, "*Beowulf:* The Monsters and the Critics," *Proceedings of the British Academy* 22 (1936): 245–95, rpt. in *The Beowulf Poet,* ed. Donald Fry, (Englewood Cliffs, N.J.: Prentice-Hall, 1968): 23.

2. R. J. White, *A Short History of England* (Cambridge: Cambridge University Press, 1967), 37.

3. Stanley Greenfield in "A Touch of the Monstrous in the Hero, or Beowulf Re-Marvellized" (*English Studies* 62 [1982]: 294–307) has offered refutation of Fred Robinson's thesis that the supernatural aquatics of the hero make him inappropriately monstrous ("Elements of the Marvelous in the Characterization of Beowulf," *Old English Studies in Honor of John C. Pope,* ed. Robert B. Burlin and Edward B. Irving, Jr. [Toronto: University of Toronto Press, 1974], 119–37). Greenfield demonstrates that Beowulf is not what Northrop Frye would call a "mimetic hero"; he is marvelous and has, indeed, something of the monstrous, quite in keeping with other Germanic heroes. Independently S. L. Dragland ("Monster-Man in *Beowulf,*" *Neophilologus* 61 (1977): 606–18) had reached the same conclusion. Yet Nora Chadwick was the first: "The Monsters and Beowulf," *Anglo-Saxons,* ed. Peter Clemoes (London: Cambridge University Press, 1969) 171–203.

4. Dragland, "Monster-Man in *Beowulf,*" 608.

5. Ibid., 613.

6. See L. L. Schucking, "The Ideal of Kingship in Beowulf," *An Anthology of Beowulf Criticism,* ed. Lewis E. Nicholson (South Bend: Indiana University Press, 1963) 35–49; Robert Kaske, "*Sapientia et Fortitudo* as the Controlling Theme of *Beowulf,*" *Studies in Philology* 55 (1958): 423–57.

7. F. H. Whitman, "The Kingly Nature of Beowulf," *Neophilologus* 61 (1977): 278.

8. Strong reasons argue against love, sapience, humility, and courage as moral themes in the story. None of them succeed. Moreover, were Beowulf a Christian exemplar, the reward of an afterlife would be stated in the work, and the heavenly and earthly cities would more clearly be in conflict. One need go no further than Bede or the tales about Andreas and Guthlac to find that the rewards of valor are personal salvation and the assurance of a divine reward. Moreover, if a hero's religious valor is salutary for the community, it is so in that it offers an example to others—not of how to survive in this world, but of how to prepare for the

next. Faced with the negative implications of the work, some critics argued that the work suggested the failure of masculine ideals and the salvation of the feminine. Martin Camargo writes that "the only hope for sure peace, the poet clearly implies, lies in the love and compassion which Christianity offers as its idea and which the women in *Beowulf* seem to symbolize": see "The Finn Episode and the Tragedy of Revenge in *Beowulf*," *Studies in Philology* 78 (1981): 133.

9. Dragland, "Monster-Man in *Beowulf*," 606.

10. Jane Acomb Leake, *The Geats of "Beowulf"* (Madison: University of Wisconsin Press, 1967).

11. I use here E. Talbott Donaldson's translation (New York: W. W. Norton, 1966) because, although it is not fully literal nor fully accurate, it chooses a sense of the story that emerges for me when I read the original. In all other places the translation is mine. Numbers refer to lines in the R. W. Chambers and A. J. Wyatt edition of the poem (Cambridge: Cambridge University Press, 1920).

12. Arthur Brodeur argues that in Beowulf's relationship with Hygelac, Beowulf's "unequaled strength and courage in his victories over formidable monsters . . . [are] enhanced by the revelation of his deep and emotionally justified concern for those in whose interest he fought," thus giving Beowulf "the roundness, the moral dimensions, and the human warmth of an epic hero": see *The Art of "Beowulf"* (Berkeley: University of California Press, 1959), 80.

13. Bernard Huppé in *The Hero in the Earthly City* (Binghamton, N.Y.: Medieval & Renaissance Texts & Studies, 1984) believes that polarity typifies the poem (47); Fred C. Robinson in *Beowulf and the Appositive Style* (Knoxville: University of Tennessee Press, 1985) contends that "in *Beowulf* we see . . . opposition of artifice and nature" (72). Recently some critics have argued that "*Beowulf* is to an extent a poem of impulse and idiosyncrasy": see Clara Kinney, "The Needs of the Moment: Poetic Foregrounding as a Narrative Device in *Beowulf*," *Studies in Philology* 82 (1985): 299.

14. Bruce Moore calls these forces "perverse" ("The Thryth-Offa Digression in *Beowulf*," *Neophilologus* 64 [1980]: 127); Robinson sees it as "malevolent" (*Beowulf and the Appositive Style,* 71).

15. J. J. Anderson shows that "good" (Beowulf) and "evil" (Grendel) contain "the same level of elementary violence," which he connects with their pursuing feuds ("The *cupe folme* in *Beowulf*," *Neophilologus* 67 [1983]: 128–29). In this reading, feuds are not a viable, social conduit for the violent nature of men, thus raising the question about acceptable violence.

16. Ward Parks in "Flyting and Fighting: Pathways in the Realization

of the Epic Contest," *Neophilologus* 70 (1986): 292–306, argues that contests are socially sanctioned forms of violence that without social sanction would destroy society, and that through these contests the hero proves a "self-worth and manhood" that is constituted by society (302–3). The argument is based upon Walter J. Ong's *Fighting for Life: Contest, Sexuality, and Consciousness* (Ithaca, N.Y.: Cornell University Press, 1981). Ong sees contest as the ritualization of competition as a socially acceptable way to meet a biological need.

17. Helen Damico makes a similar argument about Wealhtheow in her excellent book, *Beowulf's Wealhtheow and the Valkyrie Tradition* (Madison: University of Wisconsin Press, 1984). She see Grendel's dam and Wealhtheow as "antipodal" and "contrapuntal" (21) but fused at the core in a relationship in which Wealhtheow represents the positive side and Grendel's dam the negative side. In a sense the dichotomization is a suppression of identity; in the same way, the prototypes of Wealhtheow are also suppressed.

18. This is, of course, not the only possible way to view this "ecology"—as "world-open" animals, humans modify their environment and their environment modifies them. The term "world-open" derives from the work of Arnold Gehlen, *Der Mensch—Seine Natur und Seine Stellung in der Welt* (Weisbaden: Athenaion, 1975), which is important to the arguments in Karl Peter and Nicholas Petryszak, "Sociobiology versus Biosociology," *Sociobiology Examined*, ed. Ashley Montagu (Oxford: Oxford University Press, 1980), 39–81; as well as to Peter Berger's *Social Construction of Reality: A Treatise in the Sociobiology of Knowledge* (Garden City, N.Y.: Anchor, 1967). Some feminists, in fact, have argued for an "eco-centric" view of life.

19. In part because of the monster debate, those critics who have recognized Beowulf's failure have redichotomized the struggle this way: society can go only so far in coping with perverse nature (even the most heroic attempts fail); therefore, we have a contest between Christian (spiritual armor) and pagan (physical armor) in which the pagan is shown to be insufficient: see Robert Finnegan, "Beowulf at the Mere (and elsewhere)," *Mosaic* 11, no. 4 (1978): 54; Alan K. Brown, "The Firedrake in *Beowulf*," *Neophilologus* 64 (1980): 454; Huppé, 47.

20. Damico notes that traditionally the mother had a more intimate relationship with the son than did the father (*Beowulf's Wealhtheow*, 20); however she does give the counter example of the father's lament for the lost son (2444-2462) (p. 191n). In the relationship of Grendel's dam to her son Damico sees a commentary on the evils of familial intimacy (113f.).

21. Rosemary Cramp, "*Beowulf* and Archeology," *Medieval Arche-*

ology 1 (1957), 57–77; rpt. in *The Beowulf Poet,* ed. Donald Fry (Englewood Cliffs, N.J.: Prentice-Hall, 1968): 133.

22. David Herlihy describes the disappearance of the *sippe,* a medieval and pre-medieval Germanic social organization based on family and kinship, in *Medieval Households* (Cambridge, Mass.: Harvard University Press, 1985), 44–48.

23. Joseph Campbell suggests that horsemanship signifies the "male-oriented patriarchal order" in its victory over Goddess religions. *The Masks of God: Creative Mythology* (New York: Viking Press, 1965), 208.

24. This is certainly at the back of a similar passage in Shakespeare's *Henry IV part 1* when passionate Hotspur turns away from his pursuing wife, Kate, to take his horse. As he rushes madly about the scene, Kate implores him to tell her what is taking him away. He replies, "My horse, my love, my horse" (II.iii.73–76). Later, horse will become car and motorcycle, and men, especially young men who are undergoing the awakening of conscious erotic desire, will spend much of their time working on machines and driving very quickly in them.

25. My discussion here uses Talcott Parsons, *Societies: Evolutionary and Comparative Perspectives* (Englewood Cliffs, N.J.: Prentice-Hall, 1966), and Clifford Geertz, "The Impact of the Concept of Culture on the Concept of Man," *The Interpretation of Cultures* (New York: Basic Books, 1973), 33–54, in which Geertz modifies the Parsonian model. This approach is not a "functionalist" one, a thoroughgoing critique of which may be found in Nancy Chodorow, *The Reproduction of Mothering: Psychoanalysis and Sociology of Gender* (Berkeley: University of California Press, 1978), 36–38.

26. Geertz, echoing Max Weber, so defines a semiotic idea of culture in "Thick Description: Toward an Interpretive Theory of Culture," *The Interpretation of Cultures,* 5.

27. Parsons points to this when he writes, "Skill is the internalization of certain elements of the culture" (*Societies,* 15n). Fred Robinson, following Dorothy Whitelock (*The Anglo-Saxon Chronicle* [London: Eyre and Spottiswoode, 1961]), notes that in *Beowulf* there are "pervasive identifications of men with artifacts." He sees "artifacts as allies of men and the forces of good": "The human essence is to be found in the artificial, and the works of men's hands not only express but actually help implement their desire for natural control" (*Beowulf and the Appositive Style,* 73–74).

28. The Dragon as *wyrm* is connected with death. In *Judith* and *Vǫluspá* hell is described as a worm-hall. In *Soul and Body* worms eat the corpses of men. Sigemud must go under the ground alone to slay his

wyrm, and Beowulf finds his in a barrow, from which he draws it forth. Satan turns to a *wyrm* to fetch the apple for Eve in *Genesis B.* In keeping with the traditions of the Bible, the conflation of the deadly worm with Satan is one which was obvious, suitable, and convenient. If the Dragon is Christianized in *Beowulf,* it is only partially and imperfectly, and it makes little difference, ultimately, whether that moral meaning has been added to the worm or not. The worm stands for a danger outside society, one which society is not sufficiently prepared for and one which it cannot adequately subdue.

29. The fear of abandonment, of dying alone, was real in the Middle Ages, according to Philip Aries, *The Hour of Death* (New York: Alfred A. Knopf, 1981), 11.

30. This is the thrust of the Christian-pagan analysis of Huppé, Brown, Robinson, and others. John Niles still adheres to Tolkien's, Schucking's and Kaske's original line: "The poem's controlling theme is *community:* its nature, its occasional breakdown, and the qualities that are necessary to maintain it," i.e., the hero and the heroic code: see *Beowulf: The Poem and Its Tradition* (Cambridge, Mass.: Harvard University Press, 1983).

2

Sir Gawain:
Touches of Flesh

But you, Jesus, good lord, are you
not also a mother? Are you not
that mother who, like a hen, collects
her chickens under her wings?
—Anselm of Canterbury (A.D. 1109)

AT THE MOMENT in *Beowulf* when each Geat warrior thinks to
meet his death, his mind turns not to king, rewards, or bravery. His
mind turns to home: "None of them thought that he would ever seek
his beloved dwelling again, his people or free-city, where he had been
nurtured [*afeded*]" (691–93).[1] More particularly, each warrior turns
his affectionate thoughts to that place where he had been nurtured. In
small moments throughout *Beowulf*, the poet opens a chink in the
armor through which a fuller experience of the men in the story may
be glimpsed. *Afeded* gives us one such picture in which a word that
could suggest warriors at feast with their king conjures moments of
mother and child. Doubled ironically in that word is the idea that
their role of securing a feasting hall had, in effect, cut them off from
home and nurturing.

In *Beowulf* these few words form one of the few introspective and
psychologically intimate passages; they give a rare view of a homelife
usually kept in the background or suppressed. That thoughts of the
suppressed private household emerge at such a crucial juncture and
that these thoughts exert such power over the men encourages specu-
lation about the crucial part that the experience of nurture plays in
fashioning the masculine ideal and in connecting men to that ideal.

Often tales of knighthood turn on questions of nurture. *Sir Gawain and the Green Knight* is such a tale. In it ideas of hospitality become embroiled with ideals of masculinity. In the midst of the Christmas feast at King Arthur's court a green knight of churlish aspect challenges the hospitality of the court: he begs that someone deal him a blow that he may return. Gawain agrees and severs the knight's head from his body. The knight gathers his severed head, which raises its eyelids and speaks to remind Gawain that he must find repayment a year and a day hence. On the day after All-Hallows' Gawain begins his search for the Green Knight to receive the return blow. But the Green Knight has gone without a trace and Gawain knows not the way to the knight's castle. When the returning Christmas season overtakes him, Gawain is nearly dead from the hardships of his quest. Suddenly, a castle presents itself to him. The bulk of the middle of the work deals with the comforts and temptations of that castle. Finally Gawain is shown on his way to the place where the Green Knight awaits him.

At the end of his quest, an odd passage similar to the one in *Beowulf* appears. At the crucial moment when Gawain expects to lose his head, the Green Knight's axe merely nicks his neck. Gawain's overflowing joy is described thus: "Never since he was *burne* born of his mother / Was he never in this world *wyʒe* half so blithe" (2320–21).[2] These words are not without ambiguities: does *burne* mean "baby" or "knight?" Does *wyʒe* mean "man," in the sense of a stalwart, brave, or doughty man, or does it mean "creature" or "child?" This is the first time in the tale that any mother, besides Mary, and any birth, besides Christ's, has been mentioned. The invocation of Gawain's birth makes the meaning of *burne* and *wyʒe* more confusing.

But ultimately it matters not whether one sees Gawain as never half so happy as a child, man, or creature. Regardless of whether one views it as a rebirth[3] or rite of passage,[4] the experience brings Gawain back to the origins of his life, to his mother, to his childhood. Among its other possible meanings the passage points out that Gawain has never known complete joy since he was a child with his mother. Somehow the world at birth had been joyous and promised joy that he now remembers only indistinctly. The adult world has been joyless in its tainted and suspect joys. But the joy of being spared, the joy of being alive, the joy of being, is, for Gawain of the poem and for the poet imagining Gawain, pure.

In this context of remembering the most tender moments of his life, Gawain's expression of recollected joy may seem chilling:

> He sprit forth span-foot more than a spear length,
> Had hotly his helmet & on his head cast,
> Shot with his shoulders his fair shield under,
> Bares out a bright sword & brimly he speaks. . . .
>
> Cease, knight, of thy roughness I bide no more.
> I have had a stroke in this stead without strife,
> & if thou reaches me more I readily shall require
> & reply readily again (& thereto you may trust)
> & fierce.
>
> (2316–19, 2322–26)

Having been compelled to bow his naked neck quietly before the axe, Gawain in one movement points himself with arms and words. Gawain expresses joy, connected with birth, with a time of passive vulnerability,[5] by swinging heavy arms—metal extensions of the body—from behind the iron walls of his carapace. Gawain's expression of joy recounts the language of hardness that he has learned since those early days, a language that makes joy infrequent and fleeting.

Moreover, the cut Gawain receives, which testifies to his vulnerability, his rootedness in experiences of the flesh, closes, rather than opens, the possibility of future joy:

> But in sign of my surfeit I shall see it often
> When I ride in renown, remorse to myself.
> The fault & the frailty of the perverse flesh,
> How tender it is to entice touches of filth.
> Thus when pride shall prick me for prowess of arms,
> The look of this love-lace shall soften my heart.
>
> (2433–38)

For Gawain the flesh has proven frail because it has proven perverse, perverse because frail. This fault, only discovered now, as Gawain observes, has ever been in himself (2382). Such soft flesh invites touches of impurity. Since hardness cannot totally temper human softness and softness cannot protect from a hard world, a knight must remain aware of his softness and guard against it. Lost is the possibility of a pure childish joy that for Gawain constitutes the ideal world.

Lost is that joy in the very moment of its recovery, making more poignant the male journey between childhood and maturity, raising questions about the process by which one becomes the other.

Sir Gawain's theme seems to elaborate the theme of masculine arming expressed in *Beowulf.* But here the abstract passions seething symbolically and monstrously outside the men and silently and treacherously within have been replaced by the acknowledged presence of the flesh. *Sir Gawain,* unlike *Beowulf,* observes the flesh and senses that reside in the armor. The world inside and out is described in sensitively sensual language. The world of senses, sensuality, flesh is called "softness." It is the discovery of men's softness that the work concerns itself with. The concepts of fertility, nurture, affection touched in this work are not abstract. They are pressing, present, and pleasing—even though they are shown to be repressed and threatening.

Gawain's trials all advance upon this discovery of underlying softness. The poem moves from a world of hardness and hardship to one of warmth and softness, where armor seems unnecessary, and back to a hard world in which exposed softness is probed, a cut is given, and the need for armor demonstrated. Gawain, unlike the Green Knight, cannot afford softness: "though my head fall on the stones / I cannot it restore" (2282–83). While an uncovered Green Knight can lean amusedly on his axe to watch Gawain's gyrations of knightly defiance, he can do so only because he is invulnerable. He can literally and figuratively lose his head without hurt. He may, as critics have often averred, stand for the world of fecundity that Gawain's society conceptualizes as lying above and below the lot of men, as signified by the birth of Christ in the winter world and by the immanent resurrection of nature.[6] But because Gawain finds the lot of men different, he finds that although they may need to love and be loved, to procreate, to trust, to know joy, they also must guard against suffering and death that haunts the very places where they should find joy.[7]

In *Beowulf* the masculine concern is centered on establishing a space in which the processes of life can be stabilized. In *Sir Gawain and the Green Knight* not only flesh but time, to which flesh is subject, dominates the concern of men. To have soft flesh in Gawain's world means to be susceptible to touches of mortality. In Gawain's world a man must be hard, inside and out, should he wish to endure. Thus the perceptions of flesh and time produce a different armor and ethic.

Men must find new ways to endure, to live. In Gawain's language "life" means what is "left" when everything else changes, and in his world only the hard offers the possibility of endurance. Whereas in *Beowulf* God is often called *Metod*, the measurer, in *Sir Gawain and the Green Knight* God is almost exclusively called *Dryȝtyn*, the lord, the soldier, the hard, the enduring.[8] Ideally the soft and changing male is to be *dryȝe*.

The adversary time and temporality haunt the poem: softness seeps into every episode as fragility, mortality, decay.[9] Time rushes around men, wearing them and all their civilizations down. And time is inside men as well, in their nativity, their sexual longings, their desire for home, their impending age. Thus men live in time and against time trying to salvage a life, which is somehow a journey or a time outside of time.

The poem begins with a description of the working of time on civilizations past, suggesting the problems that even hardness encounters in eluding change:

> Since the siege & the assault was ceased at Troy,
> The walls broken & burnt to brands & ashes,
> The knight that the trammels of treason there wrought
> Was tried for his treachery, the truest on earth.
> It was Aeneas, the noble, & his high kin
> That since forced down provinces & fathers became
> Well nigh of all the wealth in the West Isles. . . .
>
> & far over the French flood Felix Brutus
> On many banks full broad Britain he sets
>>> with joy,
>> Where war & wrack & wonder
>> Together have dwelt therein,
>> & often both bliss & blunder
>> Full swift have shifted since.
>
>>>> (1–7, 13–19)

The city of Troy represents a desirable moment protected by hard walls that nonetheless are broken and burnt.[10] Historical time seems a succession of walled cities destroyed, a unity fragmented over time. Time has brought, as the bob and wheel summarize, swift successions of wars, griefs, and marvels that work joy and confusion. Here, in the poem's beginning, the central paradox of hardness and softness emerges: if history suggests that individuals and societies must be strong to survive, the political, natural, and spiritual histories that surround Gawain's story in part constitute exempla of the insufficiencies of hardness. They warn that men must also be soft, not indiscriminately, but soft nonetheless.

Hardness, for instance, does not preserve Troy; reproduction does: Troy survives when Aeneas becomes a father, literally and figuratively. But reproduction means displacement, losing the original shape to retain the original shape: London becomes the "new Troy." As the profound center of the poem, the celebration of Christ's birth also makes birth (and, paradoxically, death) the central act of salvation, or survival:

> On that morn when each man's mindful of that time
> That *dryȝtyn* for our destiny to die was born,
> Joy waxes in each home in the world for his sake,
> So did it there on that day through many dainties.
> Both at meals & larger feasts full quaint,
> Hard men served the guests upon the dais.
>
> (995–1000)

The Gawain-poet sings the praises of a *dryȝtyn*, the one who endures, born to die for our endurance; he claims that the mystery of that death/birth is the key to living/remaining. This mystery calls forth joy and nurture ("meals & larger feasts") and transforms "hard men" to soft and humble servants. At Bercilak's castle, where the celebration occurs, the "ancient wife" sits in the highest place in deference due to the celebration of nativity.

In the same way, the catalog of the succession of seasons suggests that softness as well as hardness is necessary to pass through time, where ends do not conform to beginnings and life conduces to death:

> A year passes full swiftly & yields never likeness.
> The final fits the first so seldom. . . .
> Then the weather of the world struggles with winter,
> Cold shrinks down, clouds uplift,
> Shining falls the rain in showers full warm,
> Falls upon fair fields. Flowers there show.
> Both grounds & the groves green are her weeds.
> Birds busk to build & brimful sing—

For solace of the soft summer that ensues thereafter
    by banks;
    & blossoms bulge to blow
    By rows rich & rank.
    Then notes noble enough
    Are heard in wood so fair.

After, the season of summer with soft winds,
When Zephyr sighs himself on seeds & herbs;
Joyous is the plant that waxes thereout,
When the dropping dew drips off the leaves,
To bide a blissful blush of the bright sun.
But then hastens harvest & he hardens soon.
Warns him for the winter to wax full ripe. . . .
Wroth wind of the welkin wrestles with the sun. . . .
& thus passes the year in many yesterdays.

                        (498–529)

Passing through a time of struggle with cold to a time of warmth, softness, joy, and birth, the year reverts to hardness, "wroth wind," and wrestling. The poet crafts these passages on the passing year with sensual beauty. As a result, the recollections of exquisite celebrations of youth and procreation in spring and summer intensify the cold winter world through which a knight must travel. The portrait of time and nature in the poem suggests that men cannot avoid the lot of living things—birth, death, procreation, hardship, desire, nurture—or the emotions of pain and joy attendant on them. It further implies that no single stance for a man is appropriate.

The hunting scenes further exemplify this.[11] The death that pursues the animals in each of the three hunts cannot be avoided regardless of the character of the animal pursued. The does and hinds that flee in terror, exemplifying their soft and timid natures, cannot escape. The fox, treacherous and stealthy, "steals out full still," thinking to escape death, but stumbles on a hunting station (1710ff.) and "*stiffly* start[s] aside / With all the woe on life" (1717; my emphasis). But neither craft nor stiffness helps him evade his fate. Ironically, despite the emblematic thrust of these encounters, the hunters do not read their own lives in the fox's desperate struggle to avoid death. The lines describing the hunter's perspective, however, echo with uncanny differences previous lines: "Then was it lust to live to listen to the hounds" (1719). Being on the other end of pain, being the ones causing, rather than receiving, blinds the hunters to the wheeling of reciprocity that the poet discloses. The "lust to live" for the "stiff" springs from this illusion of control, difference, distance, knowing emphatically that one is not the victim.

Among those hunted beasts, the boar causes most suffering and most closely resembles the hunters' ideal hardness. He is described as an iron-clad, if churlish, warrior. "Grim" (1442), *brim* (violent) (1580) arrows cannot pierce his "shields" (shoulders) (1456). He thrusts as he fights (1443), and "by turns, he startled the *stiff*est" (1567; my emphasis). When Bercilak and the boar collide and fall together in the river, the mirror image of hunter and hunted fuse. Then Bercilak "set sadly the sharp in the slot even / Drove it up to the hilt that the heart shattered" (1593–94). As a reflection of the hard men who hunted him, the boar suggests that even the stiffest man has one soft and vulnerable place through which his heart may be shattered—the "slot." The slot, which is the soft hollow where neck joins body, becomes the pervasive site of vulnerability in the story. Gawain fears to lose his head; the hunters eviscerate deer through the slot before they "unbind" them. "Slot" is a term that also refers to the concavity between the breasts, suggesting the nurturant or sexual, as in the erotic décolletage of Bercilak's lady. The slot, which, then, refers to the area between mid-breast and mid-throat, is also the vulnerable area for Gawain.

The poet shows that every animal has a "slot," a defenseless area of natural tenderness and vulnerability. In this context, the dressing of the "hard" boar becomes a striking lesson. Carving the boar is "unlacing" it, and the first lines make the boar and the task seem soft and easy: "To unlace this boar lovely begins" (1606). The word "unlace" ("cut up") is delicate, echoed in the word "lovely." It will be echoed again by the word "love-lace," the name given both the girdle and the cut ("lace") that Gawain receives, for Gawain's fate also echoes the boar's: the discovery of the vulnerable heart that conduces to death. So too after the beautiful line about the boar follows the grim reminder: "First he hews off his head" (1607). The unlacing that begins with the head grates in sound and sense: "& since then rends him all rough under the spine, / Drags out the bowels" (1608–9). The poem allows no escape from either view: the unfolding of life in time is lovely and harsh, sweet and unlovely. Men in the poem are inescapably forced to experience both.[12]

The inadequacy of hardness alone to cope with temporal existence is shown in other ways as well. Before setting out on his search for the Green Knight, the "*stiff* man" Gawain (570) hasps himself in arms, the fifty-line description of which stresses hardness: "the *steel* in hand" (570), "the *steel* sabots" (574), "His legs lapped in *steel*" (575), "his knees *riveted* with *knots*" (577), " his *thick thongs*" (579), "the *braided hauberk* of bright *steel rings*" (580), the "well *burnished* arm-pieces" (582), "gloves of *plate*" (583), "rich *coat-armor*" (585), and so forth (my emphasis throughout). No wonder, for the winter world of cliff and forest, roaring water and rock offers hardship upon hardship that only Gawain's own hardiness can overcome:

> At each shore or water where the wight passed,
> Marvel it were if he found not a foe him before
> & that so foul & so fell that fight him behooved.
> So many marvels by mount there the man finds
> It were taxing for to tell of the tenth dole.
> Somewhile with worms he wars & with wolves also;
> Somewhile with wood-wild ones that waited in the knars;
> Both with bulls & bears & boars otherwhile;
> & giants that him pursued on the high fells.
> Had he not been doughty & enduring [*dryȝe*] & *dryȝtyn* had served
> Doubtless he had died & been killed full oft.
>
> (715–25)

Beyond Camelot's protective walls threatens a harsh world for which the hardness of society has been inculcated.[13] Yet Gawain's arms, symbol of his society's hardiness, nearly kill him:

> When the cold clear water from the clouds sheds
> & freezes ere it fall might to the pale earth,
> Near slain with the sleet he slept in his irons,
> More nights than enough in naked rocks.
> There as clattering from the crest the cold stream runs
> & hung high over his head in hard icicles;
> Thus in peril & pain & plights full hard,
> Through country carries this knight till Christmas eve.
>
> (727–34)

In the harsh winter, when swords of once flowing water hang over Gawain's head and ice "clatters" like the hunters or the Green Knight over the rocks, Gawain's armor becomes his enemy, turning from steel to iron, from saver to oppressor and slayer.

In this hard world only warmth and home can save him. Oppressed doubly by his and the world's hardness and by the knowing it is the time of Christ's birth, he "crie[s]" (760) and begs to be led to "some home" (739). Mercy is what he desires, softness and warmth—just what the nativity requires. It is to "Mary that is mildest mother so dear" (754) that he directs his prayer. And it is to Bercilak's castle that she leads him.

Sir Gawain and the Green Knight in part studies the masculine ideal of endurance, exposes both the claims and limits of hardiness and softness, and records what seems to be the more or less total displacement of softnesses by hardness advocated in the Arthurian construction of masculinity. Seen thus, the poem reveals the adversities men experienced in following the time's ideal masculinity and the necessities that bound men to that ideal.[14] Gawain confronts his fears about his own vulnerability, in particular his fears associated with softness, flesh, nurture, childishness, eroticism.[15] The poem suggests that regardless of their stance men must be born, be nurtured, desire, die. Men can protect themselves sometimes, but they cannot eradicate what is seen as their natural history. In dealing with this vulnerability by denying it, Gawain's story suggests that men in his age were not happy being hard but that being soft conjured equally unpleasant anxieties. Fickle time, nature, and existence make every stance problematic.

In this society, hardness becomes the way to express softness, and Arthur's court suggests this pattern. At the beginning Arthur's court in its "first age" (54) throngs joyfully with "beardless children" (280). Arthur, still "somewhat boyish" (86), is "jolly of his joyfulness." Yet even in this beginning that relates joy and childhood, these youthful males are praised for being "stiff": Arthur "stands up *stiff* in stall" (104); he is a "*stiff* king" (107); Arthur's knights are praised as the "*stiffest* under steel-gear on steeds to ride" (260); Gawain is "the *stiff* man" (570); even the helmet that protects Gawain's vulnerable head is "stapled *stiffly*" (606; my emphasis throughout). The Green Knight seeks Arthur's court because he has heard they are "hardy" (285), "bold" (286), and bear themselves "stiffly" (287). Arthur's knights are not physically powerful, but they are tough, as the king advises Gawain on how to defeat the Green Knight: "heart & hand should hardy be" (371). Even in its youth, Camelot inculcates stiffness as an attitude, a sentiment, a moral behavior.

Moreover, Arthur has already learned to express the remnant of childish joys in hard ways, suggesting that the ideal of a stiff manhood early shapes the vocabulary of beginnings:

> But Arthur would not eat till all were served,
> He was so jolly in his joyfulness & somewhat boyish.
> His life liked him light. He loved the less
> Either to long lie or alone sit,
> So busied him his young blood & his brain wild.
> (85–89)

Arthur's childish vitality and carefree feelings do not make him, like Bercilak, lose his head and dance around or play frivolous games or seem drunk (1086–87). Nor does Arthur in his joy seem soft or easeful. Instead, with "face so proud / He stands stiff in stall, / Full bold in that New Year. / Much mirth he makes with all" (103–6). Arthur's wild joy, like Gawain's later, vents itself in a macabre desire: Arthur wants to fight someone to the death as a way to exercise and exorcise his youthful spirits (91–99).[16]

This displacement of softness by a masculine hardness occurs throughout the poem, distorting the diction of birth and nurture. It provides a picture of the early training men receive: "And when this Britain was built by this rich knight, / Bold ones bred therein that loved strife" (20–21). According to the poet, British men were "bred" to be bold. "Bred" in its root means "born" and through its etymology implies warmed and protected, as in the related word "brooding." Previous concepts of birth and nurture seem to have been replaced by institutional ideals that reflect the need for "stiff" men. We can see a similar displacement in the use of "gentle," which means "soft" and implies something "softened" or nurtured from its brutal nature. Yet at root the word "gentle" also means "born" and suggests that softness comes from being well-born, that selective reproduction leads to a mollification of the harsh elements in human nature—the idea behind a hereditary social elite. However, "Jousted full jollily these gentle knights" (42) illustrates that in Arthur's world "gentle" does not refer to birth or to softness; instead, "gentle" is appropriated for praising highly valued social qualities: prowess, hardness, and violence.

Because of such transubstantiation, Gawain can be called "that fine father of nurture."[17] Men have become the nurturers because "nurture," as used here, no longer has anything to do with breast feeding. Men have become mothers who reproduce without sexual congress, without birth, without nursing. Birth and nurture here express social qualities borrowing from, but inimical to, previous "soft" ideas that we see expressed in the birth of Christ or the seasonal cycle—qualities usually associated with and requiring women.[18] The type of joy that Gawain is shown to have known as a child with his mother, the type of intimacy, warmth, and protection exemplified in the birth of Christ and in the invocation of Mary, have been redirected to other types of activities which, as when Gawain receives his cut, perversely express those distantly remembered experiences and desires, while the experiences themselves of heedless (headless) joy and play, intimacy, and nurture are feared and fought against. This condition of the male "nurtured" and "gentled" and "bred" in Britain explains the form of Arthur's own childish behavior and the hardiness of his knights.

Yet when Gawain accepts the game of decollation, he suggests that he is more effeminate than the others of Camelot: "I am the weakest I know and of wit feeblest / & least. . . . & since this business is so nice, nought it falls to you" (354–55, 358). The game is a "nice" or *ny-wys* one: it requires no wit for it is heedless or headless. Gawain suggests that the game does not require the hardiness, strength, or wit of the masculine world. While Gawain's modesty may imply its opposite, Gawain was traditionally thought to be "softer"—more prone to discourse than battle, to the arms of Venus than Bellona.[19] This ambiguity in Gawain's character of feminine softness and masculine hardness informs the tale. Weakness and folly are what the Green Knight's game means to try, and Gawain will find out that in speaking well he had spoken more wisely than he knew. As Gawain says presciently when he sets out, "What may man do but find out?" (564).[20]

Gawain's first experiences on setting out are cold, harsh, and, but for the intercession of Mary, fatal. Having found the limits of his hardiness, Gawain seeks the warmth of home, a search fulfilled, almost magically, just as Gawain begins it:

> He had not signed himself but thrice
> Ere he was aware in the wood of a home within a moat
> Above the land on a knoll, locked under boughs
> Of many surrounding burly trunks by the ditches,
> A castle, the comeliest that ever knight owned.
> Pitched on a prairie [*prayere*], a park all about.
>
> (763–68)

Wish and realization are so compact that the *prayere* (prayer) in which Gawain rides becomes the *prayere* (prairie) on which his desire's fulfillment is pitched. Considering Gawain's need, the wildness of the spot, and the hardship of the previous night, any dwelling would seem comely. This one, however, is "comely" in both that word's senses: being congruent to Gawain's desires and being beautiful, in this case fantastically beautiful (785–802). Set on a hill, encircled by water, the castle is made "full gay" and "love-like" by the shining white towers, carved pinnacles, and chimneys that interrupt the "hard" walls of "hewn stone." Appearing "pared out of paper purely," as the knight thought, the place suggests not military strength, but wonderful delicacy, hospitality, and nurture: it resembles the ornaments used to decorate food at feasts.[21] Chimneys dominate the lofty and magical living spaces, a sign of the warmth within.[22]

Bercilak's castle corresponds to Gawain's fantasies of softness in the same way that the wilderness corresponds to his idea of hardness. Just as he "finds" beasts to quell, he also "finds" the castle.[23] A porter immediately opens the gates to the stranger and a throng of people bow before him. Moreover, the lord of the castle, without knowing his guest, embraces him and announces, "You are welcome to wield as you like. / That here is all as your own to have at your will and wield" (835–36). And whatever Gawain likes does appear, from "sauces so sly" (892) and amorous ladies to a lifesaving green girdle and directions to the Green Chapel. If the castle indeed represents what Gawain likes, then Gawain likes softness. Not that the idea of softness is an unambiguous good to him. As our own dreams are rarely unalloyed pleasure or pain, but an ambiguous com-

pound of both in which desire and dread meet, so too this castle for
Gawain.

In the castle, where the word "free" is more frequent than "stiff,"
Gawain experiences an environment of ease. Despoiled of his armor,
he receives a robe whose "flowing skirts" (865) contrast to the frozen
water of his last wintery night. "All his glowing and lovely limbs [are
exposed] underneath" (868). His new clothes make him seem "ver-
nal" and himself the bearer of spring, with its implications of warmth,
growth, fecundity, and sensuality (866). To add softness to softness,
Gawain, seated by a chimney on a quilt-covered, cushioned chair, is
wrapped in an ermine mantle and served a warm meal of his favorite
foods. When he retires, it is a bed "full soft" (1120). And there is a
lady, "fairest of hair, of flesh & of face," who, like the castle, conforms to his desires:[24] "Her breast & her bright throat, bare displayed, / Shone sheerer than snow shed on hills" (942–45, 955–56).
Gawain thinks she is "lickerous . . . to like" (968), suggesting that he
finds her another form of nurture.[25]

Yet Gawain's ambiguous feelings towards the woman, and perhaps
towards his desires generally, seem to be represented by the old and
loathsome crone who accompanies her.[26] The old woman's "milk-
white" veil suggests an aged nurse. The older companion thus might
represent what has become a terrifying sense of maternal nurturing
that shadows all his pleasures connected with nurturing. The ancient
mother also represents the other repressed aspects of erotic drives:
birth, nursing, age, death. She is a memento mori or *amoris*. Inhibi-
tions such as those represented by the ancient mother apparently me-
diate Gawain's desires. For instance, the snowy whiteness of the desirable woman associates her with the inhospitable world of Gawain's
journey; thus the metaphor for physical perfection also suggests a
monitory image of distance and hardness. Gawain's comparison of the
whiteness of the lady's breasts to cold snow imperfectly veils his interest in the hidden hills on which the snow lies. Gawain finds the "slot"
a place of intense desire and dread, and the images that cluster around
this emblem of vulnerability, softness, nurture suggest an uneasy alli-
ance in the ideal male's mind between maternal nurture and sexual
desire, a relaxation of distinctions that could bring joy or death. In
the final and successful seduction attempt the lady returns in this first
costume.

Gawain's liking calls forth the soft environment, and his developing passivity seems appropriate for that environment. It is interesting, therefore, that his society's prohibitions against this environment actually encourage his passivity. For Gawain uses passivity to help him distance himself morally from his pleasures. Because Gawain permits himself to view the lady as the cause of his desires, as an active agent, Gawain believes that the young creature attacks him: her visits parallel the hunting scenes and partially invert the relationship of pursuer to pursued and the imagery of love portrayed in them.[27] However, the poet insists that the castle and its contents merely manifest Gawain's desires. His passivity, then, is simultaneously distancing and enticing, cold and warm, hard and soft.

Throughout the scenes in Bercilak's castle, Gawain fears the lady's ability to soften him and thus to efface his masculinity and his moral rigor. He sees her as the active agent and himself as the passive victim. Such masculine fear underlies many medieval works.[28] Throughout *The Art of Courtly Love*, for example, and especially in book 3, "The Rejection of Love," Andreas argues that women act as immoral agents, forcing men to submit passively to desire. Love, according to Andreas, enslaves men to women and thus lowers men to the level of beasts.[29] For Andreas love is a criminal excess that leads to others, such as perjury, homicide, and war. So Andreas writes about even sexual reproduction: "Many evils come from love, but I do not see that anything that is good for men comes from it; that delight of the flesh which we embrace with such great eagerness is not in the nature of a good, but rather, as men agree, it is a damnable sin which even in married persons is scarcely to be classed among the venial faults which are not sins, according to the word of the prophet, who said, 'For behold I was conceived in iniquities and in sins did my mother conceive me'" (193–94). Along with moral weakness sex brings physical weakness: "By love and the work of Venus men's bodies are weakened, and so they are made less powerful in warfare. . . . Since, therefore, bodily strength is a great and especial gift to man, you will do wrong if you strive after things which can for any reason cause this particular gift to fail in you or to be in any way decreased" (198–99).[30] Sex also causes mental weakness.

In sum, loving women robs men of their hardiness. Men become soft and women rule them.[31] *The Romance of the Rose* echoes the moral about the distance that a knight should preserve between himself and all women:

All damsels and all dames
He ought to honor, but small confidence
Repose in them, for no one is too good,
However she may seem. Such gentleman
Should have the name of true gentility.[32]

In this section, entitled "Nature Discusses Gentility," the distance between men and women defines "gentility."

In Chrétien's *Perceval* and Wolfram's redaction, however, Gornemant of Gohort's niece is not held in moral reprobation when she
comes uninvited to Perceval's room. Perceval invites her to share his
bed, she accepts, and later they marry.[33] In fact, in the Perceval stories,
while knights soften through the agency of women, those tales do
not present feminine-identified places of softness and masculine-
identified places of hardness antithetically. They are presented anti-
phonally, exclusive but related responses to each other, morally equal
but opposed. In Chrétien's *Perceval,* when Perceval decides to leave
home to become a knight, his mother has good reason to dissuade
him, for, as we learn, Perceval's father and brothers have all died in
feats of knighthood. As Perceval rides away, ignoring the calls to return, his mother collapses and dies. Ironically, Perceval's quests and
adventures eventually arise from his desire to regain the home he had
left. For Perceval, home remains incomplete when it comprises just
mother and child; yet his leaving simply adds to the pattern of
destruction.

Perceval's case suggests that men of his era, culture, and station
could not enjoy both masculinity and home. As children they seem to
have been taught that women do not allow boys to become men, partially because manhood was defined as something that occurred outside home. *The Romance of the Rose,* for instance, shows this specifically in the case of Gawain, "Who from the cradle practiced all his
life / Nobility, largesse, and chivalry, / Nor e'er was pleased to take
ignoble ease, / But rather was a man before his time" (397). "From
the cradle," "before his time," a male child finds that the ideals of
masculinity invade his place and time of nurture, cast him out of
home, away from women, harden him. As we have seen in *Sir Gawain*
too, in displacing the virtues of the cradle, masculinity posits itself as
an antithesis that coopts the rhetoric of birth, transforms the activities
of home, and uses those new activities, in part, to satisfy and repress
the ones that have been displaced. And yet, in both the Perceval and

Gawain stories, home, which masculinity has made unattainable, remains the object of knightly longing.

Moreover, knighthood, which is the mechanism of escape from home, paradoxically is also the mechanism by which longing for home is expressed. As the only mode for effective masculine action, knighthood becomes the only available means by which men can recover what their masculinity has displaced. For the male so defined, taking ease requires vigilance, no lying down. When what have been marked as masculine values and actions replace what have been marked as feminine values, the soft reappears as something hard, even when men directly take on the feminine role, as in the knight's relationship to Christ. For example, in *The Art of Courtly Love*, the masculine bride awaits the "Bridegroom" Christ in a non-feminine way: his lamp filled, his room illuminant, neither sitting or lying. He stands ever roused, ready and watchful. He labors (211–12). Thus the age portrayed masculine displacements of nurture, breeding, and gentility.[34] Of course, knighthood thus circumscribed could never recover home, and home could never recover men. That is Perceval's problem: he cannot use his knighthood to return home, because his knighthood destroys home, a home that in part is not a home because it contains no men.

Within these paradoxes of masculine and feminine, knighthood and home, hard and soft, sleeplessness and sleeping, Gawain first encounters the woman who appears as both dreaded and desired temptress. Gawain lies in bed—passive, prone, the antithesis of the "stiff man" waiting for Christ the lover. As "in softness he slumbers," Gawain hears the woman steal to his door and rouses to find her "full softly on the bedside" (1182ff.). Her first words laughingly remind him of the ease, openness, and thus vulnerability in which she finds him: "you are a sleeper unsly that one may slide hither" (1209). And she adds, "You are welcome to my body / Your own pleasure to take. / It behooves me of fine force / Your servant to be & shall" (1237–40). Although Gawain laughs at this and states, graciously, "I shall follow your will & that likes me well" (1214), he also wishes to rise from the bed and dress. When the knight acts "with defence" (1282) to this "attack," he seems to fear the passivity of his role, the sense of imprisonment and tameness. Yet, although Gawain is disquieted by the encounter, there is nothing to suggest that he does not enjoy it.[35]

In this first encounter with Bercilak's lady, Gawain experiences the tension between his desire for the ease of sexual union and his dread of transgressing knighthood. In parodying the nocturnal tryst between Perceval and Gornemant of Gohort's niece, the encounter seems to fit an acceptable pattern of chivalric romance. From the beginning, wish-fulfillment aspects predominate: she comes to him in sleep; she is soft like sleep; she may even be a dream. In context of the imagery of love that the companion hunting scene provides, Bercilak's lady acts like the doe, the female lover. However, Gawain suspects that the lady's doe is forcing him to act the hunter. In this masculine reconstruction of seduction, the hunter is also the victim, while the would-be victim is also the hunter—each alternately masculine and feminine. Although he announces that his will and hers are the same, Gawain feels himself victimized by the desire that she represents and that he also has conjured.

In the second encounter the phantom of Gawain's desire proposes that he may reconcile the stiffness of knighthood with the softness of ease: "You are stiff enough to constrain with strength if you like / If any were so villainous that you deny would" (1496–97). The knight rejects this line of argument: "Thus to him pleaded that free one & tempted him often / For to have won him to woo [or woe]— whatsoever she thought else—/ But he defended himself" (1549–51). Yet, even as he defends himself against succumbing to the woman's advances, the game remains for them both a satisfying flirtation: "He defended himself so fair that no fault appeared, / No evil on either half. They knew only bliss" (1551–52). Despite all his manly posturing, the undercurrent of sexual excitement arouses them both. Gawain has clearly progressed in his enjoyment: he remains hard, wary, and virtuous at the same time that he is titillated and titillating. And this becomes evident in the evening. Warmed and softened by fire, meal, song, and dance, the two continue to flirt:

> & ever our love-like knight the lady beside
> Such semblance toward him seemly she made
> With still stealthy countenance that stalwart to please
> That all wondering was the wight & wroth with himself.
> But he would not for his nurture turn against her
> But dealt with her all daintily howsoever the deed turned
>   towards.
>
>   (1657–63)

The lady's pleasing countenance suggests enjoyment of an intimate knowledge that she and the knight alone share. Yet Gawain is confused and angry with himself, for he wants to stop enjoying this flirtation, but he cannot. His defense here is like that of the morning.[36] Willingly against his will, by means of his very defenses, he is allowing himself to draw closer and give in.

The growing arousal promoted and forestalled by Gawain's defense culminates in the last visitation. After a night of restless dreaming, Gawain sees her as he had first in church:

> so glorious & gaily attired
> So faultless of her features & of so fine hues
> That welling joy warmed his heart
> With smooth smiling & soft they melt into mirth
> So that all was bursting bliss & happiness between them
> & joy.
>
> (1760–65)

The lady embodies a sensual experience that throughout the poem has been identified with repressed "nurture": "welling joy," "warm," "heart," "smooth," "soft." Characteristically, the poet's warning heightens the sensual and sexual tension of the moment: "Great peril between them stood" (1768). He continues to build the sense of arousal and imminent sexual contact: "For that princess of prize pressed against him so thick, / Urged him so nigh the thread, that need him behooved / Either to latch her love or loathly refuse" (1770–72). Through sounds, images, and secondary meanings the passage accumulates a sense of Gawain and the woman's pressing together, coming to the very edge of gratification: "thick" and "thread"; "urged," "nigh," and "need"; "latch," "love," and "loathly refuse." To withdraw now would be repulsive, Gawain realizes, as to continue would be loathsome. "God shield me," he cries in his dilemma (1776), re-arming himself through his invocation, hardening just when he would have softened.

In this scene the re-arming stiffness of the hero clearly displaces sexual energy. In Gawain's world, where sex is thought to make men passive, soft, and feminine,[37] where men do not lust but become the helpless victims of women's lust, to keep from being aroused involuntarily, men willfully take on the characteristics of their aroused sex organs. They are to be continually "aroused" in the sense of "wakeful" as they displace the hardness and excitement of their penis to the rest of their muscles in order to protect themselves from softness— which is associated with sexual arousal. This final passage is inflected with nuances of male sexual arousal: "stood," "thick," "thread," all of which suggest that Gawain's penis is stiffening, thickening, and lengthening. "Latch her love" sounds like copulation, "loathly refuse" sounds like ejaculation. His cry "God shield me" seems the groan of orgasm that displaces this subtextual eroticism to a moral, masculine hardening.

In this context the woman's next lines counter the stances of "enduring" man: "blame you deserve / If you love not that life that you lie next to / Before all the wights in the world wounded in heart" (1779–81). As the representative of what men desire, the lady of the castle presses home what Gawain has lost: the soft, warm, and open, that which is precious just because it is vulnerable to wounding. Here Bercilak's lady becomes the victim. Her "wounded in heart" echoes the wound that the boar receives through his one soft spot, recalling too that the hunters mirror their victims, separated only by the illusion of distance. She reminds us of the earlier theme: that the "life" of intimacy, procreation, warmth and softness, while fragile, not only allows endurance, but also makes endurance estimable. Of course, Gawain could not accept this "life" of his desire without great blame to his knighthood. But we can imagine that it is not without effort and even pain that he pulls back from the encounter with this other life.

Yet even as the sexual dimension of his encounter with the lady closes, Gawain's desire for "life" that she and the castle represent remains strong. Therefore, when she offers, he accepts her green girdle that represents "life," a girdle referred to ambiguously as beautiful, delicate, injurious: a "love-lace," a "cut."[38] The girdle, which is fastened around the lady's "sides," under her mantle, in a warm and intimate place, is green like growing things, implying fecundity. Its circle suggests female genitals and regenerating cycles of seasons. The girdle, looped around her ribs, over her heart, next to her breast is the final sign of the soft, the vulnerable—as if a softer, more feminine, more fecund life can be lifesaving, as if hardness were not all. The girdle is an interesting symbol of life, for through it Gawain is both spared and not spared, triumphant and shamed. The sign of this "life" is a "lace," a cut, perhaps the navel, the emblem of recurrent nativity, of having parents and being destined to be parents, of the need for nurture, of the need for softness, of life in time, fleshiness, impending death.

Gawain is punished, ultimately, for not keeping his word to his friend, for not exposing their common "lace." Instead Gawain tries to cover up his own frailty, his love of life. Yet, as the Green Knight says, "for you loved your life, the less I you blame" (2368). And within his armor Gawain feels weak and shamed: "That other stiff man in study stood a great while / So aggrieved for grief he trembled within / All the blood of his breast bled into his face / That all he shrank for shame that the other talked" (2369–72). His quivering, the blood of his breast, his grief, all suggest this vulnerable life and the shame he, inside his stiff cover, feels at it.

Gawain's journey from hardness to softness, a journey into the male heart, dreams, and fears of his age, is further defined by his relationship to the Green Knight, whose appearance precipitates Gawain's journey. That green can represent both death and fertility suggests that the two are not strictly dissociable in the Gawain-poet's society.[39] Moreover, that the narrative was shaped by combining a tale dealing with death and a separate one dealing with fertility reinforces that notion.[40] Nor is such a combination of death and fertility unfamiliar.[41] Thus in the tale the Green Knight seems to represent indeterminately both death and fertility, insofar as birth implies death, as the nativity of Christ in which the narrative is set suggests. This connection helps illuminate why life was thought to require hardness. If one wished to endure, one needed to step outside of the circle of birth and death. This also explains why nurture becomes hardened in Gawain's society, for nurture symbolizes all time-related processes that make one vulnerable. Because the ideals of endurance repress the processes of birth and death, for men of Gawain's world, "life" had developed two subtle shadow meanings, each capable of startling men with anxieties about the other.

A feast of birth celebrated by Camelot's stiff men calls forth the Green Knight, who, as a folk figure of fertility, shocks the company by his phallic virility. In a world prizing masculine stiffness, the Green Knight displays undoubted virility with his broad shoulders, huge thighs, and small waist and stomach; in fact, "it seemed as no man might / Under his dint endure" (201–2). Yet, despite this apparent fierceness, he appears connected with peace:

> Yet had he no helmet nor hauberk neither,
> Nor any breastplate nor any piece that pertained to arms,
> Nor any shaft nor any shield to shove or to smite,
> But in his one hand he had a holly bob
> That is greatest in green when groves are bare.
>
> (203–7)

And his words confirm this meaning:

> You may be sure by this branch that I bear here
> That I pass as in peace & no plight seek,
> For had I journeyed arrayed in fighting wise
> I have a hauberk at home & a helmet both,
> A shield & sharp spear shining bright,
> And other weapons to wield I know well also
> But as I wish no war my weeds are softer.
>
> (265–71)

The Green Knight plays his game to test those whom he has heard are "stiffest under steel-gear" and "manliest" (260, 261). However, his test requires passivity, acceptance, and resignation. In the Green Knight's game, moreover, unlike the Christmas joust or war itself, none wins or loses. This is beyond the imagination of the court. That the Green Knight survives without struggle, through softness, through passivity, indicates the qualities he represents—qualities the court cannot understand, qualities they fear. Peace and passivity frighten knighthood. The Green Knight as a masculine fertility figure offers an uncanny and fearful prospect: peaceful virility.

The tremendous size, strength, and power of the Green Knight, of course, also frightens the court. But the Green Knight never uses these attributes, so that they seem simply to represent the importance and power of the forces he represents—death and sexuality—and their "natural" connection with men. Through this portrait the poet develops a masculine imagery for forces that have been repressed in masculine ideals and defined as feminine. The Green Knight gives those forces positive value; he portrays masculine sexuality.

Indeed, the Green Knight has specific phallic resemblances. The knight and horse are said to resemble each other: "great & thick / A steed full stiff to restrain" (175–76). Bushy hair and beard encircle the Green Knight's head, and "The stiff man him before stood on high" (332). These glimpses invite us to see the Green Knight as an erect penis taunting a silent, shamed, and fearful court, a court catching similar uncanny glimpses. Moreover, like the *pudenda* (the place of shame) and the *os innominata* (the unnameable bone), the Green Knight has no proper name nor nameable dwelling, although any knight can find him. He tells Gawain, "thou shall seek me thyself whereso thou hopes / I may be found upon land" (395–96). Even after he announces that many know him as the knight of the green chapel, "[t]o what region he went knew none there, / No more than they understood from whence" (460–61), a line oddly repeated when Gawain and the Green Knight part for the last time. So the male genitals are an unacknowledged but well-known country. And its representative is feared, in part because the associations of peace, passivity, and softness, of being a willing victim, cluster around male genital desire as portrayed in the story-poem, in part because the penis, like the Green Knight, can stand up in the middle of any banquet, asserting what in Camelot was a primitive, powerful, and frightening presence.[42]

In this connection, when Gawain claims the diversion because he is the weakest at court, Gawain's suggestions of latent feminine qualities creates a tableau representing the masculine view of the threat of women in sexual play: when the feminine Gawain plays with the phallic Green knight, he cuts off its head. This picture suggests that orgasm is castration, loss of reason and life, all of which cluster around the masculine views of heterosexual engagement in Gawain's society. For a man to engage in sexual activities is to be vulnerable, and vulnerable to a woman who, at the very least, will trim his hair (as in the case of Samson), thus depriving him of his strength and masculinity. In further loops of irony, Gawain's femininity is another masculine substitution in the feared domain of softness. In this substitution one finds Gawain using softness as a disguise for a hard masculine power so that he can conquer. This is also the implication of Gawain's earlier mock modesty: "I am the weakest," for which read "I am the strongest." Under the guise of weakness, Gawain wishes to retain his hardness; under the guise of friendliness, he wishes to do the unfriendly thing; under the guise of peacefulness, he seeks to kill.

This of course only mirrors his anxieties about the Green Knight's softness, friendliness, peacefulness. In this encounter, we see the men of Gawain's time and place encountering themselves. Through this we can begin to see that the idea of softness is thoroughly mitigated by the intrusion of masculine uneasiness that turns even the soft into a disguise for the hard.

At the same time, the Green Knight shows that the softness that men construct includes them. Considering this, Gawain's imposition of the knightly ethic on the sexual reality does not succeed. As Arthur, speaking more wisely than well, states, "& as thou foolishly has asked, it behooves to find" (324). A "fool" fits the sport, for sex is literally folly, "fool" being related to pejorative Latin and Italian terms for the scrotum. Cleverness is not needed, desirable, or successful for erotic play. The game is "nice" in the archaic sense of that word, "not wise": it literally and figuratively requires no brains. Seen in this light, the decapitation of the Green Knight suggests that when you engage in sexual play you "lose your head," but that you do not die when you "lose your head"—when you have an orgasm. Nor do you die when you engage in "heedless" activities. But men do confront their fear of death and they are brought into closer contact with mortality.

However, by being heedless men also may gain or renew life—like the holly, like the resurrected Green Knight, like the birth/death of Christ—through procreation, through softness. It is a risk. It requires passivity, not hardness, and a courage that no one in King Arthur's court has. It is, the Green Knight shows, difficult to be soft. Softness requires much more courage than hardness does. For one imbued in the masculine ethos of Arthur's court, to be soft means that one must endure shame, guilt, and a sense of one's own mortality. Of this truth the great exemplar is Christ, and his season is the one at which the Green Knight comes. So too Gawain's trials show that it is difficult to be hard, for life yields more pain than simple hardness can cope with. Hardness can not hold back death, relieve loneliness, or heal wounds.

Thus, Gawain's journey of following his sexuality ultimately leads to the chapel of the Green Knight, which, like other hills in the story, seems to represent a female anatomy displaced and repressed. The chapel is "a little mound on a field" (2172). More, "it had a hole on the end & on either side." This mound is covered with a pubescent growth. And "all was hollow within, nothing but an old cave / Or crevice of an old crag" (2181–83). The Green Chapel seems pelvic. Certainly if this description pictures the female genitalia—the proper home for the Green Knight ("Well it beseems the wight wrinkled in green" [2191])—the view is a fearful masculine one: an old cave, an old hollowed-out place, an old crevice. And as Gawain waits his thoughts become even harsher: "Here might about midnight / The devil his matins tell" (2187–88). Of course, as Andreas, echoing St. Jerome, tells us, "The Devil is really the author of love and lechery" (195). Gawain goes even further: "It is the cursedest / coarsest kirk that ever I came in" (2196)—no twentieth-century pun intended.

This view of female sexuality seems to connect, not with Bercilak's lady, but with the ancient dame, her companion. And it is quite fitting that it should, for while Gawain's desire aimed towards the young woman, it fled the old, as the same woman in a separate guise. In this way too the connection of female sexuality and witchcraft or devil worship, so evident in this passage, makes sense.[43] The passage evinces an underlying Arthurian dread of the female genitalia as a wrinkled crevice out of which and into which men crawl.

To strengthen this point, the Green Knight reveals that the old woman was Gawain's maternal aunt and so Gawain's surrogate mother—Morgan the Goddess. If, as has been alleged, Bercilak's lady was Morgan in another guise, then the seduction was incestuous, one played between mother and child. This would seem to strengthen Gawain's mental linking of sexual and infantile desires. In this configuration too, Bercilak becomes Gawain's father, threatening punishment for the boy's sexual desire and saving him. Bercilak in age has the relation of father to Gawain, and as instructor and punisher he fulfills that role. Moreover, this reading is in keeping with the *Caradoc* redaction from which, in part, the story derives.[44]

The old woman, who seems to personify for Gawain the disgusting and repulsive aspects of sexuality—its infantile associations, its reproductive consequences, its temporal inevitabilities—stands in a similar kin relationship to both Gawain and Arthur, suggesting that both Arthur and Gawain have her blood in them, blood that to them seems procreative, erotic, irrational, and temporal. In this context, that Morgana La Fay has been the guide to the adventure seems fitting, she of whom Bercilak states, "Wields none such high haughtiness / That she can not make full tame" (2454–55). She has wanted to test the *surquidre* of the knights, to deprive them of their "wits," and to scare Guenevere to death with the spectacle of the Green Knight, all of which could be conceived to happen when the court is confronted with their repressed version of genital eroticism. Moreover, she attained her supernatural powers, neither from books nor from the example of others, but from "ma[king] love full sweet sometime / With that cunning clerk" Merlin (2449–50), a method of acquiring knowledge suitable to the knowledge acquired. The figure of Morgana connects sexuality and irrationality and shows them to be powerful and ominous forces in the lives of men. And so, in the mind of the poet and the court to whom and about which he is writing, she would be, for she represents powers that knights must constantly try to restrain but which, living in the world, they cannot.

Among other lessons that Gawain learns is that men must acknowledge the full extent of their being in order to have some power over it. To pretend that his sexuality does not exist is to allow himself to fall into traps that his desires set:

> For care of thy knock, cowardice me taught
> To accord me with covetise, my kind to forsake
> That is largesse & loyalty that belongs to knights.
> Now am I faulty & false & afraid have been ever.
>
> (2379–82)

He sees that his softness has made him act with *covetise*—desire, lust. He clings to the notion, even here, that his "kind," his nature, is that of a knight; yet he acknowledges (if one places the period after "ever") that he is afraid he has always been faulty and false. This, indeed, seems to be what he finds out: that despite the "nature" of a knight, he has another "nature" that will undermine his knighthood if he allows it to.[45] He fears sensuality, mortality, eroticism, and softness generally, yet these compound his being, as the "love-lace" must remind him—the green girdle and the scar.

Yet while the poet points to this dysfunctional dichotomy of hard and soft that men create and live, he can offer no escape, save through the mystery of the life and death of Christ. When it comes to dealing with earthly matters, he seems trapped in the same web of language and association that Gawain is. His language, while acknowledging the exigencies of "softness," displays what throughout the poem is a masculine doubleness that turns back on softness and undoes it. We find such doubleness, for instance, when after having described Gawain in a soft, flowing robe, with the face of spring, and glowing limbs moving freely under the garment, the poet comments:

> That a comelier knight never Christ made
>   they thought.
> Whence in world he were
> It seemed as he might
> Be prince without peer
> In field where wild men fought.
>
> (869–74)

The images of war remind the listener that, regardless of how pleasant life seems at one moment, it is at the same time unpleasant. One may dally in bed, but beyond the walls the hunt goes on, a hunt that uncannily resembles dallying. This is the method of the poet: not to make choices but to pose problems. The poem operates paratactically, by juxtaposition, by constantly exposing, as if to make a choice would be to choose finally between hardening and softening and thus would be to harden the poem.

While the poem seems to approach its own ideal of the cyclical, of a transcendental temporality, the poet ultimately, like Gawain, chooses the knightly ideal. His own words about his verses show this:

> I shall tell it at once as in town I heard
>   with tongue
> As it is staid & standing
> In story stiff & strong
> With loyal letters locked
> In this land as it has been long.
>
> (31–36)

In *Sir Gawain* men may desire "softness"—a category that contains the idealized joyous moments of "home," with its infancy, intimacy, and fragility, its desired moments of eroticism and sensuality—but they recognize the cost: the loss of manhood, the disdain of society, and the imperilment of body. The soft becomes so highly desirable in part because the ideals of hardness prohibit it while also taking it over, underscoring its importance.

A sense of the flesh and the senses arises within the armor of endurance. A series of behaviors devolve on men as the result of the roles which they have been taught: fear of intimacy/infancy, fear of erotic heedlessness, fear of disclosure, fear of passivity. So men in Gawain's world, separated from nurturing women and homes that include men and taught instead by hard fathers outside the home in a hard society, have come to inhabit a world that, by calling forth and repressing the world of "soft" childhood, fills that world with uncanny reverberations.

Gawain's is not a world that men find joy inhabiting, and yet it is the world that, given the chance to choose, they cannot but choose, for that world already defines what they see, limits their perception and their expression, their choices. This is the world that Beowulf's dissociation of home and society has made Gawain heir to. Caught in the trammels of a design he is forced to reproduce, Gawain and the other knights make a world where toughness pays, but so do the tough, in which softness is a powerful and seductive shadow-presence, feared, despised, desired—and remembered. In Gawain's world men express the joyous recollection of birth by a show of swords and a spate of threats. But as Gawain says to the Green Knight, if I were invulnerable, I would not fear being soft. Ironically, if he had not feared being soft, he would not have been so vulnerable.

Notes

1. In Beowulf's society "home" comprised people (*folc*), treasure (*hord*), and town (*burh*), but not household as such.

2. Line numbers refer to the Charles Moorman edition in *Works of the Gawain Poet* (Jackson: University Press of Mississippi, 1977). In translating this work, I have tried to stay close to the original language, merely modernizing spelling where possible, making substitutions where the root word no longer exists in English or where I have wished to emphasize one particular meaning.

3. The circumcision motif is connected with spiritual rebirth. On circumcision see, e.g., Richard Allen Shoaf, *Poem as Green Girdle: Commercium in "Sir Gawain and the Green Knight"* (Gainesville: University Press of Florida, 1984), 3, 53–54. As the venerable Bede writes in *On the Feast of Our Lord's Circumcision,* "Our true and complete circumcision" will take place "on the day of judgment, all souls having put off the corruption of the flesh" (qtd. in Leo Steinberg, *The Sexuality of Christ in Renaissance Art and in Modern Oblivion* [New York: Pan-

theon, 1983], 53). In Augustine's *On Marriage and Concupiscence*, circumcision, like baptism, signifies a reborn soul cleansed of original sin (Steinberg 50). The idea of spiritual rebirth in Gawain is commonly seen as an important theme, most recently in Victor Yelverton Haines, *Fortunate Fall of Sir Gawain: the Typology of "Sir Gawain and the Green Knight"* (Washington: University Press of America, 1982), and Lynn Staley Johnson, *The Voice of the Gawain-Poet* (Madison: University of Wisconsin Press, 1984). Johnson interprets these lines as expressing "true renewal, a model for the process of spiritual rebirth" (67). While the allusion to Gawain's birth may suggest rebirth, my own reading suggests that rather than supplanting the time of birth, this new moment suggests the perfect joy of that time, a joy not recoverable even at the moment of the cut.

4. The first discussion of this theme occurs in Charles Moorman, "Myth and Medieval Literature: *Sir Gawain and the Green Knight*," *Mediaeval Studies* 18 (1958): 158–72; Moorman finds this ritual admission to chivalry a ritual admission to manhood.

5. The passivity necessary to survive has long been acknowledged in *Gawain* criticism, but it has been connected with a movement from the active chivalric life to a contemplative spiritual life, as in Ina Rae Hark, "Gawain's Passive Quest," *Comitatus* 5 (1974): 1–3; see also Haines, *Fortunate Fall*, 103–5, and Johnson, *Voice of the Gawain-Poet*, 67, 86ff.

6. This is a well-known motif, first proposed by Jesse Weston in *The Quest for the Holy Grail* (New York: Barnes & Noble, 1964) and *From Ritual to Romance* (New York: Peter Smith, 1941). For important contributions see R. S. Loomis, *The Celtic Myth and Arthurian Romance* (New York: Columbia University Press, 1927); Johns Spiers, *Medieval English Poetry: The Non-Chaucerian Tradition* (London: Faber & Faber, 1957).

7. The idea of the contingency in life that underlies the code of knighthood and calls it into question has been remarked upon in a number of recent studies: see Wendy Clein, *The Concepts of Chivalry in "Sir Gawain and the Green Knight"* (Norman, Ok.: Pilgrim Books, 1987); Shoaf, *Poem as Green Girdle,* 7. In many writings, the vulnerability of Gawain demonstrated his insufficiency as a knight: see William Goldhurst, "The Green and the Gold: The Major Theme of *Sir Gawain and the Green Knight*," *College English* 20 (1958): 61–65; Donald Howard, "Renaissance World-Alienation," *The Darker Vision of the Renaissance: Beyond the Fields of Reason,* ed. Robert Kinsman (Berkeley: University of California Press, 1974): 64–75; Johnson, *Voice of the Gawain-Poet:* "Heroes may choose . . . to fall . . . through ignorance, self-interest, and luxury" (91).

8. *Dryȝtyn*, meaning Lord, suggests a soldier. Its connection with the Old English *dreogan* implies hardness. See "dree" in Ernest Weekley, *An Etymological Dictionary of Modern English* (New York: Dover Publications, 1967) and *The Oxford Dictionary of English Etymology*, ed. C. T. Onions (Oxford: Oxford University Press, 1976).

9. For Johnson, the poem is predominantly about time—cyclical, degenerative, redemptive (*Voice of the Gawain-Poet*, 39ff.). She sees the movement from a temporal perspective to a spiritual one (86). Traditional studies that emphasize a vegetation myth also assume the centrality of time.

10. The lines further imply that through the treachery of men Troy has been destroyed. The story, like Gawain's, involves a woman; moreover, although Antenor was at one time honored for his righteous counsel to return Helen and reconcile with the Greeks, such weakness turned him into the type of the traitor in the Middle Ages.

11. The hunting scenes are perhaps among the most analyzed; however, they are primarily analyzed in their contrapuntal relationship to the bedroom scenes. The original article about the precision of the hunting scenes and their significance was written by H. L. Savage: see "The Significance of the Hunting Scenes in *Sir Gawain and the Green Knight*," *JEGP* 27 (1928): 1–5. See also Peter McClure, "Gawain's *Mesure*: the Significance of the Three Hunts in *Sir Gawain and the Green Knight*," *Neophilologus* 57 (1973): 375–87; Avril Henry, "The Temptation and the Hunt in *Sir Gawain and the Green Knight*," *Medium Aevum* 45 (1976): 187–99; W. R. J. Barron, *Trawthe and Treason: The Sin of Gawain Reconsidered* (Manchester, U.K.: Manchester University Press, 1980). The latest works do not seem to have progressed much beyond reiteration of the original insights: see Gerald Morgan, "The Action of the Hunting and Bedroom Scenes in *Sir Gawain and the Green Knight*," *Medium Aevum* 56 (1987): 202, 213–15.

12. Lawrence Besserman, "The Idea of the Green Knight," *ELH* 53 (1986): 219–39.

13. One may say that Gawain "finds" these foes, that they are not inclined to find him, that the battles and the necessary hardness are the result of his desire, his actions, his decisions, that the world is hard because he has made it such. And this is at least partially true. But however Gawain and this harsh environment are brought together, Gawain's hardiness and his iron armor undoubtedly save him.

14. "The poem dramatizes Gawain's discovery of the tensions inherent in his personal ideology" (Clein, *The Concepts of Chivalry*, 37).

15. Steinberg sees death and generation as the definitive attributes of incarnate existence for Renaissance artists and others (*The Sexuality of Christ*, 13ff.)

16. This might remind one of Clint Eastwood, whose line "make my day" is roughly equivalent to the good humor inspired by this scene. Arthur, then, seems close to a type who in our society is alternately worshiped and despised: the wise-cracking tough guy—perhaps more James Bond than Dirty Harry, but the same.

17. Shoaf (*Poem as Green Girdle*, 8) suggests "nurture" is a transactional sign that mediates the ideal and the experiential. Thus as nurturer Gawain "incarnates the ideal." Gawain's posture here would be in keeping with the one Caroline Bynum elaborates in her fascinating book, *Jesus as Mother: Studies in the Spirituality of the High Middle Ages* (Berkeley: University of California Press, 1982). In this reading, Mary is no longer maternal but transacts the maternal, not as experiential mothering, but as ideal mothering incarnate. Shoaf does not remark on the odd subversion of one group's signification by another—that is, female by male.

18. Caroline Bynum suggests that Christ was maternalized among the Cistercians because they sought to reject actual mothers (*Jesus as Mother*, 145) and displace personal affective ties to the community (166). As she notes, frequently those whose mothers were most influential become virulent antifeminists.

19. Such behavior piques the ever-piqued Kay in Chrétien de Troyes's *Perceval*:

> Sir Gawain addressed the King: "Sire, so help me God, it is not right, as you know and have always said, for one knight to disturb another's thoughts for any cause. . . . Perhaps the knight was brooding over some loss or was cast down because his lady had been stolen from him. Now, if it is your pleasure, I will go to observe him, and if I find that he has stopped brooding, I will request him to come here."
> At these words Kay broke out in anger: "Ah, Sir Gawain, you expect to lead the knight here by the hand, even if he is reluctant. That will be a gallant deed. . . . Indeed you could carry out that errand in a silken gown, without drawing sword or breaking lance. You may well pride yourself that if your tongue is able to say: 'Sir, God save you and give you joy and health!' he will do your will. . . . Then people will say: 'Now Sir Gawain is waging a fierce battle!'"
> "Ah, Sir Kay!" said Gawain, "you could surely speak more kindly. Do you think to get your revenge by pouring out your fury on me? In faith, good friend, I will bring him back, and without a broken arm or a dislocated collarbone, for I do not like such wages." (Trans. Roger Sherman Loomis. *Medieval Romances*, Ed. Roger Sherman Loomis and Laura Hibbard Loomis [New York: Random House, 1957], 76–77.)

20. This line is usually translated, "What may man do but try?" "Trial" is another name for experience.

21. See *The Pearl* in *Works of the Gawain Poet*, ed. Moorman, line 1408.

22. As Charles Moorman writes in his note on this line, "the main purpose of the image is surely to suggest a magnificent imagined artifice, a child's dream of a castle" (*Works of the Gawain Poet*, 802n). Larry D. Benson, too, talks in his book about the dream-like nature of the narrative in this part (*Art and Tradition in Sir Gawain and the Green Knight* [New Brunswick, N.J.: Rutgers University Press, 1965]).

23. The meaning of Bercilak's castle has been variously assigned. Howard, for example, finds it the immoral worldly ("Renaissance World-Alienation," 66–69). On the other hand, Robert Blanch and Julian Wasserman think that "Hautdesert is founded upon good will." Yet for them that means "a principle of limited volition or will harnessed by reason and modification" ("To '*Ouertake your wylle*': Volition and Obligation in *Sir Gawain and the Green Knight*," *Neophilologus* 70 [1986]: 121). My own account suggests that will is not restrained here.

24. It has been argued that women have been formed to male desire in courtly literature: see Joan Ferrante, *Woman as Image in Medieval Literature* (New York: Columbia University Press, 1975), 95.

25. This sense is still retained in the word "likkerish," which quite naturally became associated with "liquorish" or "sweet."

26. It is common to find these two as aspects of the same person, a point made originally in 1903 by Lucy Allen Paton. Her studies in *The Fairy Mythology of Arthurian Romance*, 2d ed., ed. Roger Sherman Loomis (New York: Burt Franklin, 1960), discusses the various roles and shapes that Morgain assumed (see, e.g., 8). See also Mother A. Carson, "Morgain la Fee as the Principle of Unity in *Sir Gawain and the Green Knight*," *MLQ* 23 (1962): 5–9.

27. For instance, the doe or hind of the first hunt should represent the beloved female whom the male lover pursues. Here, however, the woman is the pursuer, Gawain the pursued. See note 11, above.

28. For instance, Jean de Meun's satirical portrait of women painted by the jealous husband in *The Romance of the Rose* (pp. 171–91) exposes this side of women's nature: see E. William Monter, "The Pedestal and the Stake: Courtly Love and Witchcraft," *Becoming Visible: Women in European History*, ed. Renata Bridenthal and Claudia Koonz (Boston: Houghton Mifflin, 1977), 119–36.

29. Andreas Capellanus, *The Art of Courtly Love*, trans. John Jay Parry (New York: W. W. Norton, 1969), 188–97. The transformation of men to beasts gives the trope of Gawain as the hunted a moral grounding quite different from the usual views of the hunt.

30. Since making war is considered particularly masculine and since sexual liaisons make one more prone to war, it would seem that "love" is sinful because it enhances masculinity. Oddly, also, "love" conduces to war while it weakens them so that they cannot fight. Andreas portrays a battlefield filled with aroused men who cannot get their axes up. The odd complexities of all this would be well worth pursuing if length permitted.

31. The actual intention of the "Rejection" has been debated. For an interesting view of women as text and the problems of misogyny, see R. Howard Block, "Medieval Misogyny," *Representations* 20 (1987): 1–24.

32. Jean de Meun and Guillaume de Lorris, *The Romance of the Rose*, trans. Harry W. Robbins, ed. Charles W. Dunn (New York: E. P. Dutton, 1962), 396.

33. "While he slept peacefully, she, who had no defense in the struggle which went on within her, brooded, turning and tossing, till at last she donned a short mantle of scarlet silk over her shift, and set out on a bold enterprise. . . . Leaving her bed, she issued from her chamber, perspiring and trembling in every limb with terror. She came to the bed where the knight was sleeping, wept and sighed deeply, and knelt so that the tears wetted his face; she did not dare to be bolder. At last he woke, startled and wondering how his face was so wet, and found her on her knees beside the bed and her arms around his neck. He had the courtesy to embrace her in turn, and drew her toward him, saying: 'Fair lady, what do you wish? What has brought you here?'

"'Ah, gentle knight, have mercy! I implore you for God's sake and for His Son's not to take me for a vile thing because I have come to you thus, and though I am nearly nude, I have no light, wicked, or coarse design' " (*Medieval Romances*, 40).

34. The picture of a feminized male in relationship to an inspiriting Christ can be found in thirteenth- and fourteenth-century religious writings. Bynum quotes a sermon in which an abbot describes himself in the third person as a woman who, "despite her desire to bask in the bridegroom's presence, . . . is entrusted with cares of begetting and rearing children" (*Jesus as Mother*, 118). Bynum notes that this feminization exists along with a harsh antifeminism and masculinism. Consider this example given by Bynum: "[God the Father] draws [the wretched] into his very bowels and makes them his members. He could not bind us to himself more closely, could not make us more intimate to himself than by incorporating us into himself" (qtd. in Bynum, 121). Here, by implication at least, the incoporation of the wretched into the body of Christ suggests that the suppliants come to share Christ's paternal power. As begetters of good works, the wretched become inseminating "members" of God. At

the heart of the theological trope one finds a sense of men wrestling with maternal and paternal aspects of divinity and of themselves.

35. Joseph Gallagher has shown that Gawain's speeches to the Lady are as erotic as hers to him: see *"Trawthe* and *Luf-Talkyng* in *Sir Gawain and the Green Knight," Neuphilologische Mitteilungen* 78 (1977): 362–76.

36. This phrase is usually translated "however, he turned it aside" or "however, it went against the grain," but it seems to mean "regardless of where her actions were taking them."

37. "Passion" and "passive" share a common link—the root *patior,* which means both "to suffer" and "to undergo." "Passion" has, therefore, often been considered a form of suffering that one was subjected to, rather than a pleasure one initiated.

38. The girdle is said to represent a new covenant, although the meaning of that covenant is disputed. The dominant motif at the end of the poem shifts from shield to girdle: see Donald Howard, "Structures and Symmetry in *Sir Gawain," Speculum* 39 (1964): 425–33. Lynn Johnson finds this a change from the chivalric to the spiritual, although the green girdle signifies that Gawain "defines himself, now, as a man [i.e., human]," the wearing of it shows "his acceptance of the remedy for the human condition, penance" (*Voice of the Gawain-Poet,* 89). This ties the "cut" to the "circumcision" rather than to the whole narrative of birth, ties it to separation rather than the union and separation encoded in the full narrative. The girdle in the story seems to enact a desire for union and a fear of separation.

39. The history of criticism of *Sir Gawain and the Green Knight* is replete with attributions of meaning for the Green Knight. Perhaps the most common—that the Green Knight is a fertility god—has the longest history. In both *The Quest for the Holy Grail* and *From Ritual to Romance* Weston describes the sacrifice of a fertility god that transforms the wasteland from its frozen, dry, hard, sterile aspect to the warm, flowing, soft, fecund land. While in keeping with the kind of imagery, diction, and plot, no such transformation takes place. If the Green Knight represents fertility, that concept has been transformed by the Gawain-poet's society and culture. The opposition of hard and soft, infertile and fertile, is made problematic by the conditions of life and the roles prescribed by society.

Another common theory maintains that the Green Knight represents death: see, for instance, Heinrich Zimmer, *The King and the Corpse: Tales of the Soul's Conquest of Evil,* ed. Joseph Campbell (New York: Pantheon, 1948), 67; J. A. Burrow, *A Reading of "Sir Gawain and the Green Knight"* (New York: Barnes and Noble, 1966), 26–28. Several important pieces of evidence support this position: the traditional association of the color green with death, the fact that the Knight carries a holly sprig, which can represent death, and the fact that the Knight slays but cannot be slain. The text adduces additional supporting information in the tumulus that turns out to be the Green Chapel and in the caution of Gawain's guide who tells him that all who approach the chapel are slain regardless of their age or social position. Yet this theory faces problems similar to the fertility theory. Gawain does not die, nor does the Green Knight take much pleasure in hurting him. Moreover, the Green Knight's anger is mitigated because Gawain loves life.

On the other hand, one cannot say that the story gives an example of how to triumph over death. For Gawain commits, as some have argued, what could have been, considering the position of *troth* in medieval society, a fatal sin. As the poet states, his letters' "loyalty" is a source of their endurance. Yet it is obvious that part of the Green Knight's aspect involves death, or at least fear of death, a sense of mortality.

Another theory identifies the Green Knight with the devil: see Dale B. J. Randall, "Was the Green Knight a Fiend?" *Studies in Philology* 57 (1960): 479–91; Malcolm Andrew, "The Diabolical Chapel: A Motif in *Patience* and *Sir Gawain and the Green Knight*," *Neophilologus* 66 (1982): 313–19. The diabolical readings find the Green Knight vicious, full of "fear, self-regard, deceit and pretence" (Andrew, "Diabolical Chapel," 318–19).

40. One way to reconcile these has been recourse to a "vegetation myth," as in William A Nitze, "Is the Green Knight Story a Vegetation Myth?" *Modern Philology* 33 (1936): 251–366.

41. Far from it. Even as late as the so-called metaphysical poets, the word "die" was used to stand for orgasm, as in Donne's "The Canonization": "So, to one neutral thing both sexes fit. / We die to rise the same, and prove / Mysterious by this love" (ll. 25–27), *The Complete Poetry*, ed. John T. Shawcross (Garden City, N.J.: Doubleday & Co., 1967).

42. One can contrast the Green Knight with the "bride knight" of *Andreas*. Although in many ways the two are comparable figures in the phallic stiffness, the "bride knight's" softness and passivity is really a form of hardness, while the Green Knight's hardness is really a form of softness and easiness.

43. See Monter, "The Pedestal and the Stake."

44. This, according to Larry Benson, is the redaction to which it most closely conforms (*Art and Tradition*, 16–36).

45. Or as Richard Shoaf puts it, "untruth" is the human "imperfect" and "mortal" condition (*Poem as Green Girdle*, 76).

3

Mothers and Fathers: Change and Stability in Hamlet's World

So while thy beautie drawes the heart to love,
As fast thy Vertue bends that love to good:
'But ah,' Desire still cries, 'give me some food.'
—Sir Philip Sidney, Sonnet 71

Are not the sexes altered?
Contrary to that in *Deut.* 22.5?
—Thomas Walkington, *Rabboni*

THE SHIFT FROM abstract passion to tangible flesh continues in *Hamlet,* where details become increasingly intimate and psychological, as the play revisits the castle, bedroom, and bed which had been so crucial in *Sir Gawain.* By the time of *Hamlet,* however, the cultural symbolism and usefulness of armor had nearly been exhausted. Hamlet experiences anxiety both because of the dysfunction of previous masculine roles and because of his shame at their loss, a loss he holds himself accountable for. In this vulnerable situation, without a male guide, Hamlet sees himself as charged with creating a new masculinity. In part he finds his task is to resurrect his father and reestablish the lost masculine powers of his father.

On the battlements of Elsinore, a symbol of masculine ideals like Heorot or Camelot, *Hamlet* begins.[1] As it did those other fortresses, danger surrounds Hamlet's castle. But inside too, unseen pitfalls and enemies make the castle insecure: devils may lure one into the ever-changing flood, and the crumbling wall or clumsy step may throw one from the parapet. The opening words question identity: "Who's there?"[2] And the threat of instability no longer comes exclusively from without, but from the intimate within. This is the problem for men of Hamlet's world:

> So, oft it chances in particular men
> That some vicious mole of nature in them,
> As in their birth, . . .
> Oft break[s] down the pales and forts of reason.
>
> (I.iv.23–34)

As in the other stories, the space of masculine virtue has been invaded, but the intruder is neither a monster of untamed nature nor a god of fertility. It is the ghost of Hamlet's father, the king of Denmark, an exemplar of knightly nurture who has been quietly murdered. The unsuspected killer, Hamlet's uncle, has married Queen Gertrude, Hamlet's mother. When the ghost of Hamlet's father reveals his story to Hamlet and forces his son to swear vengeance, Hamlet tries to gather evidence to substantiate what he fears might be a hell-sent apparition. At the same time he is driven mad by the tale which his heart had foretold. For Hamlet the process of finding out becomes an unpleasant journey behind the timeless ideals of knighthood, kingship, and marriage to the changing bodies, minds, and emotions that those ideals overlay. Hamlet finds within the castle and within himself that which disturbs all stability and undermines the foundations of a fortified society.

In *The State of England Anno Dom. 1600*, written the year of *Hamlet*'s writing, Thomas Wilson pictured the new relationship of individual to social stability in a world without protective walls: "Since no force is found able to withstand the subtlety of man's invention they are not of the opinion that walles and fortifications can helpe them, but that the best fortifications is one the fortitude and faythfuylness of subjects' hearts."[3] In an age that looked upon "the fashioning of human identity as a manipulable, artful process,"[4] in an age in which walls and armors were inadequate, institutional continuity was thought to rest solely on the behaviors and dispositions of men. Only the constancy and consistency of men's behavior was thought to enable society to endure.[5] In Shakespeare's other plays, when men and women deviate from acceptable behaviors—when Bolingbroke rises against Richard or Regan and Goneril against Lear—disorder reigns, for their actions violate the shared shape of social order that orderly behavior creates and exemplifies.[6] Misbehavior exposes a palpable fiction of order that, for Shakespeare, thinly disguises a grimmer and less certain nature of man and world.

Thus the security of one's beliefs and, hence, the predictability of one's social performance became the most crucial social components. Without consistent personal belief, words were thought to lose meaning, institutions lose shape, people lose identity. The masculine ideal became constancy, change its antithesis. That a father reproduce himself in his son became less urgent than that the son reproduce his father. If a man should fail to reproduce his father, he lost the title of son and thus lost the world created by his father as well as the title conferred upon his father, including the right to entitle himself a man. Failure of a son to reproduce his father would mean loss of virtue, position, manhood. Stability and manhood became synonymous.

In Hamlet's world, the highest praise one can confer is "A was a man, take him for all in all" (I.ii.187; cf. II.iv.62). "Man" does not refer to a biological male; it refers to a model of human virtue. The ideal man combines the attributes of Jove, Hyperion, Mars, and Mercury (III.iv.56–62). Manhood elevates one above the "human" condition, as Hamlet states in his praise of Horatio

> As one, in suff'ring all, that suffers nothing,
> A man that Fortune's buffets and rewards
> Hast ta'en with equal thanks; and blest are those
> Whose blood and judgment are so well commeddled
> That they are not a pipe for Fortune's finger
> To sound what stop she please. Give me that man
> That is not passion's slave.
>
> (III.ii.66–72)

When Horatio would act the antique Roman and follow Hamlet to death, Hamlet conjures him, "As th'art man / Give me the cup" (V.ii.347–48). That is, a man does not change in a changing world. A man exercises self-control, subdues passion, ignores the knocks of the world at the door of his mind. This fixity and self-control confer the name of man on him, make him valuable, make him virtuous. Such is the man Hamlet aspired to be and was, if we credit Ophelia's report—courtier, soldier, and scholar, the "mould of form" (III.i.153–55).[7]

Hamlet's discourse on the dignity of man also discloses the desire for fixity that controls his notion of masculinity. Hamlet summarizes the cosmological view into which such a man fits and which derives from the presence of such a man who takes his place in "this goodly frame the earth": "What a piece of work is a man, how noble in reason, how infinite in faculties, in form and moving how express and admirable, in action how like an angel, in apprehension how like a god: the beauty of the world, the paragon of animals" (II.ii.303–7). The description of the perfect man, stressing form, mind, fixity, relies on a metaphor of man as art, particularly a work for the theater (cf. III.ii.46–47).[8] This appears in Hamlet's instructions to the players, which recapitulate the masculine role Hamlet had praised in Horatio: "In the very torrent, tempest, and, as I may say, whirlwind of your passion, you must acquire and beget a temperance that may give it smoothness" (III.ii.5–8). One "begets" one's self, tempering tempests, taking the rough edges off of passion. "Discretion" should be the tutor (III.ii.16–17). "Suit the action to the word, the word to the action, with this special observance, that you o'erstep not the modesty of nature" (III.ii.17–19). According to Hamlet, the masculine role refashions nature, makes it stable and rational. It is clearly a role that the best actors—men—play.

Antithetically, to be subject to change, to change, to perceive change is to be immoral, irrational, "mad," for madness, rooted in *mutare,* suggests "change."[9] Moreover, as stability constitutes the preeminently masculine virtue, so instability becomes the preeminently feminine vice. Thus conflict arises between the internalized values of a stable masculine identity, typified by the father, and the temporal and conditional world, typified in *Hamlet*—and in Tudor England—by the mother, a term that referred indifferently to parents, witches, and prostitutes.[10]

As developed in *Hamlet,* conflict between a stable order and a changeable world originates dramatically in English domestic and homiletic tragedy, in which, as in *Hamlet,* it is dramatized as a battle between mothers and fathers for control of sons.[11] Consistently mothers are viewed as the cause of male degradation. One of the oldest "interludes" of the Tudor period, *The Four Elements* (1519), presents the moral basis that underlies subsequent domestic drama.[12] In *The Four Elements,* Studious Desire teaches Humanity to learn the causes of the universe, how all is "engendered" (17). Despite terms like "engendered" and explanations of generation that suggest change, such as the following: "These elements, which do each other penetrate, / And by continual alternation they be / of themselves daily corrupted and generate" (13), Humanity learns that a masculine father-god "made" him (15). Moreover, the desire to learn this truth also defines manhood: "For the more thou [Humanity] desireth to know anything, / Therin thou seemest the more a man to be" (15). Opposing Studious Desire's effort to bring Humanity to manhood is Sensual Appetite, who leads Humanity to Taverner and satisfaction of his lusts:

> If ye will touch
> A fair wench naked in a couch
> Of soft bed of down,
> For to satisfy your wanton lust,
> I shall appoint you a trull of trust,
> Not a fairer in the town.
>
> (44)

By 1560, in *The Disobedient Child,* the ingredients of the interlude have been given a domestic situation: Father tries to direct his child towards education, while Son wishes to follow his natural desires, identified here with his wife.[13] Ultimately Son must choose between an order of virtue—God the Father, who after all has no wife Himself—and the temporal world—the rule of subsistence in which pleasure and pain sit close together. By choosing Wife, by leaving Father, Son becomes a beast. The fault, we are told by Perorator, lies in the Son's wantonness (316–19), which the father must curb.

In *Lusty Juventus,* the prologue summarizes the general lesson of the morality play, now applied to the household:[14]

> For youth is frail and easy to draw
> By grace to goodness, by nature to ill:
> That nature hath ingrafted, is hard to kill.
> Nevertheless, in youth men may be best
> Trained to virtue by godly mean;
> Vice may be so mortified and so supprest,
> That it shall not break forth, yet the root will remain.
>
> (45–46)

In this domestic psychomachia, masculine virtue rejects "nature," which it identifies with images of growth ("engendered," "ingraft," "root") and thus with biological origins and women-wives-mothers. Fathers admonish sons to accept a sexless masculine authority as the guide to virtue—an authority identified with themselves.

Thus in *The Disobedient Child* the only parent present is the father, and wantoness is said to be "of mischief the mother" (316). Jack in *Jack Juggler* declares that "of my mother I have been taught / To be merry when I may, and take not thought" (113).[15] In *Calisto and Melibaea*, Melibaea's virtue rests on the instruction of her father Danio, whereas sensual desire is represented by Celestina, a bawd, who according to the fashion of the time is regularly addressed as "mother," even by the virtuous Melibaea.[16] In fact, Celestina seems to have had a role in the birth and rearing of several of the characters. Melibaea, on the verge of succumbing to the blandishments of Celestina, states the dilemma aptly in protest: "Wilt thou . . . / make me lese the house of my father, / To win the house of such an old matron" (83). Save for her father's timely intervention, Melibaea would have accepted her mother's house.[17]

These domestic dramas commonly depict mothers as bawds who easily give in to enjoyment of their desires. In *Hickscorner,* Imagination finds that his mother has lain with Sir John (166), and therefore Imagination wishes to be revenged on all his comrades.[18] Pity, however, stops Imagination:

> Lo, Lords, they may curse the time they were born,
> For the weeds that overgroweth the corn . . .
> Lo, virtue is vanished for ever and aye;
> Worse was it never.
> We have plenty of great oaths,
> And cloth enough in our clothes, . . .
> Alas, now is lechery called love indeed,
> And murder named manhood in every need.
>
> (174–76)

In lines which become clichés of the genre and which we will find echoed in *Hamlet,* mothers, who symbolize a world of uncontrolled growth, coddle their children, rearing them to resemble themselves, leading their sons from lechery to murder.

Perhaps the most striking example of this theme of a mother's aberrant influence occurs in *Nice Wanton,* published in 1560.[19] In this "pretty interlude," as it was termed, Prologue argues that children's "natural wont" is "evil" and that mothers should be punished for allowing nature to take its course (163). The interlude concerns "two children brought up wantonly in play, / Whom the mother doth excuse, when she should chastise" (163)—Dalilah and Ismael. A third brother, Barnabas, has, in spite of his mother, a "fatherly" God (175). Although all three children have been sent to school, only Barnabas takes instruction there and through it achieves moral superiority. In the end, Ismael turns a thief and is hanged, while Dalilah turns whore and is

> Full of pain and sorrow, crooked and lorn:
> Stuffed with diseases, in this world forlorn.
> My sinews be shrunken, my flesh eaten with pox:
> My bones full of ache and great pain:
> My head is bald, that bare yellow locks;
> Crooked I creep to the earth again.
>
> (173)

Barnabas comforts his sister in her misery:

> Consider, Dalilah, God's fatherly goodness,
> Which for your good hath brought in this case.
> Scourged you with his rod of pure love doubtless,
> That, once knowing yourself, you might call for grace.
>
> (173)

Barnabas summarizes the fatherly method of upbringing: fatherly love chastises, self-knowledge reveals disease.

This motif of father and mother was tenacious. *The Witch of Edmonton,* written sixty years after *Nice Wanton,* follows the same pattern.[20] In this play, Frank Thorney murders his troth-plight Susan Carter because he has been "witched" by "Mother" (V.iii.20). "Mother" Sawyer is the only mother in the play, although there are several wives and maids, and virtuous fathers abound. Contrary to the previous plays, however, "Mother" insists that she has been turned into a scapegoat or symbol for evils that pervade the lives of all men and women:

> Men in gay clothes,
> Whose backs are laden with titles and honors,
> Are within far more crooked than I am,

And, if I be a witch, more witchlike. . . .
A witch! Who is not?
Hold not that universal name in scorn then.
What are your painted things in princes' courts,
Upon whose eyelids lust sits, blowing fires
To burn men's souls in sensual hot desires,
Upon whose naked paps a lecher's thought
Acts sin in fouler shapes than can be wrought? . . .
These by enchantments can whole lordships change
To trunks of rich attire, turn plows and teams
To Flanders mares and coaches, and huge trains
Of servitors to a French butterfly.
Have you not witches who can turn
Their husbands' wares, whole standing shops of wares,
To sumptuous tables, gardens of stol'n sin?

(IV.i.116–45)

In the end, Frank Thorney prays to God for forgiveness, which the other men believe he may be granted. Mother neither seeks nor is given forgiveness. The son has strayed, but the mother reveals her truly hellish nature by her end: sons are accidentally evil; mothers, essentially.

By the time of *The Witch of Edmonton*, plays showing the struggle between mothers and fathers for the souls of sons had endured for one hundred and fifty years on the English stage.[21] So when *Hamlet* dichotomized the universe between father and mother, virtue and vice, stability and growth, the play called forth a network of moral associations with which its audience would have been familiar.[22] These associations would have been encouraged by other allusions to the interludes and moralities, such as Horatio's scholarship and Claudius and Gertrude's decision to keep Hamlet from school. That latter opening gesture, for instance, unfolds a whole series of conceptual associations that would have labelled the uncle and mother as descendents of Sensual Appetite, representatives of a changing, natural world. Strings of homiletic images, such as the unweeded garden, reinforce the thematic conflicts between a stable, ideal father-centered world and an unstable, natural mother-centered world.[23] To restore the interlude order, Hamlet must extirpate growth and reproduction, all features that the tradition allied with change and with women.

Thus Hamlet's compulsion to enforce stability on the unstable, to suppress change, aims both actually and symbolically at a mother who is conceived as the agent of change. Hamlet, in other words, must deal with the world of change that has killed his father and now reigns in the persons of his mother and uncle.[24]

Viewing Hamlet's situation in light of the interludes, an Elizabethan audience would have expected Hamlet to act the soldier-scholar son of a virtuous father and punish appetite, reshaping society to its previous form. Yet what is different in *Hamlet,* what Shakespeare seems to insist upon in the opening scenes, is the antagonistic paradox underlying the interludes: the recognition that men have two parents and two aspects, nature that rebels against virtue and virtue that tries to pare down and even extirpate nature. That is, masculine idealism seems founded partially on self-hatred. To be a man, according to the opening images of the play, is to cut one's self off from what lies outside the fortified version of the self and to repress what lies within the fortified version of the self. To fit, one must squeeze tight or else excise protruding members. The repressed family of *Beowulf* and *Sir Gawain* comes back to haunt and harass masculine idealism in the form of the ambiguous father—biological parent and ideological representative. Hamlet's father's injunction, "Remember me" (I.v.91), suggests both: the rules of a father that a son must obey and a shape dismembered by masculinity, which the son must repair.

In Hamlet's world, men find that dichotomy has become an ambiguity they must surmount. The masculine role, closely allied to the acting in *Hamlet,* seeks to describe a nature that is orderly. When Hamlet remarks that drama should "hold as 'twere the mirror up to nature; to show virtue her feature, scorn her own image, and the very age and body of the time his form and pressure" (III.ii.22–24), his words suggest that the mirror, rather than reflecting nature, creates an image of nature that superimposes upon the world an idea of nature's shortcomings. The mirror exerts a "form and pressure" that shapes "the body of the time." That is, the view of nature that Hamlet espouses is an artful one. It is a nature that has been pruned by the shape of the mirror exactly as the character Humanity prunes back the feminine nature in the morality genre.

Both claim, however, that what appears in the mirror is truly nature. This claim, which becomes identified with masculinity, can only be made through a violence done to nature. In the closet scene, for instance, Hamlet proposes to "set up a glass / Where you [his mother] may see the inmost part of you" (II.iv.18–19). To this the Queen cries, "What wilt thou do? Thou wilt not murder me?" (20–21). Hamlet's mirror seems to promise to incise when it displays nature. The lines, in fact, strongly suggest that Hamlet has drawn his sword—perhaps to kill the "rat" he has heard. This sword (real or metaphorical) is the mirror in which Hamlet invites Gertrude to "see the inmost part of you." He will not cut her open; he "will speak daggers to her" (III.iii.387).[25] In other words, masculine violence to nature begins in the "objective" view of nature found in the masculine mirror, a view used to authorize subsequent violence. The ideal of acting becomes the source of mutilation. Hamlet also holds such a mirror up to himself.

The image of the mirror-dagger dominates a scene in which Hamlet forces intimate disclosures by verbal and physical violence. Gertrude cries: "O speak to me no more. / These words like daggers enter in my ears. / No more, sweet Hamlet" (III.iv.94–96), and "O Hamlet, thou has cleft my heart in twain" (158). Shaping nature, identified with his mother, into abstract virtue, represented by his father, requires swords; it requires excisions and dismemberments to fit what is to what should be. The mirror, then, offers in its artificial view a violent refashioning. In his swordplay and wordplay and hints of sexplay, Hamlet reveals a man desperately trying to reproduce the masculine ideal.

Unlike the interludes, *Hamlet* exhibits the glaring disjunction between intent and action, between ideal and practice. The trick of successful self-division that the heroes of the interludes exhibit evades Hamlet. For even though Hamlet tries to get the moral upper hand by reducing his mother to the type of vice and viewing himself as a type of virtue, he cannot disengage from his own passionate side:

> QUEEN. What have I done, that thou dar'st wag thy tongue
> In noise so rude against me?
> HAM.   Such an act
> That blurs the grace and blush of modesty,
> Calls virtue hypocrite . . .
>
> (III.iv.38–42)

In answer to the Queen's personal question, Hamlet strives for moral objectivity. If, on one hand, Hamlet's moral diatribe tries to make Gertrude submit to her role, it reveals Hamlet's inability to submit to his own. Irony arises because the tone of the sermon is so passionate, so howling, so revealing of an inability to live within limits, to follow the precepts of manhood, to staunch the pain of passion and of madness. Moreover, Hamlet mounts his exhortations to virtue in the presence of Polonius's corpse, undercutting Hamlet's polar virtue and making the literary figures of violent fashioning more threatening as they merge with everyday violence. Violence directed towards vice becomes violence directed promiscuously towards life; the separation of so-called vice from so-called virtue in human life can kill.

The scene also strengthens the connection between the masculine ideal and acting, a connection that the scene anatomizes. When, after having addressed the body of Polonius to blame it for its own death, Hamlet turns back to his mother, he checks her emotions at seeing an old friend killed and knowing her son the murderer by repeating his instructions to the actors:[26]

> HAM. Leave wringing of your hands. Peace, sit you down,
> And let me wring your heart; for so I shall
> If it be made of penetrable stuff,
> If damned custom have not braz'd it so,
> That it be proof and bulwark against sense.
>
> (III.iv.34–38)

Hamlet instructs Gertrude how to act, apparently because, like a bad actor, her impulsive behavior oversteps the bounds of nature. And yet Gertrude's response seems natural, in that it seems proportionable to the act and testifies that her heart is "made of penetrable stuff," that it is easily wrung. Hamlet's instructions to his mother would appear patently absurd (she already behaves as he wishes) if they did not reveal the crucial position of acting in the moral configuration. Acting cedes control to author, actor, and director.[27] To Hamlet, loss of control—his mother's loss, his loss—is unbearable. Hamlet's aversion to a nature that appears uncontrollable and his preference for the acted in this scene reaches perhaps its dizziest height.

Hamlet's desire for control and restraint, his excess of violence and virtue apparently derive from his sense that the masculine world—with which these all connect—and masculine identity generally are in danger.[28] While the desperate frenzy of the closet scene suggests Hamlet's desperate attempt to impose a masculine ideology on the world, his excesses also suggest the emergence of powerful aspects of his personality that have long been suppressed behind the masculine ideal and that are now being released because of the change in his perception of the conditions of life. The passion that Hamlet seeks to repress echoes a passion emergent in his own actions. Change, passion, and intimacy suffuse Hamlet's attempts to make his mother reject a vicious nature conceived as change, intimacy, and passion.[29] And again the excesses derive partially from stress fractures in the male role, in Hamlet's mutually exclusive, and thus self-destructive, attempts to repress and express simultaneously.

Perhaps Hamlet clings to his masculine behaviors all the more desperately because he is aware of the mother's world that he both desires and dreads. Ironically, his desperate grip drives him further from the masculine stoicism he desires. Perhaps for this reason acting mad appears the way to save himself. True madness would be excessive; acted madness he could control. Yet because he blinds himself to his madness, to the strong emotions and changes fraying the edges of his stability, Hamlet has none of the actor's ideal control. Instead he mercilessly hacks at the world as if he were imparting some order, as if he had a method, as if his every action were not informed by dread, doubt, pain, abomination, and self-loathing.

Hamlet's madness arises from his oscillation between his longing to *be* and his longing to be *a man*. The shifting contradictions in and among Hamlet's various speeches exhibit longing for a fixed, harmonious, and virtuous world, a realization that for men that world is enacted through violence and stoicism, and a contradictory but deep desire to express and display adequately what he feels.[30] The "To be or not to be" soliloquy typifies this. Beginning with a scholarly parsing of the matter which reduces "being" to a choice between the masculine poses of stoic suffering and armed opposition, the speech unfolds alternatives that undermine the original assumptions, so that, as the speech progresses, even death becomes a kind of being.

This process of a firm starting premise's becoming wrapped in contradiction appears again in Hamlet's confrontation of Ophelia at prayer. In the central portion of the scene, Hamlet's troubled viewpoint slips from position to position: (1) a general disquisition of the relationship of beauty to honesty; (2) accusations against men, himself in particular, as sinners; (3) accusations against women as sinners; (4) accusations against women as the *cause* of men's sins. This speech suggests that because men have no power, control, or will in sexual affairs, women must bear the responsibility for male virtue or lack of it. If women could remain virtuous, men would as well.

Hamlet's attempt to reassert men's moral superiority in this way does not relieve him, for he creates a circle in which men and women are complicit. At the end he feels a fuller measure of self-loathing than at the beginning: "Go to, I'll no more on't, it hath made me mad" (III.i.148). The utterance, like the problem, takes the form of a fused and irresolvable choice: "Get thee to a nunnery, farewell" (III.i.138–39, 141, 151). "Nunnery" as a convent or brothel (both ruled by "mothers") simultaneously suggests abstinence and promiscuity. Nor is Hamlet clear about which alternative he is proposing. At every moment the utterance undoes itself by taking a point opposite to its previous meaning. One can imagine Hamlet accidentally hitting on this catchphrase, a line so full of ambiguity and even emptiness that it can only be conceived as a howl of pain that in its unbearable, irresolvable dichotomy looses meanings which explain Hamlet's pain and explain why those meanings can be expressed only in words that tear themselves into a howl. Hamlet is mad. He is unstable and sees the world as unstable. The world of his father seems inaccessible to him.

Hamlet's problem arises from his experiences in a world where paternal love embodies, rather than resolves, the tormenting dichotomy of ideal and nature. Paternal love is said to be love's most "noble" form (I.ii.110–12), yet in Hamlet's world its nobility rests upon the suppression of natural affection. "Noble" implies an orderly masculine behavior that sons must reproduce. Thus, Polonius's list of precepts becomes the conduit for affection between him and Laertes (I.ii.55–81).[31] Ironically, this means of expressing affection also suppresses affection and teaches its suppression. The tension between lively expressive behavior and measured inexpressive behavior flows from a supposed antithesis between what are symbolically labeled maternal and paternal qualities.

In desiring the stable, father's world, Hamlet accepts a vision inimical to affection and, as we will see, to growth, what a later age might call "life."[32] To Hamlet, his father had been "Hyperion" (I.i.140) or "Hercules" (I.i.153), the proper epitome of manhood (I.ii.187). Even as a ghost his father displays those manly qualities that confer moral, aesthetic, and physical beauty: in his armor he appears "fair and warlike" (I.i.50). Yet while in his guises of Hercules, Hyperion, Mars, Mercury, Zeus, the father embodies a moral rule, an order of unreachable perfection; it is one from which the son, who is Nemean lion to his father's Herculean self, is excluded. Not only must Hamlet be subdued by the father's rule, but as the metaphor makes clear, the father must kill some part of the son.

The revelations of the father's ghost apparently align father worship with a kind of dismemberment, self-destruction and death.[33] The play associates Hamlet's father, alive and dead, with the "unnatural," the sterile, and the deadly. Throughout the play, for instance, Hamlet's father is associated with cold: "sledded Polacks" whom he slaughtered and "eager" (sharp) air in which his ghost appears. The play connects cold with death and sterility as when "*cold* maids" (chaste) call "long purples" "*dead* men's fingers," while the "liberal shepherds" call them dog's cods (IV.vii.168–70; my emphasis). The freedom of the shepherds, who accept a larger view of nature and reproduction, is contrasted with the pretended chilly morality of the frigid maids.[34] Also, the ghost in his military aspect "usurps" that time most allied to death (I.i.49). Hamlet's father appears "in the dead waste and middle of the night" (I.ii.198), connecting him with "waste," death, and night. Significantly, the line, echoing an earlier line about Rosenkrantz and Guildenstern, suggests that Hamlet's father causes the waste and death.[35] Hamlet's father occupies the sexual parts ("waist") of night and death. The line portrays Hamlet's father as siring death, as reproducing sterility.

So we find that in his first speeches Hamlet's superabundance of filial affection makes him reject life: he is "too much in the sun" (I.ii.67); he wears the livery of night (68); his lids are veiled; he seeks for his father in the dust. His colors ally him with the "graveness" of age, rather than the carelessness of youth. Hamlet has put himself in the world of night, darkness, death, ghosts. Opposed to this in his first speeches are the worlds of sun, day, the living, the present.

As suggested above, the emphasis on death arises because it reduces, simplifies, stabilizes, and orders what appears to ooze and grow involuntarily. At the end of the play, for instance, bodies of the dead become readable ciphers, symbols of history, subjects of a tale. Hamlet is drawn to death. Only in the grave can Hamlet declare his love for Ophelia. Only when death has deprived the body of life can he adore the ghost of his father, the skull of Yorick. The dead body, then, aids Hamlet's conceptualization of life. Combat—the warfare of Fortinbras or the duel of Laertes and Hamlet—would seem the perfect means to reduce life to order.

And yet the gravedigger scene that begins act V shows how the natural end of human life undoes the work of society. Hamlet sees the end to which the politician, courtier, lady, lawyer all must come (V.i.89). The gravedigger's words show that life is movement and change. On one hand, he points out that a woman is not a woman when she is dead, when she can no longer move, laugh, breathe, speak. However, while death destroys the signifying power of "woman," destroys language, destroys the notion that life is stable, death is no more stable than life. Hamlet notices the "fine revolution" when he takes up the cases of Alexander and Caesar. Seen from this standpoint, life and death join in a dance of motion. Hamlet finds that death is a "return" to something "base" (V.i.196)—that is, it involves a return to the elements, the dust, of which we were composed.

This cyclical rather than static or progressive view of life and death is seen in one of Hamlet's riddles: "We fat all creatures else to fat us, and we fat ourselves for maggots. Your fat king and your lean beggar is but variable service—two dishes, but to one table. . . . A man may fish with the worm that hath eat of a king, and eat of the fish that hath fed of that worm. . . . To show how a king may go a progress through the guts of a beggar" (IV.iii.21–31). Here is a description of the cycle of life that even more deftly undercuts the notion of social order. Although Hamlet's tone is meant to offend his auditors, Hamlet certainly shares their revulsion, so that later in considering Alexander's and Caesar's dust he does not have it nourishing flowers (as Laertes imagines Ophelia's to do) and thus joining the circle; he has it used by society to stop a beer barrel (V.i.205) or "stop a hole to keep the wind away" (207). The circle or cycle must be filled in by society. The "O," the hole which expresses "nothing," creates a pitfall for society, and so it is appropriate that the dust should plug up the beer barrel (an emblem of appetite) or that it should keep the wind (intruding nature, undifferentiated breath) out.

Of course, the figures primarily indicate that Hamlet has reduced the monuments and works of the world's two greatest warriors to the smallest scale possible. But while he has chosen two ideal men and shown how life and death have belittled their accomplishments, their ethos, and their *techne*, Hamlet finds this work of death repulsive. He fears the open hole, whether cycle or revolution. It sickens him, as he states. Even as he recognizes the ability of death to level and to make meaningless the ideas men have labored over, he needs to feel that monuments are possible, meaning is available, control may be exerted. He needs to feel that he can give shape to his life, that his father's world will endure.

As virtue and masculinity are associated with death in the sense that they are associated with life-denying attributes and activities, life and life-giving attributes and activities are associated with sin and femininity, even when those activities and attributes appear undoubtedly a part of male experience. From the standpoint of masculine idealism, growth destroys man-made distinctions and meanings on which order rests.[36] Sexual reproduction, when not controlled for economic and social benefit, kills—as weeds kill a garden. Throughout *Hamlet,* as in the interludes, sex involves death through a series of overlapping images. The quibble on the "nothing" between maids' legs connects the female genitalia with the threat of meaninglessness and with the emblem of the cycle "O." The "O," which for Hamlet signifies the birth canal, the vagina, and the consummation of desire, is also the yawning grave that undoes manhood.[37] In Hamlet's vision of the bunghole that the dust of Caesar may stop, the appetite, represented by the barrel, is clogged by the insertion of dead matter, so that the picture suggests defecation into a barrel, as it also suggests antiintercourse and antibirth.[38]

"Fat," which is used pejoratively throughout the play, offers a particularly interesting look at this fear of changing bodies because it suggests not only luxury and appetite, which Hamlet excoriates, but also sweat, seminal discharge, and sexual reproduction. As above, to live in ease is to provide "fat" for maggots, while "fatness of these pursy times" (III.iv.155) suggests economic and physical satiety. "Pursy" also suggests the scrotum, and Hamlet connects sexual satiety with fat. For instance, the uncle and the mother are compared to swine in their fornications, and their sheets are "enseamed" (greased with fat):

> Nay, but to live
> In the rank sweat of an enseamed bed,
> Stew'd in corruption, honeying and making love
> Over the nasty sty!
> (III.iv.91–94)

The association of "enseamed" with semen is clear, as is the association of "fat" generally with semen, as in this example from *The Faerie
Queene:* "As when old Father Nilus gins to swell / With timely pride
above th' Egyptian vale, / His fatty waves do fertile slime outwell . . ."
(I.i.21). In his pejorative use of the word "fat," Hamlet rejects activities generally connected with the changeable state of humans, connected with bodies: feeding, resting, excreting, reproducing.[39]

Masculine revulsion against natural growth, expressed in images
of seminal discharge, is particularly noticeable when Laertes warns
Ophelia to "keep . . . in the rear of your affection / Out of the shot
and danger of desire. / . . . Virtue itself scapes not calumnious strokes"
(I.iii.33–38). Later he again mixes a genital-war metaphor with a
flower-genital one:

> The canker galls the infants of the spring
> Too oft before their buttons be disclos'd,
> And in the morn and liquid dew of youth
> Contagious blastments are most imminent.
>
> (I.iii.39–42)

So the flower of youth must withstand the blastments–shots–disease-
ful semen of desire. Laertes also puts it this way: Do not "your chaste
treasure open / To his unmaster'd importunity" (I.iii.31–32). The
flower is a commodity whose profuse growth undermines its economic value. The masculine attitude towards "nature" is reflected
quite fully in Ophelia's associations with flowers, which make her a
representative of sexual reproduction and natural growth.[40]

The abhorrent world of sensuality and sexuality is most frequently
figured by images of nature, fecundity, and growth—weeds (which
means all uncultivated plants, including wildflowers), flowers, and
beasts. Ophelia is a "rose of May" (IV.v.157); Hamlet himself is a
flower (III.i.158–62), although a "blasted" one. Sins are "blossoms"
(I.v.76), the Uncle a "mildew'd ear" (III.iv.64). Hamlet's father warns
Hamlet against becoming a "fat weed," and when Hamlet sees his
sexual side most clearly he blames it on "the old stock," an image that
harkens back to the interludes, drawing plant proliferation and animal breeding together.

One reaction to natural fecundity, to sexual reproduction, which
Ophelia represents to her father, is to control it.[41] Thus, Polonius
speaks of owning his daughter (II.ii.106) and, turning farmer, offers
to "loose" her to Hamlet (II.ii.162). In this context man is a maker of

order out of natural fecundity, by cutting away, controlling, owning; this meaning is preserved in the word "husband," which means both master of the household and the one who controls production and distribution (IV.v.138).[42] The imposition of order on the natural world means marking off productive from unproductive.

This commerce in flowers relies on weeding and lopping off seed cases—the masculine tasks of excision that turn nature to a garden. When Hamlet states that "things rank and gross in nature / Possess" the world (I.ii.136–37), the words "rank" and "gross," meant to be morally opprobrious terms, also retain their meanings of "growing luxuriantly" and "fertile." Thus he rejects fecundity and fertility, as when he earlier decries the world as an "unweeded garden / That grows to seed" (I.ii.135–6). A garden—whether the plot of farmer-father Polonius or the verses of the poet-courtier—thrives by its sterility, by not allowing plants to go to seed, by not allowing desire to be fulfilled, regardless of whether the produce is flowers, vegetables, sonnets, or children. The cutting away of the reproductive part, the seed, the semen, enables a stable order. The image of a society retaining its virtue by cutting away its capacity naturally to reproduce comes from homiletic drama. But in *Hamlet* the farm becomes a garden, which suggests an even more decorous and even decorative order imposed on nature.

Hamlet, the exponent and victim of the repressive dichotomy of male/female, cannot develop a therapeutic attitude towards his sexual energies, his bodily functions, his changes, in part because he views them as the inheritance of his mother, evoked by women generally. The sword-penis imagery of the play reinforces this. The penis becomes a lance, the vagina a canker, the semen pus. Gertrude as the embodiment of desire has replaced the "rose," symbol of the female genitalia, with a "blister" (III.iv.40–45). It has become an "ulcerous place" (III.iv.149). The ulcer image seems to derive from *De Rerum Natura*, book 4, on "Sensation and Sex,"[43] where Lucretius writes, "*Ulcus enim vivescit et inveterascit alendo*" (For the ulcer [of desire] rouses and strengthens with feeding).[44] There Lucretius offers the following advice: "Vent the seed of love upon other objects. By clinging to it you assure yourself the certainty of heart sickness and pain. . . . Your only remedy is to lance the first wound with new incisions; to salve it, while it is still fresh, with promiscuous attachments; to guide the motions of your mind into some other channel."[45]

Although in Lucretius repressed desire (not fulfilled desire) becomes a disease, discharge of the seed is healthy. In *Hamlet* the flow of seed is the pus or "matter" from the ulcer. He rejects the life-giving, healthy alternatives to repressed sexuality. The rejection is so profound that Hamlet cannot bear to think about a flower that "grows to seed" (that produces semen, that reproduces itself sexually) (I.ii.136). In the bedroom scene Hamlet denounces sexual activity as spreading "compost on the weeds / To make them ranker" (III.iv.153–54), using images that make fertility and the powers of growth vicious and that echo with his earlier lines (I.ii.135–37).[46]

For Hamlet, therefore, channeling does not provide a cure for passion; only excision does. Thus the "lance" becomes a "sword" and is directed at others. The sword that lances the ulcerated vagina clearly connects all the other swords with the violence and conflict of repressed sexual functions. As the means of controlling reproductive functions, swordplay ironically becomes the channel for release of sexual energies. The sword displaces the penis, and masculine social intercourse—the male reproductive act—becomes a death-dealing parody of sexual intercourse.[47] When Hamlet quips to Ophelia's remark ("You are keen, my Lord, you are keen"): "It would cost you a groaning to take off my edge" (III.ii.243–44), he not only conflates stabbing and sexual intercourse but also exposes the witty riposte, verbal swordplay, as another displacement of sexual activity.

The dichotomy of feminine nature and masculine virtue, which seems to control the choices men make in Hamlet's society, has little relevance to the experience that Hamlet has of himself or what he discovers is the similar experience of other men. We can see how men slip across the lines of their own moral opprobrium if we re-examine Laertes's and Polonius's lectures to Ophelia. Given the underlying male interest in controlling sexual desire and the revulsion at reproduction, one may be surprised by the obscene innuendoes that chock the "virtuous" advice of Polonius and Laertes. The men deploy these double entendres to test Ophelia's innocence. Can she understand "buttons" and "blastments," or Polonius saying " 'Tis told me he hath very often of late / Given private time to you, and you yourself / Have of your audience been most free and bounteous. / . . . What is between you?" (I.iii.91–98)? Although both men obviously have a full stock of sexual awareness, desire, and stratagems (a similar awareness displayed by Hamlet in the innuendo of his talk generally and in the ribald accosting of Ophelia in particular), they believe that women furnish this knowledge. They attempt to degrade the women of the play for their sexual knowledge, their eruptions, their provocations of desire, their infectious diseases, at the same time that this encompasses part of their own experience.

This certainly is the case with Hamlet's father as well. For instance, in its sexual meaning, the ghost's appearance "in the dead waste and middle of the night" (I.ii.198) suggests that Hamlet's father is the devil-mate to a witch-like night. Hamlet must be profoundly shocked when he discovers that his father suffers in purgatory for sins of appetite (I.v.9–13, 79–80). It is King Hamlet, not King Claudius, who had been "Cut off in the blossoms of my sin" (I.v.76). Therefore, although Hamlet promises not to mix the memory of his father "with baser matter" (I.v.104), he can hardly be unaware of the resemblance of father and uncle, brothers, after all, sprung from a single root.[48] Hamlet refrains from killing his uncle at prayer because "A took my father grossly, full of bread, / With all his crimes broad blown, as flush as May" (III.iii.80–81). "Bread" connects his father with the "poison" in man's nature that "o'erleavens" the rest (I.iv.29–38), as the flower images, "bloom" and "blown," connect his father with what he must regard as the feminine—sensuality, appetite, and lust. It is in like condition that Hamlet hopes to take his uncle.

So too the equation is present when Hamlet calls his uncle "a mildew'd ear / Blasting his wholesome brother" (III.iv.64–65), echoing the disease-semen-violence of "blastments." Yet though Hamlet wishes to suggest that his uncle's rottenness killed his father, he suggests instead that his father was infected with the same moral rottenness. Interesting, of course, is the "ear" image, because although referring to corn or the garden untended again, and turning lust into disease, it also echoes the "ear" as the place of vulnerability, one which, for instance, in Hamlet's speaking daggers to the queen, becomes vaginal. The uncle may be a diseased strumpet who has infected (and killed) the father. Yet it is at Hamlet's father's ear that the poison entered—he was receptive to the "poison" of sexuality that courses through bodies, the poison with which the sword-penis is envenomed.[49]

The important revelation, however, is that Hamlet's father was, take him all in all, not a "Man," but that poor pitiful thing—a man.

The revelation of resemblance between father and uncle is the revelation that Hamlet himself, that all men, have aspects that masculine tradition assigned to the mother.[50] While Hamlet's uncle is connected with "mother" through his "witchcraft" (I.v.43) and harlotry (III.i.51), Hamlet's father has been revealed to have a similar connection. The failure of the mother/father dichotomy shows through in Hamlet's riddling farewell to his uncle: "HAM. Farewell, dear mother. / KING. Thy loving father, Hamlet. / HAM. My mother. Father and mother is man and wife, man and wife is one flesh; so my mother" (IV.iv.52–55).

Similarly, when "mouse," the uncle's term of endearment for Gertrude (III.iv.185), appears in the title of the play "Mousetrap," Hamlet seems to confuse his uncle with his mother. "Mouse," of which "muscle" is the diminutive form, in the Renaissance was associated with the penis that running in and out disturbs the steady thoughts of men—as in the solemn silence of the opening scene, not disturbed by a mouse.[51] Masculine images and feminine endearments fuse, so that male and female, mother and father, cause and effect can not be extricated: "wise men know well enough what monsters you make of them" (III.i.140). The inseparability of wisdom and monstrosity seems to be Hamlet's inheritance. The triumph of the mother reveals that the "Father" as masculine ideal is dead and that, therefore, his uncle is his father.

Hamlet cannot avoid seeing himself as implicated in this process of breeding, of desire, growth, reproduction, death. He had written to Ophelia that "I have not the art to reckon my groans" (II.ii.119–20), thus exposing his own illness and allying him with groaners, with utterers of "O," with women. So he sees himself as a sinner, "for virtue cannot so inoculate our old stock but we shall relish of it" (III.i.117–18). "I could accuse me of such things that it were better my mother had not borne me" (III.i.123–24; cf. "would it were not so, you are my mother," III.iv.15). "We are arrant knaves all, believe none of us" (III.i.129–30). The maternal side, the side most visibly represented by his mother's actions, now seems to him to dominate in himself. Hamlet is thus implicated in the death of his father. And Hamlet's anger that arises against the sexuality of others therefore really arises against himself.

Ironically Ophelia—symbolically "nature" and more particularly the "woman" of Hamlet's desire—believes men, not women, bring instability to sexual love.[52] "Men will do't if they come to't" (IV.v.60), she sings, speaking of men's use of the promise of marriage as a way to satisfy their appetites, after which they are no longer interested in marriage; in fact, the lover is gone. So the lover "Robin"—a character from the fertility rites and sometimes a euphemism for the penis (cock-robin)—who "is all my joy" comes crossed in Ophelia's mind with this song:

> And will a not come again?
> And will a not come again?
> No, no he is dead,
> Go to thy death-bed,
> He never will come again.
> (IV.v.84–88)

All this is explicitly about the death of an old man or a lover whom she had longed for but who is absent, dead and never able to return. Yet it is also about the death after orgasm: the death that orgasm was supposed to cause—the loss of seed, blood, and spirit, as well as the death of the penis (its lying down, thus the death of desire) and the disappearance of the lover. The lover will not come again because having come once he leaves, hides. Such songs may indeed seem nonsensical yet profound to the courtiers who listen.[53]

Hamlet's sexual nausea[54] not only aims at women but also suggests disgust with his own sexual being:[55] a typically male Renaissance problem, encoded in all the interludes, amply expressed in *Hamlet,* observed in Ophelia's songs and concisely articulated in Sonnet 129:

> Th' expense of spirit in a waste of shame
> Is lust in action: and, till action, lust
> Is perjured, murd'rous, bloody, full of blame,
> Savage, extreme, rude, cruel, not to trust,
> Enjoyed no sooner but despisèd straight;
> Past reason hunted, and no sooner had,
> Past reason hated as a swallowed bait,
> On purpose laid to make the taker mad:
> Mad in pursuit, and in possession so;
> Had, having, and in quest, to have, extreme,
> A bliss in proof, and proved, a very woe,
> Before, a joy proposed; behind, a dream.
> All this the world well knows; yet none knows well
> To shun the heaven that leads men to this hell.[56]

Hamlet's difficulty in dealing with desire, seminal discharge, and change seems reproduced in the many readings that state that this sonnet concerns the impact of an external and desirable object on a man: its ability to inspire with despicable lust.[57]

Such readings tend to repress one unmistakable point of the poem:[58] the poem describes the mental and emotional effects of ejaculation. According to this verse, sexual union brings delight; orgasm is "a bliss in proof." Before "lust in action," however, a man will lie, murder, do bloody, blameful, savage, extreme, rude, cruel things to achieve the bliss of orgasm. Don't trust a man with an erection, Shakespeare says. Such a man will despise the object of his lust because he will blame her (or him), the poem seems to say. Bliss of the achievement, the union and orgasm, is followed by shame, letdown, and woe, self-hatred and hatred of the object of desire: "Th' expense of spirit in a waste of shame / Is lust in action." Later, however, the moment will regain its "dream"-like erotic power. The orgasm itself is a "heaven" that leads to "hell," because of the trauma that surrounds it, as well as the morality founded in part on that trauma. Although the poem represents lust externally, it purports to describe male experience. Moreover, it proclaims that this experience has been projected on the outside world.

The inability of Hamlet to accept his own sexuality separates him from a principle of *eros* that is not simply a principle of desire here, but of growth as well, of nature and natural reproduction. It is not simply *sex* that Hamlet rejects; the "maternal" in this play encodes reproduction and growth, change and instability, death and the body, indefiniteness and blissful ignorance, as well as the orgasm itself which engages all these and calls in question masculine ideals of excision, castra-tion ("fortifica-tion"), ideation, poeticization. Through Hamlet, the play depicts men as trapped in violence flowing from a perverted reproductive activity that cannot achieve either growth or order, "mother" or "father."

Hamlet does not represent some adolescent aberration carried into adulthood. The age "thirty" derives as much from the wish to mark Hamlet fully adult, the age of Adam, as from the wish to place Gertrude beyond childbearing. For Hamlet's "madness" stems from the cultural condition of his masculinity in its untenable dissociations from sexual identities, from positive reproductive capacities, from mortality, from emotion, from what G. Wilson Knight distinguished from "the exquisite music of the soul" as the "trivial things of life that blur our mortal vision"—the mundane conditions of life.[59] Men like Knight have entrapped Hamlet in a construction that devalues sexual union, reproduction, sensual pleasure, the round of life and death as the "fardels" that the "disobedient son" bears. These come short of the glories of battlefield death, the good fight, the monument. This much persists in our own view.

Yet Hamlet exhibits the excruciating discomfort that men may feel when asked to polarize themselves so absolutely, to be virtuous, to see (and reject) life.[60] This tension creates the magic of Hamlet's first soliloquy:

> O that this too too [sallied] flesh would melt,
> Thaw and resolve itself into a dew,
> Or that the Everlasting had not fix'd
> His canon 'gainst self-slaughter. O God! God!
> How weary, stale, flat, and unprofitable
> Seem to me all the uses of this world!
>
> (I.ii.129–34)

Hamlet describes death as if it were sexual union. He wants his body to dissolve, to evanesce. And yet, regardless of what is explicitly stated, he wishes for union, which he imagines as the evanescence of the body into an excretion, into water, into dew. The image implies dew and sweat of sexual intercourse. This rhapsody made lovely, soft, and powerful by its faint evocation of sexual union, aims at effacing that connection with its own music, aims at death. The "flesh" is "sallied," indicating that Hamlet desires physical union without flesh, sex without getting dirty.[61] And given this desire the alternatives are "death" or the "uses of the world." The endpoint for Hamlet's sensual meditation on the limits of sensuality superimposes sexual union on death, an unsettling fantasy arrived at by way of his own dislocated, and therefore beautiful, desires.

What discomfits Hamlet is his internalization of a system of values that stands in opposition to life, that has infected his view of life. What he rejects is growth; what he desires is death itself and death in its various social aspects. Yet Hamlet's fixation on death conveys the very opposite of what it seems to convey—he wants a life of growth. His words imply it and power his other ideas, and the obstacle is the view of the world that he inherited from his father, a view that paradoxically he is asked to uphold not through the systems of justice but through the passion of kinship. That is the paradox: he obeys his father's rules because he loves his father; he loves his father, not because his father's rules are so virtuous and wonderful, but because his father is his father. That is the dilemma of Hamlet's position, a dilemma that tears him down the middle. The passion of the play seems to swell from Hamlet's uncontrollable affection for his father, mother, and Ophelia. When Hamlet displaces this passion into ideas about hypocrisy, lust, pride, and coxcombry, those themes affect us because we recognize the subterranean torrent of Hamlet's passion—his howl.

In the end, it would appear that Hamlet does make birth and nature central.[62] For instance, he rejects Hercules: "Let Hercules himself do what he may, / The cat will mew, and dog will have his day" (V.i.286–87). In this figure Hamlet dismisses the idea that man can bring nature into perfect order. In fact, nature will out. This is part of a pattern that finds Hamlet moving away from notions of rigid social order to ones of nature. He invokes the idea of rebirth: he states that he is "set naked" on the kingdom, that he is "alone," that this is a "sudden and more strange return" (IV.vii.42–45). With the centrality of this birth image also comes the centrality of "rashness" over "discretion" (V.ii.6–24): "Let us know / Our indiscretion sometimes serves us well / When our deep plots do pall" (V.ii.7–9). Hamlet chooses not to divide and categorize. He submits to a fate that lies outside himself and that is indifferent to the craft and art of men to shape nature: "There's divinity that shapes our ends, / Rough-hew them how we will" (V.ii.10–11).

At the end Gertrude tries to calm Laertes with the image of a maternal Hamlet: "Anon, as patient as the female dove / When that her golden couplets are disclos'd, / His silence will sit drooping" (V.i.281–83).[63] Her image is in striking contrast to Laertes's image of his nurturing self: the "kind life-rend'ring pelican" (IV.v.146) who impales itself so that the young may feed from its blood.[64] And it contrasts with Rosenkrantz's and Guildenstern's asseverations that the king, like a nurse caring for the subject-children, needs to be strong and well-armed to do the tough job of caring (III.iii.8–23). In the case of both male versions, birth has been transformed into a masculine vision of care.

Yet Hamlet explicitly rejects Gertrude's vision of a feminine self in a passage that glances at Nashe's rejection of feminine patience as just another version of sloth:

> Am I a coward?
> Who calls me villain, breaks my pate across,
> Plucks off my beard and blows it in my face,
> Tweaks me by the nose, gives me the lie i' th' throat
> As deep as to the lungs—who does me this?
> Ha!
> 'Swounds, I should take it: for it cannot be
> But I am pigeon-liver'd and lack gall
> To make oppression bitter.
>
> (II.ii.566–74)

So in *Pierce Penniless* under "The Effects of Sloth" Nashe writes, "If he . . . sit dallying at home, nor will be awaked by any indignities out of his love-dream, but suffer every upstart groom to defy him, set him at nought, and shake him by the beard unrevenged, let him straight take orders and be a churchman, and then his patience may pass for a virtue, but otherwise, he shall be suspected of cowardice, and not cared for of any. . . . The only enemy to Sloth is contention and emulation: as to propose one man to myself, that is the only mirror of our age, and strive to out-go him in virtue" (111). Here the use of "mirror" is apposite with its use in *Hamlet*, as is the notion that one fashions oneself in the mirror of another "true" man. Patience is just part of what Nashe describes as "these degenerate effeminate days of ours" (113).[65]

In other words, Hamlet does not at the end adopt the feminine view or surmount distinctions between masculine and feminine, father and mother. In his accommodation of himself to nature, Hamlet finds new ways for men to displace women and all the aspects of dependence that they signify.[66] Men can, in the end, give birth to themselves. In his thickly allusive words "deep plots do pall" (V.ii.9), Hamlet recognizes that the systems of men are deadly. But he refuses to accede the universe to a more androgynous notion. Instead he seeks a new isolation, cutting himself off from everyone, mother and father, for although fathers can no longer embody a perfect external, moral philosophy, Hamlet can find a more perfect paternal force in nature. The heavenly aspects of Hamlet's earthly father are conferred upon a heavenly Father who can in the apparent disorder of nature encompass order. King Hamlet will die on earth, only to rise to rule in Heaven. The father has been apotheosized: Hamlet's father will be Zeus.[67]

Ultimately in *Hamlet* the institutional forms of masculinity, of male roles imaged in the father-warrior-ruler do not explain the whole man. Those aspects of masculinity that had been confined to and allied with the "mother" seem to have asserted themselves through a new awareness of the body, of time, of nature. For whatever reason, the sexual, "natural," de-castrated[68] aspects of men were emerging into consciousness. At the same time the family was becoming—as in the novel of the next century—the center of conflict and drama. Yet no models existed for men, like Hamlet, to incorporate the new relationships and revelations. The ending repeats the ending from homiletic drama, the rejection of worldly parents, the discovery of the divine Father. But it rewrites that ending, by making Hamlet pass through the dysfunction of the dichotomy on which the triumph of the Father rested. It did so by exposing Hamlet to the "mother" that resides in the "father" and in himself, to the excruciating bonds of love, desire, life, and growth that tie him to the bodies of the world. The *deus-pater ex machina* must encompass this new awareness, heal this new wound. In part, the puritan theologians of the time were allowing the body its sexuality without depriving it of its morality, making marriage and family central.

But this, of course, was only possible under the aegis of a paternal God. Men, reared in their fathers' system of language that put them into a neurotic relationship with themselves and others, needed and desired to retain the power that their fathers' structures conferred upon them. The end of the play reifies the ideal of fatherhood by discovering a paternal God who assimilates nature, passion, growth in his persons. Such faith reaffirms the rights men have given themselves to control themselves and others, as it also reasserts the ideals of chivalry and arming, the dichotomies of male and female, reason and passion, love and sex. Such faith, while apparently accommodating the new awareness, also attempts to rebury men's uncertainty about their sexual desires and so attempts to create the conditions for the energy of that sexuality and that denial to reemerge in a variety of perverse and violent forms. In this new construction, men can embrace "Fortune" and "change," as Fortinbras does, but, like Machiavelli, they arrive fully armed, ready to grab Fortune by the forelock and ravish her. In Hamlet's world there is no peace from his father's masculinity, no peace with it, and no way to replace it. That masculine ideal remains the source of death, rage, and violence in the childless and womanless land of Elsinore, in the fortress of men.[69]

Notes

1. Quotations from *Hamlet* come from the Arden edition, edited by Harold Jenkins (London: Methuen, 1982).

2. Critics have long noted that the beginning of *Hamlet* poses a question about identity: see Roy Walker, "*Hamlet*: The Opening Scene," *Shakespeare: Modern Essays in Criticism*, ed. Leonard F. Dean (New York: Oxford, 1961), 216–21; Maynard Mack, "The World of Hamlet," *The Yale Review* 42 (1952): 502–23; Salvador de Madariaga, *On Hamlet* (London: Frank Cass, 1964). David Leverenz in "The Woman in Hamlet: An Interpersonal View," *Representing Shakespeare: New Psychoanalytic Essays*, ed. Murray Schwartz and Coppelia Kahn (Baltimore: Johns Hopkins University Press, 1980), 110–28, begins with this same question. His approach is Jungian-existentialist, following R. D. Laing's *Divided Self* (New York: Pantheon Books, 1969). He distinguishes his reading from that of Alex Aronson's strictly Jungian reading in *Psyche and Symbol in Shakespeare* (Bloomington: Indiana University Press, 1972). There are similarities between Leverenz's reading and my own; however, I do not take the dichotomies of masculine and feminine either as universal or as necessarily confined to the meanings he ascribes to them. Moreover, I believe that the relationship of masculinity to femininity as conceived in the work is more complex; in this I am closer to Edward A. Snow's thesis in "Sexual Anxiety and the Male Order of Things in *Othello*," *English Literary Renaissance* 10 (1980): 384–412. Snow argues that the imposition of male order leads to the apprehension of the female as unbounded appetite; "so to attribute the destructive impulses unleashed in *Othello* to man's 'bestial nature,' to the sexual impulse breaking through the civilized barrier that usually contains it, is to turn the vision of the play on its head. . . . What erupts in Othello's jealousy is not primitive, barbaric man but the voice of the father, . . . the outraged voice *of* [civilized] order" (410). Insofar as we can label masculine and feminine principles, these interact in a way that engages part of both readings.

3. Ed. F. J. Fisher. In *Camden Miscellany*, vol. 16, 3d series, vol. 52 (London: Camden Society, 1936), 43.

4. Stephen Greenblatt, *Renaissance Self-Fashioning: From More to Shakespeare* (Chicago: University of Chicago Press, 1980), 2.

5. Ian Maclean in his comprehensive work *The Renaissance Notion of Women: A Study in the Fortunes of Scholasticism and Medical Science in European Intellectual Life* (Cambridge: Cambridge University Press, 1980) writes that the virtues of the Prince were traditional masculine values that even women rulers were supposed to acquire (60–61). Maclean notes too that those who claimed that men and women had identical virtues saw that because of the differing spheres of behavior those "deep" virtues had different "surface" expressions. His implied point (and one still valid today) is that without social change "conceptual" arguments have little impact (55–57). This was the case for the woman prince, who was not a model for women, but an exception.

6. In that chain of being that Shakespeare's work invokes (see E. M. W. Tillyard, *The Elizabethan World Picture* [New York: Random House, 1959]) the chain that orders all existence stays in place only by the actions of those in the society. The belief in the chain as it is exemplified in the lives of the citizens allows the chain to give society order.

7. Peter Erickson discusses thoroughly the Horatio-Hamlet relationship. He regards it as a type of male bonding that precludes the admission of women or the "feminine": *Patriarchal Structures in Shakespeare's Drama* (Berkeley: University of California Press, 1985), 71ff. Kay Stockholder, in *Dream Works: Lovers and Families in Shakespeare's Plays* (Toronto: University of Toronto Press, 1987), sees Horatio becoming the "ideal" man because he lacks "contaminating contact with women or with family" (43).

8. Regardless of whether this notion of man as an actor derives from Pico's *De hominis dignitate,* in which men are capable of every role, including the role of angels, the metaphor is apt, considering that the definition of manhood relies on fashioning oneself to an identity which may usefully be thought of as a role.

9. See "mad" in Ernest Weekley, *An Etymological Dictionary of Modern English* (New York: Dover Publications, 1967) and *The Oxford Dictionary of English Etymology,* ed. C. T. Onions (Oxford: Oxford University Press, 1976).

10. The dichotomy of masculine/feminine, mother/father, in the Renaissance and Shakespeare has been widely noted, from the histories of the family (such as Lawrence Stone, *Family, Sex and Marriage in England, 1500–1800* [New York: Harper and Row, 1977]; Steven Ozment, *When Fathers Ruled: Family Life in Reformation Europe* [Cambridge, Mass.: Harvard University Press, 1983]; Jonathan Goldberg, "Fatherly Authority: The Politics of Stuart Family Images," *Rewriting the Renais-*

sance: The Discourses of Sexual Difference in Early Modern Europe, ed. Margaret W. Ferguson, Maureen Quilligan, and Nancy J. Vickers [Chicago: University of Chicago Press, 1986], 3–32) to psychological criticism (such as Ernst Kris, *Psycholoanalytic Explorations in Art* [New York: International University Press, 1952]; Coppelia Kahn, *Man's Estate: Masculine Identity in Shakespeare* [Berkeley: University of California Press, 1981]; Marjorie Garber, *Coming of Age in Shakespeare* [London: Methuen, 1981]) or feminist criticism (Leverenz, "The Woman in Hamlet"; Marilyn French, *Shakespeare's Division of Experience* [New York: Ballantine Books, 1981]; Phyllis Rackin, "Anti-Historians: Women's Roles in Shakespeare's Histories," *Theatre Journal* 37 [1985]: 329–44).

11. In his book on the development of domestic or homiletic drama in England, Henry Adams (*English Domestic; or, Homiletic Tragedy 1575 to 1642* [1943; New York: Benjamin Blom, 1965]) remarks that viewed one way "even *Hamlet* may be properly called a domestic tragedy" (1). Yet given Adams's description of the standard plot of a domestic tragedy, we may be justified in expunging "even": "The ordinary Elizabethan domestic tragedy presented a tale of infidelity and murder. A wife falls in love with another man and plots with him to murder her husband. The crime is delayed by various circumstances, but eventually the deed is done. The wife and her lover are quickly revealed in some natural or supernatural way to the agents of justice, are sentenced to death, and pay the penalty for their crimes" (6–7). The resemblance to *Hamlet* is clear. As interesting, though unremarked by Adams, is the place of mothers in such plots.

12. *The Four Elements* (1519), in *Dodsley's Old Plays, vol. 1,* ed. W. Carew Hazlitt (1874; New York: Benjamin Blom, 1964), 5–50.

13. *The Disobedient Child* (c. 1560), in *Dodsley's Old Plays, vol. 2,* 269–320.

14. *Lusty Juventus* (c. 1560), in *Dodsley's Old Plays, vol. 2,* 45–102.

15. *Jack Juggler* (1562), in *Dodsley's Old Plays, vol.2,* 107–57.

16. *Calisto and Melibaea* (c. 1530) in *Dodsley's Old Plays, vol. 1,* 53–92.

17. The fifteenth-century Spanish dramatic novella on which this interlude is based explores chance, change, and women's power. In that work, Melibaea's father, Pleberio, once himself a follower of "sensual desire," gives the closing speech, which describes the world as controlled by irrational forces that cannot be surmounted (*The Celestina,* trans. Lesley Byrd Simpson [Berkeley: University of California Press, 1966], 158–62).

18. *Hickscorner* (c. 1530), in *Dodsley's Old Plays, vol. 1,* 147–95.

The name (Hic[k]-scorner) may suggest some connection with the *Hic Mulier–Haec Vir* controversy; see note 21 below.

19. *Nice Wanton* (1560), in *Dodsley's Old Plays, vol. 2*, 163–84.

20. John Ford, Thomas Dekker, and William Rowley, *The Witch of Edmonton*, in *Elizabethan and Stuart Plays*, ed. Charles Read Baskerfill, Virgil B. Heltzel, and Arthur H. Nethercot (New York: Holt, Rinehart and Winston, 1934), 1445–83.

21. Here the *Haec Vir* controversy is probably at the back of this revival. The sudden appearance of a number of tracts on the feminization of men and masculinization of women is thought to reflect the growing assertion of the equality of women, reflected in their adopting male dress, and the degeneration of men, reflected in the "wanton" dress of the courtiers. For discussion of this phenomenon see Linda Woodbridge, *Women and the English Renaissance: Literature and the Nature of Womankind, 1540–1620* (Urbana: University of Illinois Press, 1984); Mary Beth Rose, "Women in Men's Clothing: Apparel and Social Stability in *The Roaring Girl*," *English Literary Renaissance* 14 (1984): 367–91; R. Valerie Lucas, "*Hic Mulier*: The Female Transvestite in Early Modern England," *Renaissance and Reformation* 24 (1988): 65–84.

22. Of course, Lawrence Stone has made the rule of fathers in Renaissance England an established fact (*Family, Sex and Marriage*). It has been applied to much of literary study: for instance, Marianne Novy points out that emotional control and self-regulation were the father's message (*Love's Argument: Gender Relations in Shakespeare* [Chapel Hill: University of North Carolina Press, 1984], 9–10); Jonathan Goldberg reports on the ideological applications in painting in "Fatherly Authority."

23. Ian Maclean concludes that between 1580 and 1630 the notion of woman was revised so that they appeared the equals of men (*The Renaissance Notion of Women*, 89); Woodbridge sees the "uprising" of women to reach its height in the years of the *Hic Mulier* controversy, 1610–20 (*Women and the English Renaissance*, 263); on the other hand, Suzanne Gossett, in "'Best Men are Molded out of Faults': Marrying the Rapist in Jacobean Drama," *English Literary Renaissance* 14 (1984): 305–27, argues that in the second decade of the seventeenth century plots ending in the rapist's marrying his victim show a devaluation of women, the corruption of their sexual instinct, and the need for marriage to keep women in line. Of course, as Woodbridge argues, this may simply be a reaction to the growing independence of women and the challenge they were seen to present to male rule and masculinity.

24. Of course the play also the connects the "murder" of the father and the adultery which, as the play-within-the-play shows, also "kills" the father: see Richard Flatter, *Hamlet's Father* (New Haven: Yale University Press, 1949).

25. The mirror/dagger is also found in George Gascoigne, *The Steele Glas. A Satyre . . . togither with the Complainte to Phylomene* (1576; rpt. New York: Da Capo Press, 1973).

26. She is often played as tremendously unmoved throughout the bedroom scenes, partially in confirmation of her callous sinfulness. Rebecca Smith, on the other hand, argues that "Gertrude's words and actions . . . create not the lusty, lustful, lascivious Gertrude that one generally sees on the stage and film productions but a compliant, loving, unimaginative woman whose only concern is pleasing others": "A Heart Cleft in Twain: The Dilemma of Shakespeare's Gertrude," *The Woman's Part*, ed. Carolyn Ruth Swift Lenz, Gayle Greene, and Carol Thomas Neely (Urbana: University of Illinois Press, 1980): 206–7.

27. Juliet Dusinberre describes Hamlet as "a player, obscuring the real woman with [his] fictions": *Shakespeare and the Nature of Women* (New York: Barnes and Noble, 1975), 190.

28. The literature on masculine violence in Shakespeare is large. The first important work seems to be Madelon Gohlke's "'I wooed thee with my sword': Shakespeare's Tragic Paradigms," *The Woman's Part*, ed. Lenz, Greene, and Neely, 150–70. For her, violence arises in part out of the awareness that men owe their life to women and the hostility of expulsion from the mother's body; thus men violently intrude on the female body (157). Marianne Novy states, "Shakespeare's tragic heroes, like the traditional masculine stereotype of our own society, are afraid of qualities within themselves that they consider female and try to deny them by asserting their own male identity through violence" (*Love's Argument*, 164). The erotic component of this aggression has often been written about: see Joan M. Byles, "The Basic Pattern of Psychological Conflict in Shakespeare's Tragic Drama," *Hartford Studies in Literature* 11 (1979): 59.

29. As critics have pointed out, his unacknowledged desire for sexual expressivity lies behind those rebukes of his mother that seem to revel in her sexuality.

30. Stephen Booth in "On the Value of *Hamlet*," *Reinterpretation of Elizabethan Drama*, ed. Norman Rabkin (New York: Columbia University Press, 1969), 164–71, has demonstrated the incoherence of this and most of the soliloquies, showing that they are held together by their texture, rather than by their reason.

31. In *Antony and Cleopatra*, Octavius and Cleopatra represent a similar polarity between nobility (a sociopolitical concept) and love (a problematically moral, aesthetic, and physical concept). Octavius's nobility is such that he disdains physical affection, while Cleopatra values emotion above safety. She appears as a glorious, sensual goddess arisen from the fertile slime of the Nile, with which she is associated. This is to

reduce these two characters—particularly Cleopatra—severely; however, they do represent the polarities of the masculine and feminine in Shakespeare. Between the two of them is Antony, indifferently one or the other, unable to yoke the two qualities together.

32. Erich Fromm would express the world of Hamlet's father as "necrophilus": *The Heart of Man* (New York: Harper and Row, 1964). Necrophiles deny both life and death; they look for a sterile alternative. Fromm offers "biophilus" as the alternative. But there is no category in *Hamlet* that means "life-loving" in the same way Fromm means it. Nonetheless, Fromm's and Shakespeare's dichotomies do have genealogical resemblances.

33. Marjorie Garber notes that the comparisons of King Hamlet to Hercules always involve a derogation of Prince Hamlet (*Coming of Age*, 199–200). For her, Hamlet's dichotomizations show an unhealthy failure to admit sameness. Modern critics would argue that the dichotomy assumes sameness.

34. Throughout Shakespeare's work the shepherds offer an alternate version of masculinity loosely allied to the pastoral tradition, especially Corin in *As You Like It*. Louis Adrian Montrose argues that the pastoral represents a "feminine" power that was masculinized for political use: "'Eliza, Queene of Shepheardes,' and the Pastoral of Power," *English Literary Renaissance* 10 (1980): 153–82.

35. This suggestion arises from the resonance of these lines with Hamlet's comments on Rosenkrantz and Guildenstern: "Then you live about her [Fortune's] waist, or in the middle of her favours?" (II.ii.232–33). Being "about her waist" or "middle" is said to make them her "privates" (234). The comparison can be taken two ways: Rosenkrantz and Guildenstern are Fortune's genitals, or their genitals make Fortune a strumpet. Again, confusion clouds who is responsible for sexual activities, men or women, and here, as usual, responsibility shifts away from the males. Regardless of who instigates the seduction, by this metaphor we are invited to view Rosenkrantz and Guildenstern as agents of strumpet Fortune's fecundity. They are opportunists who conspire to help Fortune turn her wheel. It is appropriate that having "ma[d]e love to this employment" (V.ii.57), when they "go to't" (56), that what they go to is not sexual union but their downfall and death, which is the cost of sexualizing political activity, of reproducing in society. The sexuality of their approaches to Fortune is emphasized as well in Hamlet's finding of their commission: "Grop'd I to find out them, had my desire, / Finger'd their packets" (V.ii.14–15). It sounds as though Hamlet deflowers strumpet Fortune's privates. The link between misogyny and manliness is revealed in the sexualization of this passage, according to Linda Bamber,

Comic Women, Tragic Men: A Study of Gender and Genre in Shakespeare (Stanford, Calif.: Stanford University Press, 1982), 90.

36. It has been pointed out that the father only becomes ideal because of death: see C. L. Barber and Richard P. Wheeler, *The Whole Journey: Shakespeare's Power of Development* (Berkeley: University of California Press, 1986), 243–49.

37. For a complete discussion of the "O," see David Wilbern, "Shakespeare's Nothing," *Representing Shakespeare,* ed. Schwartz and Kahn, 244–63. Wilbern suggests the "O" is "unmanly" and arouses male anxiety, so that Shakespeare seeks to fill the stage with "actor/phalli" (259). When Hamlet says that he will remember his father, he suggests that everything else will be "nothing." The suggestion is that memory is meant to fill up "nothing." It might also be said that words are "matter" (semen) meant to fill up "nothing," as in Hamlet's response to Polonius about reading (II.ii.191–95).

38. Stockholder sees the plugging of the hole as necrophilia (*Dream Works,* 61). The connection of sex and death is a feature of *Hamlet* criticism, most recently in Stockholder (45). Donne also "equated the 'excremental jelly' of semen with 'that jelly which thy body dissolves to at last' ": James Grantham Turner, *One Flesh: Paradisal Marriage and Sexual Relations in the Age of Milton* (Oxford: Clarendon Press, 1987), 195.

39. Edmund Spenser, *Poetical Works,* ed. J. C. Smith and E. De Selincourt (London: Oxford University Press, 1912). While in Shakespeare's age women were thought to emit seed during intercourse, these features of Sensual Appetite's world, though labelled as "feminine," hardly belong to the exclusive province of women and other beasts. The ideal man, however, must rise above his nature. When Hamlet says, "I know not 'seems' " (I.ii.76), he suggests that nature—and semen in particular—is responsible for duplicity, for the uncomfortable distance between word and deed, ideal and actual.

40. Linda Bamber, *Comic Women, Tragic Men,* 72–73, 81.

41. Elaine Showalter in "Representing Ophelia: Women, Madness, and the Responsibilities of Feminist Criticism," *Shakespeare and the Question of Theory,* ed. Patricia Parker and Geoffrey Hartman (New York: Methuen, 1985), sees Ophelia as the absolute Other: "Deprived of thought, sexuality, language, Ophelia's story becomes the story of O— the zero, the empty circle or mystery of feminine difference, the cipher of female sexuality" (79); she is a "blank page to be written over or on by the male imagination" (89). Bamber also sees the women in *Hamlet* as generally the Other in this way (*Comic Women, Tragic Men,* 72ff.).

42. Many writers make this point: see Bamber, *Comic Women, Tragic Men,* 71.

43. "Blister" refers to venereal disease: see Frankie Rubenstein, *A Dictionary of Shakespeare's Sexual Puns and Their Significance* (London: Macmillan, 1984). "Ulcer" is not listed in her book, and the word is peculiar to *Hamlet*.

44. Book 4, line 1068, ed. Martin Ferguson Smith (Cambridge, Mass.: Harvard University Press, 1975). In the Galenic-Epicurean ideas of reproduction current in the Renaissance, both men and women produce seed, and the image of the ulcer in Lucretius describes genital swelling. This same image seems to underlie Horatio's remark that there appears "strange eruption to our state" (I.i.72).

45. Trans. Ronald Latham (Baltimore: Penguin, 1951), 162–63. We might ask why the neo-stoic Hamlet (see Sidney Shanker, *Shakespeare and the Uses of Ideology* [The Hague: Mouton, 1975], 81ff.) should invoke an Epicurean text. Throughout the play the tension of father/mother is also a tension of stoic/epicure since stoicism is conceived as *the* masculine philosophy. That may explain Shakespeare's use. The explanation of Hamlet's use does not need to be more complex: Hamlet has within him the same confusions that the play dramatizes. That he read and was attracted to Epicurean philosophy, while an unnecessary fiction, is one that fits.

46. According to Gohlke, Macbeth's violence comes from the fact that procreation confers power (158). To support this, she quotes from the play: "The *seeds* of Banquo kings!" (III.i.70; my emphasis).

47. Here is my divergence from Snow ("Sexual Anxiety"). The patriarchal Renaissance structure meant to keep sexuality in check not only makes female sexuality seem excessive, but releases male sexuality in perverse ways. This is neither civilized nor uncivilized man.

48. The idea of Claudius and King Hamlet as two aspects of the father which the son must reconcile has a long history, from Ernest Jones (*Hamlet and Oedipus* [New York: W. W. Norton, 1949]) on, a point repeated by Kirby Farrell, *Shakespeare's Creation: The Language of Magic and Play* (Amherst: University of Massachusetts Press, 1975), 175; Barber and Wheeler, *The Whole Journey*, 254; and others. Most recently Kay Stockholder suggests that there are several fathers: (1) the idealized martial father (Ghost Hamlet); (2) the satyr (Claudius); (3) the old man, fool (Polonius) (*Dream Works*, 43ff.). Stockholder, like the others, thinks that Hamlet's ambivalence about sexuality is represented in this split (45); yet she also thinks that by killing all his fathers, Hamlet "reclaims his own sexuality" (64). Of course, she disregards the important point that in order to have a "sexuality," one needs a public, social model for self-expression: see Terence Eagleton, *Shakespeare and Society* (New York: Schocken Books, 1967).

49. Stockholder notes that the lazar-like body of the poisoned king is an image of the sexualized father, Claudius (*Dream Works,* 45).

50. This is certainly typical of Shakespeare of this period (see Sonnet 144), and a well-known idea in Shakespearean criticism (see Jones, *Hamlet and Oedipus,* 88, 106). For Leverenz ("The Woman in Hamlet"), this is not just what Hamlet learns, but what the reader learns from *Hamlet.*

51. This pun is missing from Frankie Rubenstein's dictionary. The *locus classicus* would seem to be Dürer's *Fall of Man* (1504), in which the painter "delight[ed] in paralleling the tense relationship between Adam and Eve to that between a mouse and a cat crouching to spring": Erwin Panofsky, *The Life and Art of Albrecht Dürer* (Princeton: Princeton University Press, 1945) 84. The cat sleeps curled around the legs of Eve, while the mouse sits, tail stiff and straight, between the legs of Adam. As images of the male and female genitals, they also suggest the Renaissance view of the fallen relationship between the two: the consuming female ready to trap the masculine mouse.

52. John Hunt in "A Thing of Nothing: The Catastrophic Body in *Hamlet,*" *Shakespeare Quarterly* 39 (1988): 27–48, sees the play about Hamlet's "despairing contempt for the body" (27); he concludes that Hamlet comes to accept the body as a limit (44).

53. For the sensuality of Ophelia's song, see Caroll Camden, "On Ophelia's Madness," *Shakespeare Quarterly* 15 (1964): 247–55. Much debate exists about the significance and meaning of the songs. Frankie Rubenstein in "Persistent Sexual Symbolism: Shakespeare and Freud," *Literature and Psychology* 34 (1988): 1–26, describes the bawdy in these songs and suggests that Ophelia sees herself as a prostitute "scolded and sent to the nunnery as punishment for her participation in her father's charade to entrap Hamlet. . . . Ophelia had prostituted herself when she joined ranks with her father and rejected Hamlet's lover for her and her nonny" (22–23). "Nonny" is part of Ophelia's song that engages in punning on "nunnery" and "nothing." It connects the image of the vagina and the economy of prostitution.

54. This idea goes back to T. S. Eliot in "Hamlet and His Problems," *Sacred Wood* (London: Methuen, 1920); and J. Dover Wilson, *The Essential Shakespeare* (Cambridge: Cambridge University Press, 1932). Recently the notion has been examined critically by Jacqueline Rose in "Sexuality in the Reading of Shakespeare: *Hamlet* and *Measure for Measure,*" *Alternate Shakespeares,* ed. John Drakakis (London: Methuen, 1985). For Rose, the critics who conceive of this anxiety about sex as an anxiety about femininity should realize that it is "not, to put it at its most simple, the woman's fault" (116). Although Edward Snow identifies Othello's disgust with "post-coital male disgust with the 'filthy deed'

of sexuality itself" ("Sexual Anxiety," 388), which is close to Hamlet's "anxiety," Bamber resolutely begins her discussion by stating that the play is about Hamlet's "sexual nausea" (*Comic Women, Tragic Men,* 71–72).

55. Farrell, among others, points out that the "loathing" of others is a "self-loathing" (*Shakespeare's Creation,* 175).

56. William Shakespeare, *Sonnets,* ed. Douglas Bush and Alfred Harbage (Baltimore: Penguin Books, 1961).

57. Karl F. Thompson states that "lust is imagined as a traitorous counselor, a hunted object and then a hunter" in "Shakespeare's Sonnet 129," *A Casebook on Shakespeare's Sonnets,* ed. Gerald Willen and Victor B. Reed (New York: Thomas Y. Crowell Company, 1964): 174. C. W. M. Johnson finds that the focus of the poem is that "the victim [of lust] despises what he has had and promises himself better luck next time. . . . The poem provides us . . . an ironic disparity between means and ends, between expectation and realization": "Shakespeare's Sonnet 129," *Casebook On Shakespeare's Sonnets,* ed. Willen and Reed, 174–75. In a much later reading, Roger Stilling suggests that "Love for woman has become nothing more than a lust of the blood and permission of the will and woman herself a poisoning, maddening bait": *Love and Death in Renaissance Tragedy* (Baton Rouge: Louisiana State University Press, 1976), 107. In *Captive Victors: Shakespeare's Narrative Poems and Sonnets* (Ithaca, N.Y.: Cornell University Press, 1987), Heather Dubrow writes that Sonnet 129 shows "an anguished consideration of the anguish of lust" (178).

58. Dubrow does make the appropriate point that the victims of lust are ignored by the poem's commentators (*Captive Victors,* 209).

59. Knight finds that "when [Hamlet] is alone with death; then he is lovable and gentle, then he is beautiful and noble, and there being no trivial things of life to blur our mortal vision, our minds are tuned to the exquisite music of the soul" (*The Wheel of Fire: Interpretations of Shakespearean Tragedy with Three New Essays* [London: Methuen, 1954], 45–46).

60. Many commentators, particularly Christian critics, still see the play as a battle of good vs. evil: see Henry Morris, *Last Things in Shakespeare* (Tallahassee: Florida State University Press, 1985): "Sinless for his restraint and blessed for his ultimate fulfillment of a heavenly deputizement, [Hamlet] goes . . . to his reward, the celestial coronation of the man in grace at his death" (75).

61. Cf. *Thersites* (1530), in *Dodsley's Old Plays, vol. 1,* 395–431.

62. It has been pointed out that Hamlet's quiescence on the issue of "women" occurs simply because the women leave, Hamlet withdraws,

and the question is avoided altogether (Bamber, *Comic Women, Tragic Men*, 82–83).

63. One of the most interesting redactions of the original Saxo story is the possible transformation of the Queen's father Roricus (Rorique) into Yorick. As the father of the Queen we might expect Rorique-Yorick to represent a maternal-male presence, and this is exactly what we get in the picture of Yorick: "He hath bore me on his back a thousand times. . . . Here hung those lips that I have kissed I know not how oft." (V.i.179ff.) This is the most intimate depiction of a relationship between any two characters in the play. It is not surprising that Hamlet in his jests and gibes should so resemble the man: see Saxo Grammaticus, *Amleth*, in *The Sources of Hamlet*, ed. Sir Israel Gollancz (1926; rpt. New York: Octagon Books, 1967).

64. This medieval icon of Christ's sacrifice was adopted by Queen Elizabeth. It was meant to transform feminine nurturance into masculine power: see Louis Adrian Montrose, "*A Midsummer Night's Dream* and the Shaping Fantasies of Elizabethan Culture: Gender, Power, Form," *Rewriting the Renaissance*, ed. Ferguson, Quilligan, and Vickers, 77.

65. In *The Unfortunate Traveler*, ed. J. B. Steane (Baltimore: Penguin, 1972).

66. Many modern readers see an attempt to accommodate patriarchy and protofeminism: see Marilyn L. Williamson, *The Patriarchy of Shakespeare's Comedies* (Detroit: Wayne State University Press, 1986); Marianne L. Novy, "Patriarchy and Play in *The Taming of the Shrew*," *English Literary Renaissance* 9 (1979): 280. Some see the "feminine" as triumphant: "The values that emerge from these plays are, if anything, 'feminine', values dissociated from traditional categories of force and politics, focussed instead on the significance of personal relationships, or the fact of human relatedness: the value of feeling, of kinship, of loyalty, friendship, and even romantic love" (Gohlke, "'I wooed thee with my sword,'" 161). Some see the whole question of sex difference called into question, as in Catherine Belsey, "Disrupting Sexual Difference: Meaning and Gender in the Comedies," *Alternate Shakespeares*, ed. Drakakis, 167; Jonathan Dollimore and Alan Sinfield, "History and Ideology: The Instance of *Henry V*," *Alternate Shakespeares*, ed. Drakakis, 206–27. Masculine perspectives do seem to win out in the plays, although the plays may call them into question.

67. James Calderwood notes the regressive aspects of this "Father-worship": *Shakespeare and the Denial of Death* (Amherst: University of Massachusetts Press, 1987), 116.

68. "Castra" is a walled encampment, a fort. Throughout this chapter

and the previous I have suggested that the fortification of masculinity required men to repress their sexual functions. The word "de-castration," then, suggests life outside those walls.

69. The absence of women at the end of the play is conspicuous to Carol Thomas Neely (*Broken Nuptials in Shakespeare's Plays* [New Haven: Yale University Press, 1985], 104) and Bamber (*Comic Women, Tragic Men*, 82ff.). Both see this, quite rightly, as the triumph of the masculine ethic.

4

The Sin of Origins:
Heavenly Fathers and Men Children

Les enfants sont hautains, dédaigneux, colères,
envieux, curieux, intéressés, paresseux, volages,
timides, intempérants, menteurs, dissimules; ils
rient et pleurent facilement; ils ont des joies im-
moderées et des afflictions amères sur de très pe-
tits sujets; ils ne veulent point souffrir de mal et
aiment à en faire: ils sont déjà des hommes.

Il n'y a pour l'homme que trois événements: naître,
vivre et mourir; il ne se sent pas naître, il souffre
à mourir, et il oublie de vivre.

—Jean de la Bruyère, "De l'Homme,"
Les Caractères, 1688

IN BOOK X of *Paradise Lost,* a shameful Adam momentarily echoes
Hamlet's speculations on being. Stoicism had not been able to provide
Hamlet with the iron resolve needed against the world. Instead, Hamlet's "To be or not to be" speech reflects confusion and painful struggle with a life that has somehow crawled into the armor of his roles,
philosophy, and words. As a result the speech rocks uneasily among
various alternatives: exhortation to action, renunciation of the world,
fantasy of self-slaughter. Milton uses this affecting passion to show
Adam's anguish and improve Shakespeare's lesson:

> How gladly would I meet
> Mortality my sentence, and be Earth
> Insensible, how glad would lay me down
> As in my Mother's lap! There I should rest

And sleep secure; . . .
 Yet one doubt
Pursues me still, lest all I cannot die,
Lest the pure breath of Life, the Spirit of Man
which God inspir'd, cannot together perish
With this corporeal Clod; then in the Grave,
Or in some other dismal place, who knows
But I shall die a living Death? O thought
Horrid, if true! . . .
 But say
that Death be not one stroke, as I suppos'd,
Bereaving sense, but endless misery
From this day onward, which I feel begun
Both in me, and without me, and so last
To perpetuity; Ay me, that fear
Comes thund'ring back with dreadful revolution
On my defenseless head; . . .
On mee . . .
 all the blame lights due;
So might the wrath. Fond wish! couldst thou support
That burden heavier than the Earth to bear,
Than all the World much heavier, though divided
With that bad Woman? Thus what thou desir'st,
And what thou fear'st, alike destroys all hope
Of refuge, and concludes thee miserable
Beyond all past example and future,
to Satan only like both crime and doom.
O Conscience, into what Abyss of fears
And horrors hast thou driv'n me; out of which
I find no way, from deep to deeper plung'd.

(X.775–844)[1]

All the characteristic gestures of Hamlet's speech are present in Adam's prolix prefiguration,[2] as well as many of the problems: to sleep, perchance to dream, who would fardels bear, conscience makes cowards of us all, currents run awry.

 In revisiting the throes of Hamlet's agony, Milton shifts focus away from man's problems and passions to the defects of reasoning not directed by God and to the creation of a theological framework to resolve agony. Whereas Hamlet's seemed the woe of existence, Adam's appears that of Man in the hands of an angry God. Adam's Hamlet-like ruminations are sinful, a lesson that he himself makes explicit when he upbraids Eve for having the same thoughts: "self-destruction . . . sought, refutes / That excellence thought in thee" (X.1016–17). This glancing blow falls equally on Hamlet. The stoic resolution that Adam arrives at, however, comes through submission to a Heavenly father: "He will instruct us praying, and of Grace / Beseeching him" (X.1081–82). It is this special submission that strengthens men: "that suffering for Truth's sake / Is fortitude to highest victory, / And to the faithful Death the Gate of Life" (XII.569–71). Thus Adam will possess "A paradise within" (XII.587), becoming what Hamlet could not, a good son and a happy stoic.

Paradise Lost retells the story of the first three chapters of Genesis in a verse epic-drama that tries to "justify the ways of God to men" (I.26). Satan, having been deposed from the right hand of God for rebelling, tries to revenge himself by destroying God's latest work, man. While Satan plots in hell, in paradise Adam and Eve live unsuspecting in perfect harmony, including sexual harmony. Satan, however, with God's foreknowledge and permission, manages to rise from the pit, evade the angelic guards, breach the walls of Eden and seduce Eve with ideas of knowledge and power. Satan convinces Eve to break God's commandment and eat from the forbidden tree, and, through his love for Eve, Adam is persuaded to do the same. After Christ comes to earth, drives Satan back to hell, and draws penitence from the first parents, the Father sends Adam and Eve a vision of the ultimate comedy of human history, and Michael carries out the punishment of casting them from the garden. Through his trials, Adam reaffirms what he had already known: that history is in the hands of God, who is his father, and whom he must obey. For Adam obedience means wearing the armor of virtue, ignoring desire, earthly knowledge, and earthly affiliations. His fall comes from his degrading lack of control.

Control governs Milton's epic from its formidable theme to its formidable style.[3] In *Hamlet* Shakespeare shows that the earth of itself does not produce divisions or limits. Natural growth and change instead push against the divisions and limits imposed by men. Nor does nature exist simply as an exogenous problem—like the sea outside the fort. Nature is endogenous. Men overflow with corrupt and corrupting nature. Hamlet's father, who represents a masculine order imposed on the world, is himself subject to the cycles and tensions of nature that his order tries to subdue, is himself as sensual, fertile, emotional as his Queen. King Hamlet, King Claudius, and Queen Gertrude all become equivalent in the play. As a result, Hamlet's days, like Shakespeare's, become what one contemporary writer called "these degenerate effeminate days of ours."[4] Thus man becomes, in his own eyes, feminized.

In *Hamlet* the forts, walls, armor have ceased to define the world of the adult male. Hamlet himself wears no armor. His soft garb, like Gawain's at Bercilak's castle, suggests vulnerability. In contrast, Hamlet's father appears typically armed. Yet he was murdered unarmed, an emblematic end familiar to readers of the first book of *The Faerie Queene,* for instance. A man disarms and sleeps in a garden. Relaxing his virtue, he suffers the mortal venom of the world—death, passion, sexuality—to enter his unprotected body.[5] *Hamlet* shows that without armor man enters an ambiguous state of gender identity, a state that exposes new aspects of the world and of himself.

Paradise Lost revisits the primal scene of Hamlet's misfortune— here, the garden is Eden; the poison, the serpent's. Milton's man stands totally naked and in nature while his *Paradise Lost* seeks to refit the newly exposed male body with the armor of virtue first lost in the garden when Adam sunk into the sleep of sensuality. Such a refitting, however, does not deny the importance of worldly experience to human health and existence. Instead *Paradise Lost* expresses the joy men find in the world, a joy of experience itself, but a joyful experience through which men also become subject to pain. Milton, seeking a solution to the pain that arises from worldly pleasure, finds an answer similar to the ones in *Areopagitica* and *Paradise Regained*—balance, the balance of the human state with a spiritual state resistant to pain. The idea of the fortunate fall inspires his solution, for the fall allows humans both to experience the world and to rise above the world, striking a balance between competing human needs.

Yet the tensions in the paradoxes from which balance is created—stasis with growth, affection with stoicism—can seem to underscore, rather than alleviate, the difficulties of men in the world. In part the tension in the paradoxes may seem to be exacerbated by the position of men in relationship to God. The masculinity of *Paradise*

Lost comforts men because it places them in a state of childhood, discovering the pleasures of the world while relying on the superior wisdom and security of an all-knowing and powerful elder. At the same time, such a solution partially deprives men of the power of creating actions or beings, a power that the Father correctly possesses. Milton's new Christian armor, which refashions Hamlet's armor, may help bring the changing and heterogeneous aspects of Hamlet's world under the systematic control of a fatherly God,[6] but the new masculinity, trying to rise above its paradoxes, often holds out the promise of action, experience, pleasure, of which it ultimately deprives men. Thus it threatens to divest men both of the former powers of masculinity and of the forbidden pleasures of the world. Adam's happy stoicism, then, requires a painful renunciation of what has hitherto been considered masculine as well as feminine.

As we have seen, earlier social relationships between fathers and sons required sons to imitate fathers by forgetting, excising, and dismembering aspects of their experience, by dissociating moral order from ontological observation, ideal from actual beings and behaviors, nurture from nursing. In order to surmount the difficulties created by this dissociation, Milton like many other seventeenth-century thinkers attempts to ground his polity on human nature. He attempts, therefore, to demonstrate that the relationship between the child-man and Father-God represents an ontological condition that carries a moral imperative, a truth men may ignore only at their greatest peril. As children of God, men have both a moral and ontological duty to act like children of God.[7] *Paradise Lost* proclaims the solution implied in *Hamlet:* a divine Father provides the perfect and incorruptible model.

By joining the moral and the ontological, Milton's line of reasoning allows him to include in man features of nature—growth, sexuality, death—that posed a threat both outside and within the previous systems. In order to bring nature and virtue together, however, he must repress the idea that mores originate in the imperfect human attempt to control nature and make morality a feature of the ontology of human nature itself. For morality to cease being arbitrary it must be fixed by everlasting laws above earthly corruption, and those laws must be definitive of "nature," of what it means to be human.

The excesses and deficiencies that ennobled and destroyed Renaissance heroes represented possible variations in the wide range of human nature. As in Aristotle's *Ethics,* the variety of human actions never impugned the humanness of the actor. In Milton's world, as in that of many eighteenth-century writers until de Sade, morality becomes part of the definition of what it is to be human, so that variations in human behavior raise questions, not just about the actor's morals or upbringing, but about the actor's humanness. That is, humans—but particularly men—are "created" perfect, from the standpoint of moral potential, and placed in a perfect, but inhuman, world.[8] Humans have been equipped to know their Father and obey his precepts. Should they not do these things, then they are willfully, not essentially, imperfect. By failing to follow the rules of the Father, a man does not express some repressed but essential humanity; instead he exposes his inhumanity, degrades his being, and blasphemes his Father's creation. Moreover, he becomes vulnerable to possible essential corruption of his nature, as for instance did the fallen angels who from one nature made another, becoming increasingly dull, supine, and corpulent.

To make human nature ontologically subservient to moral order, however, requires that human nature be contracted into a small sphere beyond which whatever we once thought of as natural must be considered as purely accidental. As father, God is not an inseminator, but a creator of humans who, though born of women, are made essentially perfect from the beginning.[9] Such perfection means that Milton suppresses not only mores, but local origins—conceived in terms of temporal sociocultural contexts and human biological origins.[10] Milton's conception thus clouds the need for growth in the unfolding or perfection of humans. While his conception tends to promote those aspects associated with childhood—education, trial and error, contingency, adaptation—it paradoxically also undercuts them, for the concept of childhood that could bring morality and existence together would seem to require maturity as a feature. Thus, for instance, despite the fact that *Paradise Lost* depicts three separate households— God's, Adam's, and Satan's—each household lacks elements fundamental to most families, not least of all infants. All the children in *Paradise Lost* are born as adult children. This would seem necessary, for morality, unchangeable over time, is associated with rational maturity. Following an Aristotelian as well as a patristic tradition, when Milton conceives of beings of perfect rational maturity, he conceives of men.

Yet Milton also makes it clear that the privileges maturity confers on men, although accommodating much of what men recognized as their natural impulses, have, like other privileges conferred on men, overwhelming costs. By obscuring earthly origins,[11] for instance, the masculinity of *Paradise Lost* tends to cut men off from each other, from their history, and from aspects of themselves.[12] Recognizing none but an accidental earthly origin, a man must willingly sever all ties to his past—his childhood, his parents, his experiences—and to the earth in general.[13]

The problems of a simultaneous acceptance and rejection of growth and experience helps clarify the tensions in the depictions of relationships of men to themselves, to other men, to women, and to the world in general in *Paradise Lost*. The symbol by which Raphael explains the "movement" of body up to spirit exemplifies this tension:[14]

> So from the root
> Springs lighter the green stalk, from thence the leaves
> More aery, last the bright consummate flow'r
> Spirits odorous breathes:
>
> (V.479–82)

"Consummate" seems an ugly and heavy word to crown the plant and, etymologically speaking, it is misapplied to the flower, which is not a plant's consummate part. But the tension between the beauty of the image and the ugliness of the word suggests the oscillation in the book's teachings on procreation and origins. The substitution of "flow'r" for the truly consummate part seems both to call for and to evade the crucial question: where are the seeds? By the early seventeenth century herbalists understood the growth of plants: roots spring down from seeds; the consummate part of the plant—in terms of its sexual and life cycle—is the seed. But the seeds have been repressed and a substitution made: "one Almighty is, from whom / All things proceed, and up to him return" (V.469–70). Not only does God originate everything, but he alone gives life to everything. This picture of the growing plant thus simultaneouly honors consummation even as it effaces earthly growth and the natural philosophies that explain growth in favor of a supervenient author, a Father.

The same problem occurs in the following lines, where Raphael speaks of "flow'rs and thir fruit / Man's nourishment" (V.482–83). Here Raphael reminds Adam that plants also bear fruit—though since they are not light and aery and since they assist reproduction, they had apparently previously been omitted. However, here too "flow'rs" appears ambiguous. Because Raphael uses "flow'r" both metonymically for the plant as a whole and literally for the blossom, he suggests that the plant is a "blossom." This confusion has a purpose: being close to angels, men should eat the light and aery blossoms, not the gross plants. The obscurity thus created by word order is reinforced by the line's suggestion that fruit and blossoms are also equivalent. Humans rarely eat flowers, besides broccoli, cauliflower, marigolds, and dandelions. They do eat many roots, leaves, and fruits. The images suppress any view of the plant as a whole in which the parts have vital relationships with each other, but in particular Milton ignores the root, for it suggests earthly origins, sex, growth, nourishment. Thus the exquisite beauty with which God feeds Adam and Eve represses parts of human experience, giving an illusion of earthly delights that the images simultaneously withdraw. This awful tension between the childlike delicacy granted to men and their expected moral maturity that cuts them off from certain childlike and mature aspects of experience further authorizes God the Father's intervention to solve the difficulties of human experience.

And other tensions exist. While sequential images that describe the plant suggest growth, the sequence masks and reveals deep stresses between movement and stasis. The images show the parts of a plant fully grown; they do not show a plant developing. Not only do these separate pictures fragment the plant even as they seek to integrate its parts: the images sacrifice the idea of growth in order to serve as a model of growth. In no sense does the root become the stem become the leaf become the flower. A stem is not a transformed root, nor does Milton present it as such: "Each in thir several active Spheres assign'd, / Till body up to spirit work, in bounds / Proportion'd to each kind" (V.477–79) states that each part is incapable of becoming any other part. "Up to spirit work," while implying movement and growth, also denies it. In its context the line means "until the body performs up to its capacity." Yet an ambiguous impression is created that "work" may mean "move," but then that is contradicted by the rest of the passage and is also a fallen way to view the word, since it acquired that meaning only in the early seventeenth century. Certainly Raphael evades telling Adam how likely he is to become an angel, as has been pointed out by Joseph Summers and others. Raphael ends his speech by asserting that Adam is "incapable of more" happiness. The sense of "growth" holds out the hope that, growing like the plant, Adam may eventually become capable of more; yet growth, self-help, education, training seem contradicted in the images. Men may dream of self-improvement, of growth, but at least a suspicion or anxiety lurks that where they are, they must stay except insofar as called to move by an authority above them. Thus no origin, no being, no development may seem possible beyond what they might find a constricting, though divinely given and intermittently comforting, ontology.

A related note about the phrase that culminates Raphael's speech will show how deeply the difficulty over growth and origins runs in the work: "what happiness this happy state / Can comprehend" (V.504–5), which is all that Adam is capable of. "State," like most Latin-rooted words in Milton's work, carries its "original" meaning—standing, static, not moving. Adam is "happy" in this position of non-movement, non-growth. Yet as with other non-Latin words derived from Old English roots such as "work," Milton uses the "fallen" or current meaning of the word. "Happ" originally meant "by chance," although the implication was frequently "good chance," that is, "luck." But in *Paradise Lost*, Adam's "state" is not a stroke of good luck or chance. This use of contemporary and corrupted meaning by an angel breaks the usual pattern for Latin words: before the fall "wanton" meant fertile, not lascivious; "error" meant wandering, not sin.[15] Words applied to an object according to this plan suggest something slightly less spiritual, but do not mean anything sinful—for that would imply a fallen view before the fall. By leaping over the intervening history of words to the Latin "originals," Milton suggests a prelapsarian state and subsequent corruption.

On the other hand, Milton usually presents words derived from Old Saxon, Old Norse, and Old English as if they had no history. Milton uses the word "nice" as if it never passed through Old English (*ny-wys*). It originally meant—as the title of the interlude *Nice Wanton* illustrates—ignorant, simple-minded, and had the connotation of rather unseemly foolishness. Although both the Latin and Anglo-Saxon words are, each in a different way, cut off from their historical development, from the process of growth, the rejection of Anglo-Saxon words in general and Milton's lack of concern for their origins in particular suggest that Milton, perhaps unconsciously, repressed his own identity as a speaker of English—his own historical, cultural, national, ethnic origins which are largely Anglo-Saxon. In order to save mankind and manhood, Milton appears at times to ignore himself as a product of history.

In spite of the general rejection of origins, history, growth, culture, and development that the work implies, even in the choice of words,[16] origins surface. For instance, *Paradise Lost* implies that the roles, duties, and relationships of men and women derive from eternal, natural structures laid down at the moment of divine creation.[17] The work presents humans not only as adults but also as wives-mothers and husbands-fathers, which suggests that God intended these contractual relationships to perfect male and female being. Yet this suggestion of the timeless spiritual nature of human institutions simultaneously raises the idea of their local origins. This tension is clearly presented by the description of Eden's domestic arrangements, for the archetypal behaviors of man and woman, Adam and Eve, apparently reproduce accepted contemporary notions of the sexual division of labor. Dinner preparations exemplify Milton's enjambment of divine plan and present history. Adam and Eve share most tasks, but not mealmaking:

> Adam . . . in the door . . . sat
> Of his cool Bow'r, while now the mounted Sun
> Shot down direct his fervid Rays, to warm
> Earth's inmost womb, more warmth than Adam needs;
> And Eve within, due at her hour prepar'd
> For dinner savoury fruits.
>
> (V.299–304)

Glosses do not make apparent any biblical precedent for this. Milton attempts to translate the existent social arrangement between men and women into a natural arrangement, suggesting that if change has occurred or were to occur it would be unnatural and without divine sanction.[18] Although Milton's theme would discredit the evolutions of custom, one could only with difficulty argue that this is a picture of Eden, rather than a picture of a contemporary household.[19] Nor does the following dialogue suggest the epic of first man and woman so

much as the contemporary theater of domestic relations. Adam
orders,

> But go with speed,
> And what thy stores contain, bring forth and pour
> Abundance, fit to honor and receive
> Our Heav'nly stranger. . . .
> To whom thus Eve. Adam, earth's hallow'd mould,
> Of God inspir'd, small store will serve, where store,
> All seasons, ripe for use hangs on the stalk;
> Save what by frugal storing firmness gains
> To nourish, and superfluous moist consumes:
> But I will haste and from each bough and brake,
> Each Plant and juiciest Gourd will pluck such choice
> To entertain our Angel guest.
> (V.313–28)

This scene may have been placed here, as some critics suggest, to show
Eve's incipient rebellion and her vanity about her knowledge; perhaps
it was also meant to illustrate what sometimes seems the pomposity
of Adam.[20] But regardless, Milton does seem to intend Eve's "hallow'd
mould, Of God inspir'd" to be sarcastic, and the epithet does become
ironic in Adam's actions. The irony lies not in Adam's assertion of
dominance, but in his ignorance about the running of the household,
his obliviousness to the particular nature and uses of the fruits of
Eden. While historically such ignorance may have been cultivated
among men to maintain a disequilibrium within the household, such
ignorance is difficult to understand in the being who named and knew
the nature of all things (VIII.271–76, 339–54). Moreover, it is even
less clear in Eden than outside it why Adam has earned his rest from
labor while Eve must labor on.

This displacement of current conditions of gender relations to the
ideal world of innocence seems satirical in the hands of Milton. For
Milton seems alive to the difficulties and ambiguities of his themes
and characters. Such juxtapositions were, in fact, a feature of the period's theoretical works on government—tracing the foundations of
current practice to eternal truth and biblical precedent. Such is the
argument of Robert Filmer's *Patriarchia*, for instance. And even in his
reply to Filmer, John Locke argues from divine truth while taking a

point antithetical to Filmer's and Milton's: "God . . . gives not, that I see, any authority to Adam over Eve, or to men over their wives, but only foretells what should be the woman's lot, how by his providence he would order it so that she should be subject to her husband, as we see that generally the laws of mankind and customs of nations have ordered it so, and there is, I grant, a foundation in nature for it" (chap. 5, sec. 47).[21] In the next section Locke goes on to state that even after the fall the subjection of women to men is only "the power that every husband hath to order the things of private concernment to the family . . . but not a political power . . . over her" (chap. 5, sec. 48). Locke's argument reveals just how embedded the depictions of Adam and Eve are in contemporary practice, since the Bible appears to offer no clear foundation.

Although Locke is not disencumbered of notions of sexual inequality, he does make two important points explicitly and another implicitly that use Biblical sources to contradict the Miltonic picture: (1) subjection occurred after the fall; (2) subjection concerns only husband and wife, and only insofar as they are husband and wife; (3) this arrangement is legal, not natural (although he believes there may be a natural basis), and that the legal arrangement applies only between husbands and wives, who have entered into a contractual, as well as sacramental, relationship, and not to men and women generally. Viewed from the standpoint of Locke and Filmer, then, Milton seems consciously to have entered a highly contested area. In presenting Adam and Eve as husband and wife, he boldly presents man and woman in their essence, while retaining a disruptive doubt. For in *Paradise Lost* the "institutional" relationships of Adam and Eve seem at times artificially imposed ones against which both chafe.

It would seem then that at times, in his insistence to justify the ways of God to men, Milton sought to surmount such domestic difficulties, that he wished to use the spiritual to justify the ways of men to themselves and himself, to make natural what was customary masculine behavior by giving social arrangement a spiritual origin.[22] Such telescoping of the present and the eternal occurs throughout, as in the later histories that refigure and therefore echo Satan's fall. The work's intense verticality, its dogged insistence on the "Eternal Now," squeezes the horizontal line of history so that change stands on the verge of obliteration and the universal pattern emerges, static and always present. Such threat to obliterate change in the history of men—who are the primary beneficiaries of this program—also threatens to squeeze out many of those aspects that the work suggests men cherish.

The imagery of the dinner scene illustrates how this tension we have been noting often culminates in pain for Adam, who is squeezed between two powerful and conflicting forces that dominate his life and access to either of which he is denied. In the dinner scene Adam inhabits a small space between the horizontal order (a temporality represented by Eve, the bower, and the food preparations) and the vertical order (a supervenient power represented by the noonday sun). The placement creates both pain and tension for Adam. For instance, Adam needs to escape the heavenly sun's violent inseminating force: the "Sun / Shot down direct his fervid rays" (V.300–301). Therefore, he crouches at the threshold of the temporal womb-home-bower. Inside, where Eve alone may enter, she perfects the garden's food. Adam sits uncomfortably between the sun-inseminator (masculine) and the home-womb (feminine).

To his advantage, Adam receives the food that both worlds conspire to produce without directly experiencing the discomforts of either sun or home. Yet he receives those benefits by not entering either world completely, by keeping his position, by a self-control that calls for a partial rejection of and isolation from either. Eve, on the other hand, not only prepares the meal within, but ventures into the heat to gather fresh fruits and, later during Raphael's talk, wanders through the garden alone. Eve's mobility without Adam to control her poses an incipient danger to her; yet she can do what Adam cannot. Given a purely temporal view rather than the divine one, hers in some respects seems the happier lot.[23]

In maintaining his privileged place Adam must circumscribe his actions in other ways as well. He must be obedient. Again, the imagery of the bower, with its sexual symbolism, indicates obedience to God as an alternative to procreative love. At the same time it suggests symbolically the painful sense of exclusion that, sitting at the mouth of the womb, confronting a fiery penis, a fearful child might experience. "Love" of the Father in *Paradise Lost*, according to Joseph Summers, means being "careful only of the divine pleasure," pure selflessness that has its purest expression in obedience.[24] Therefore, being obedient means that through the perfect act of will one puts oneself in the hands of a perfect, strong-willed, and all-knowing other. In terms of social relations, this submission as a form of self-restraint means putting one's self in the position of an obedient, loving, and trusting child to a perfect, loving, and trustworthy parent. Yet, although treated as a child, the child is an adult who must surmount a variety of experiences, expectations, and desires that have often defined maturity.[25] Adam's patient sitting at the threshold—as precarious and lonely as its reverberations make it—represents an acceptable outward sign of a perfect inner emotional state.

In the bower scene this divine hierarchy of will has been superimposed on a gendered world, suggesting still another threshold position that troubles Adam. Men are children of God, obedient and powerless in that relationship; yet the symbolism of the bower makes the differential relationship of Adam to the Christ-Father (the sun) also a differential relation to masculine energy (sun). That is, Adam's position excludes him from masculine potency, both in the sense that he is a child and in the sense that God, not man, makes all things. Adam, the model of masculinity, becomes nonmasculine. And yet the difference between Eve's and Adam's status in the bower scene flows from their sex/gender differences. In relationship to God, men are nonmasculine; in relationship to women, masculine.[26] The mystery of a child-man or a male nonmale—a creature perpetually on the threshold of initiation, but belonging to no group—might make sense theologically, but it appears psychologically devastating to Adam, who as adult male epitomizes masculinity, while as child loses crucial aspects of the masculine ideal.

An anxiety-producing sense of betweenness is repeatedly brought home to Adam in his displacement between God and Satan, heaven and hell, and, in this scene, Raphael and Eve. Raphael's visit suggests Adam's isolation in two ways: God sends Raphael to make clear to Adam just how precarious his position is, and God foreknows and tells that this warning will not help Adam keep his balance. Raphael's visit reinforces Adam's sense that, despite his request that God not leave him alone, he is fundamentally alone, not allowed to enter either the angel's or Eve's world, always needing to be careful about overstepping some line, as the angel's cautions make clear. In these scenes one senses Adam's anxiety in his eagerness and embarrassment in the presence of the angel, his desire to impress his superior guest without committing a faux pas. Adam, then, and in him all men are depicted by Milton as bounded, isolated, between woman and angel, between time and eternity, between masculine and feminine, rejecting while partaking of both sides of these dichotomies. This between state is man's unhappy/happy situation.[27]

The paradox of a child-man is clarified in the details of the work, particularly through the depiction of Christ. Although God has many children, only one is his "begotten" Son (III.8, 384). As the perfect Son, Christ offers a model for man's relationship to God the Father and to his own potential children. Christ, begotten perfect, needs no education or growth to raise him to a more perfect state. From the first he embodies God the Father.[28] The angels, in hymning him, call him

> Divine Similitude
> In whose conspicuous count'nance, without cloud
> Made visible, th' Almighty Father shines,
> . . . on thee
> Impresst th' effulgence of his Glory abides,
> Transfus'd on thee his ample Spirit rests.
>   (III.384–89)

The Son is the active principle of the Father, the outward manifestation of his invisible spirit.

Nor are He and his Father clearly distinguishable, so interfused is Father in Son, as the dance of pronouns in the song makes clear: "Hee Heav'n of Heavens and all the Powers therein / By thee created, and by thee threw down / Th' aspiring Dominations" (III.390–92). In this verse, "Hee" coalesces with "thee." Moreover, "by thee," no simple ablative of means, superimposes a passive on active construction—as if God the Father were the implicit subject in a passive construction in which the Son was the active agent. Further along in the hymn the referent of "hee" shifts from Father to Son and "thee" from Son to Father, so that the interfusion is complete: "Hee to appease thy wrath, and end the strife / Of Mercy and Justice in thy face discern'd . . . " (III.406–7).

Although Adam and Christ are vastly dissimilar, a similar relationship applies between God and man. To achieve perfect manhood, men, as children of God, must internalize the spirit of God, right reason, which makes them active agents for the inspiriting Father.[29] Or, to put it another way, sons never achieve their own manhood but serve as a conduit for their heavenly father's "manhood." Masculinity embodies the divine. As one result, that which arises and has its origin in man alone, from within man or the world of men rather than from without, is bad. In this sense Sin is worse than Satan, Eve than Adam. Christ has no such problem, for he comes from within God the Father who informs each part of him. Implicitly, such a system of relationship further alienates Adam from aspects of himself and from others. Through the semiotics of origin, men are alienated from paternity, emotion, sensation, desire, and experience generally.

Consider for a moment how Adam's relationship to his progeny is affected. When children come, they will not owe obedience to their parents, since things of earthly origin, though not in themselves bad, become bad when they look no further than the earth. Therefore, the relationship between parents and children becomes secondary to the relationship of children to God their Father. In this way Milton reproduces one of the points of the morality plays and interludes—the rejection of biological parents.[30] Adam's reasoning about the teleology of procreation amply illustrates this rejection:

> thy Seed shall bruise
> The Serpent's head; piteous amends, unless
> Be meant, whom I conjecture, our grand Foe
> Satan, who in the Serpent hath contriv'd
> Against us this deceit: to crush his head
> Would be revenge indeed; which will be lost
> By death brought on ourselves, or childless days
> Resolv'd, as thou proposest; . .
> No more be mention'd . . .
>   wilful barrenness,
> That cuts us off from hope, and savors only
> Rancor and pride, impatience and despite,
> Reluctance against God and his just yoke
> Laid on our Necks.
>   (X.1031–46)

"Necks," the classical icon of servitude, here incorporates a pun on the contemporary anatomical name for the sexual organs in men and women. God gives Adam and Eve a genital servitude. Procreation cre-

ates material for fulfilling divine will. The growth of the embryo resembles other types of growth, nothing in itself, only an occasion for
some greater good—food or clothes or redemption, depending on the
animal.
   When Adam is shown the slaying of Abel by Cain and is told that
"These two are Brethren, Adam, to come / Out of thy loins" (XI.454–
56), he evinces no interest that these beings who will die in hideous
fashion are his children. Their lives have only symbolic value, convey-
ing that death awaits all men. Later, in a line that critics have sometimes pointed to as an instance of bad taste, Adam shows his lack of
concern for human beings generally and for his progeny in particular
when he remarks about the destruction of the Flood:

> Far less I now lament for one whole World
> Of wicked Sons destroy'd, than I rejoice
> For one Man found so perfet and so just,
> That God voutsafes to raise another World
> From him, and all his anger forget.
>   (XI.874–78)

That Adam does not seem to have much feeling for his "sons" or, in
the case of Cain and Abel, that he does not seem to take any blame
on himself is part of the implicit dissociation of earthly fathers from
their children. Adam's response suggests a new and important ability
of men to surmount personal problems for a more universal view of
the problems of humankind—an ability of men that a little more than
one hundred years later Bentham praised and Dickens criticized.
   Yet the reader also knows Adam's terrible underestimation of the
personal element of loss and the anguish that he is fated to feel.
Against Adam's sense of the universal horror unleashed by Cain's
slaughter of Abel balances his yet unknown personal sorrow of a father for his sons' fates which may add to, rather than subtract from,
the reader's pity for Adam's predicament.
   If Adam's grand sorrow is haunted by this type of displacement,
the reason lies in part in a theory of reproduction that creates displacement. Various passages contend that in reverencing the likeness
of God—not the biological parents—in one's self, one will be whole
and wholesome. Thus the good and worthy resemble God and
through that resemblance resemble their fathers. The sinful, however,
resemble beasts or Eve:

> Can thus
> Th' Image of God in man created once
> So goodly and erect, though faulty since,
> To such unsightly sufferings be debas't
> Under inhuman pains? Why should not Man,
> Retaining still Divine similitude
> In part, from such deformities be free,
> And for his Maker's Image sake exempt?
> Thir Maker's Image, answer'd Michael, then
> Forsook them, when themselves they vilifi'd
> To serve ungovern'd appetite, and took
> His Image whom they served, a brutish vice,
> Inductive mainly to the sin of Eve,
> Therefore so abject is thir punishment,
> Disfiguring not God's likeness, but thir own,
> Or if his likeness, by themselves defac't
> While they pervert pure Nature's healthful rules
> To loathsome sickness, worthily, since they
> God's Image did not reverence in themselves.
>   (XI.507–25)

Here is an expression of the ontology of morality: to resemble God, men should follow "pure Nature's healthful rules." And yet Nature—especially in Eden—reminds one of and conflicts with *n*ature.

Adam fails to notice how marginal procreation becomes in this Natural world, which Adam represents, and how marginal it remains after the fall. For procreation merely shapes the portal through which Christ enters human history. Christ's birth parabolically dismisses any universal importance for human parenting or reproduction beyond the need to create a harvest of good souls to fill heaven. And while nobility attaches to this purpose, the consequence is to emperil Adam's relationships to his children, for in his relationship to the divine purpose Adam is cut off from his children and his children are also cut off from their parents. The individual life that from one perspective represents a glorious possibility fulfilled through spiritual education from another verges on a meaninglessness that only belief in God the Father can relieve.[31]

The passage above also underscores the related and important point by which the work restricts previous norms of male action: human beings cannot affect the course of history personally. The results of action are directly linked to the rewards or punishments of God. If part of the previous masculine ideals has been performing an action, shaping the world, shaping oneself, here that ideal—as unstable and gratifying as it was—is undercut. In the war in heaven, for instance, neither side can gain on the other by its own exertions. So too Adam and Eve sin by their own choices, but they fall as God's punishment. Nor is the fall of nature caused by the fall of man. God corrupts nature as a punishment for Adam and Eve's sin. The actions of human beings can affect how God treats them, but it cannot cause that treatment. A man can do nothing, for good or evil, without God.

Masculinity is neither creative nor procreative; it is passive. All that any man can do is keep his place by reverencing God. So Michael describes the Apostle's activities:

> [Hee] shall dwell
> His Spirit within them, and the Law of Faith
> Working through love, upon thir hearts shall write,
> To guide them in all truth, and also arm
> With spiritual Armor, able to resist
> Satan's assaults.
>
> (XII.487–92)

This is echoed by what Adam himself learns at the end:

> Henceforth I learn, that to obey is best,
> And love with fear the only God, to walk
> As in his presence, ever to observe
> His providence, and on him sole depend,
> Merciful over all his works, with good
> Still overcoming evil, and by small
> Accomplishing great things, by things deem'd weak
> Subverting worldly strong, and worldly wise
> By simply meek.
>
> (XII.561–69)

God is the one "overcoming," "accomplishing," "subverting." Men are the tools. To be powerless, meek, weak, small, dependent is, Michael tells him, "the sum of wisdom." Once again a divine emissary, by describing an obdurate meekness appropriate for men, situates men between child and adult, masculinity and femininity. Conveyed to a contemporary reader might be not only powerlessness but a loss of an ideal from which masculine power traditionally sprung. But the loss has already occurred in places like *Hamlet*. Tough meekness, therefore, may be seen as a strategy of accommodation of new awareness to an old ideal. The tough meekness helps to deal with the double perception men seem to be suffering under, of the world as resisting masculine ideals and of men as incorporating features previously thought to be feminine and even childish. As a result of man's sense of powerlessness, then, feminine, childish, involuntary features become toughened. A behavior develops which we might call passive-aggressive, reasonably stubborn, a new male response of sanctimonious virtue ("I can't talk to you if you won't be reasonable"). Through this behavior men who feel severed from both previous masculine-identified sources of power and feminine-identified sources of power—nature, emotions, nurture—strike back by speechlessly enduring, separating from parents, wives, children.

This position relies, to an extent, on the type of suppression of origins—and fear of their suppression—that runs throughout *Paradise Lost*. In *Paradise Lost* causes and effects rarely originate in the world, nor are they under the control of humans; they originate in God. Childhood has no infancy; all adults are children and children adults. Growth and stasis become confused. Humans choose actions while providence directs their consequences.[32]

Even the possibility of choice itself runs into a similar dilemma in *Paradise Lost*. Because Adam and Eve do not innately make invariably correct choices, they are given much tuition—more than four books of reasonable discourses and exemplary tales. But they are deprived of the opportunity to learn from experience, as children do, except by falling.[33] As early as the year of publication of *Paradise Lost*, Dryden satirized the work's proposal of death as a punishment for an incorrect choice, when, as a punishment, death seems too final and remains experientially mystified to Adam and Eve. In Dryden's *Tempest, or The Enchanted Island*, a 1667 rewriting of Shakespeare's play incorporating elements of *Paradise Lost*, an Adam-like character, Hippolito, speculates on death. When Ferdinand tells Hippolito that he can have Miranda only over his dead body, Hippolito replies, "How dead? what's that? but whatsoe're it be / I long to have her."[34] When Hippolito appears about to die (he is soon restored to life), his lover, the Eve-like Dorinda, echoes the lines once more:

You must not go to Heav'n unless we go together,
For I've heard my Father say that we must strive
To be each others Guide, the way to it will else
Be difficult, especially for those who are so young.
But I much wonder what it is to dye.

(75)

Dryden makes it clear that great difficulties inhere in threatened punishments that lie outside of human experience.

Partially because of the abrasion between Adam's need for experience and the abstract lessons of God, Adam finds it painful, as well as difficult, to live within the God-given rules for happiness. But for this reason, of course, there is a Christ, there is a "Fortunate Fall," there can be a justification of the ways of God to men: men must experience the world, but men must be relieved of its pains. On the other hand, even this solution can lead to the same dilemma one finds in the garden—a difficult tension between values that engage the world and values that protect one from it.

In this tension between a salvation that rests so much on paternal care and the ideas of experience, growth, or development, human paternity seems compromised. Fathers threaten to become begetters in a world in which, from birth, children are responsible for their own faults. Thus *Paradise Lost* depicts sins of the fathers visited on the heads of their children, but never sins of the children visited on their fathers. This one-way flow gives the lack of paternal care and nurture the imprimatur of divine sanction and divine similitude. The moral defects of evil children make them ontological misfires, defective from the start. The ill-fated mating of the sons of Seth and the daughters of Cain produces a race of giants (XI.683–97): "th' unaccomplisht works of Nature's hand, / Abortive, monstrous, or unkindly mixt" (III.455–56). Nature when it works by itself, and not by God's plan, produces not God's works but its own works—monsters. The moral ontology of this makes parents the cause but does not make them responsible for their children. Such definition further discredits nature and natural development and certain forms of education.

The story of Seth's sons and Cain's daughters dismisses all forms of experience and growth under the rubrics of culture and change (XI.556–627). Virtue, an exclusively male possession that defines masculinity, lies in Seth's sons who "all thir study bent / To worship

God aright" (XI.577–78). The sons of Seth concern themselves only with words of God "not hid" (XI.579). They neither search for causes nor experiment. They study what they do know—a tautological circle with no point of origin. Vice, associated with female characters and tending to define femininity, derives from earthly experiences (the plain) and from probing—finding the harmonies of melody or the metals in Mother Earth's womb and producing from them culture and society symbolized by music and tools. Whereas their virtuous studies had isolated men, their marriage produces the first social gathering and rites appropriate to society: feasting, music, dance, and, interestingly, the marriage ceremony itself. All of these are considered unmanly.

The passage, while it suggests that society arises because men have become unmanly, also reminds men of their general powerlessness. While the section censures men who invent, it also shows that the abilities of the inventors and their inventions of the hidden lie exclusively in God's power (XI.609–12). Ill nature gives the men of the plains the inclination to invent, but God gives them the ability. Following a plan to bring good out of evil, God lets men invent—thus confirming their evil—but makes their inventions benefit humanity.

Moreover, the evil of the founders of society relates to their birth. They spring from him "Who slew his brother" (XI.609). The virtuous men trace their genealogy to heaven—those "whose lives / Religious titl'd them the Sons of God" (XI.621–22). Evil comes from human birth, natural development, and change and is allied with the feminine (the daughters of Cain); good comes only from God, is stable, static, masculine. *Paradise Lost* once again suggests that ideal masculine behavior, which is spiritually correct and ontologically sound, requires that men separate themselves from their origins, from their parents, from human intercourse, society, and culture. The original sin is the sin of originating, and men, by suffering from origins and desiring to be originators, have lost their masculinity. Despite the contrary indication, it would seem that to regain this masculinity, men must live in a rugged isolation.

Why should men care to rebuild masculinity? The stories thus far seem to indicate that men of Anglo-European culture long to experience their bodies, minds, and world as controllable. While one thread of *Paradise Lost* suggests the exquisite pleasures of these elements, the work also limits them in a masculinity that can insulate men from the involuntary processes of nature, society, and culture—processes by which men may have felt victimized in the devastations, wars, and diseases of the forty years before *Paradise Lost* was written. Milton's masculinity seems to cherish things of earthly origin—emotions, parents, lovers, children, the World—as it seeks to liberate men from them.[35]

In *Paradise Lost* men have no human-earthly origins. Thus, like Christ on the pinnacle in *Paradise Regained,* men rise above circumstance and wield an authority forged from eternal abstractions, like "truth" and "right reason," not subject to change or history. This superiority dissociates head and body, reason and experience, identity and personal history, society and truth.[36] But as in *Paradise Regained,* a precarious balance becomes the key to this superiority, a balance that for men would seem to be the opposite of stressful inbetweenness. But overbalance seems too easy. For instance, in *Paradise Lost,* reason emerges as eternal, universal, and masculine, as a tool for dominance, control, and power over oneself, the world, and others. Paternity—an aspect of themselves that men have struggled with—is resolved by ceding to it an abstract authority based on God's, not man's, fatherhood, while suppressing the troublesome idea of generation and growth.

Like other words in *Paradise Lost,* "father" loses its earthly, human, experiential meaning and acquires a new meaning that denies the origin of the idea of paternity in human experience, as if "fatherhood" were understood only by analogy to heaven. In the Miltonic epic, "father" ceases to be a name children confer on men and becomes a name men confer on themselves. "Father" becomes synonymous with "patriarch," "-arch" revealing its relevance to ideas of government—a point Locke makes in reply to Filmer. The rule of the patriarch is, according to Filmer, the rule of masculine, God-given reason authorized by God in His donation to Adam as father. That fatherhood might have a historical and cultural as well as biological shape cannot be considered; that reason may differ in differing ages, that it too has a history or genealogy, cannot be considered.[37]

Throughout, ideas, symbols, rules sustain values that they simultaneously threaten to subvert. For instance, the ability to control one's circumstances in *Paradise Lost* rests on difference and superiority in a world where equality is the ideal. Milton faces these issues directly in the stories of Christ's elevation and Satan's rebellion. Yet the so-called sociable angel's conversation with Adam illustrates the difficulties in sustaining a notion of equality. In heaven, Eden, hell, chaos, and elsewhere, even before paradise is lost, relationships are almost always depicted in terms of disequilibrium. Where equality of sorts is depicted—among the angels and among the devils—one finds little of what we would call human conversation. Heaven appears unified and harmonious: angels sing and dance in unison. Milton's own foundation for utterance lies on mystical union with angelic voices who speak through him. Hell, on the other hand, appears uniformly fragmented and cacophonous: devils quarrel, hiss, harangue each other. Milton, thus, implies that *differences among equals* cause conversation and earthly relationships, and, as a corollary, that incongruent or different beings can be equal. Yet in the cosmology of *Paradise Lost* equality rarely exists without strong implications of congruity or identity—the relationship of Christ to the Father, the sexual relations of angels. Thus for Adam to break out of the boundaries placed around all the actors, to have conversation, would at least verge on the idea of improper fellowship.

Gender, of course, is depicted as different and unequal. Many of the passages examined above dubbed World "feminine," Spirit "masculine." For instance, the sins of the Sons of God, their marriage to the daughters of Cain, "from Man's *effeminate* slackness it begins" (XI.634; my emphasis). Eve or women in general cause men's sinfulness, but men's sinfulness also is considered feminine, stemming from actions and attitudes considered appropriate to "femininity." These actions and attitudes tend also to be connected with the involuntary:

> Adam . . . wept,
> Though not of Woman born; compassion quell'd
> His best of Man, and gave him up to tears
> A space, till firmer thoughts restrained excess.
>
> (XI.495–98)

Being born of woman, man inherits a part of woman that must be controlled, for womanish attributes—like compassion, emotion, tears—take manhood captive. Man "gives himself up," loses control of himself, when he weeps. And so both the activity itself and the loss of control that gives rise to it become "effeminate," kill the "best of Man."

"Excess," which literally means "departure," suggests that Adam's behavior departs from the ontology of man ("compassion *quell'd* / His best of Man" [XI.496–97]), exceeds or steps outside the ambit of manliness. Even though the passage seems to imply that Adam's behavior would be acceptable in proportion, it also implies that tears are not acceptable by suggesting that "compassion," "tears," and "excess" are apposite. It raises doubts that any effeminate action, like weeping, would seem to be essentially excessive and so would seem to discourage these traits, which *seem* to be appropriate to men "of Woman born."

When Milton writes that "brutish vice" is "Inductive mainly to the sin of Eve" (XI.518–19), "inductive" has a similar double meaning of "traceable to" and "leading into." In sinning, the man who exceeds his masculinity enters the world of Eve. The vice is "brutish" too in the double sense that it turns one from man into animal and, as the word "brute" implies, it makes one "heavy" (and immovable) as opposed to light, and deprives one of reason, which in this work is the peculiarly masculine identifier. The first passage (XI.495–98), with its suggestions for the repression of emotion, defines "masculinity" as firm, self-restrained, and rational. "Femininity" by contrast becomes soft, uncontrolled, and mindless, none of which is excessive in women.[38] Finally, the first passage suggests that having a woman as one's parent—instead of God, as Adam does—makes masculinity problematic for men, for such men will weep and feel compassion. But to express their "best of Man," to be a "man," means to control not only emotion, but mothers (origins) and bodies (nature, growth, development).

Eve, then, represents an aspect of the world and themselves that men should rule and avoid intimacy with. Her creation clearly delineates her connection with nature.[39] "Reposed under a shade on flowers" (IV.451ff.) she finds herself, in what fallen Adam calls his Mother's lap (X.775–86.) The sense of nature's womb is enhanced by Eve's being "under the shade," as she is when she prepared the food for Raphael, and by the murmuring sound from the cave. Moreover, these images link her "femininity" not only with nature, but also with art, the forbidden cultural imitation of creation.[40]

This connection is reinforced by "liquid plain," the habitation of the daughters of Cain and the point at which Satan enters Eden to seduce Eve. Moreover, the synesthesia of the passage devoted to Eve's birth enfolds her in a world of sensation—that suggests both nature and art. When she beholds herself at the lake, Eve brings together "green bank," "sky," "murmuring," "liquid," in the revelation of herself to herself. In the mirror of water all nature presses into a single place of which Eve is part and even the center.[41] What Eve sees and what the reader experiences in her and through her is nature, with Eve as its receptacle and embodiment. Only the mirror can contain all this; only the work of art could put it all together in such a unified sensual experience.[42]

Again in Eve's birth, we see a distinction between the feminine that immerses itself in the world and the masculine that sits uncomfortably on the threshold. The fallen Adam, for instance, lies on the flowers, like Eve, wishing to sleep forever secure in his Mother's lap. The images of Eve's birth become the images of Adam's death and imply Adam's desire for intimacy with the world, his mother, and his terror of the death such intimacy implies.[43] Thus the reprehension of Eve and the longing generated from the symbols and story of her birth represent a deeper set of male desires and anxieties.

No wonder, for instance, that in *Paradise Lost* women come out of men, rather than the other way around. In the only picture of normal birth order, Sin begets Death and the hounds that consume her, presenting men a cautionary picture about what sort of children women beget and what sort of women beget children, and presenting women a cautionary tale about the need to separate from their children.[44] Having a mother, in other words, is bad for children; being a mother is bad for women. Thus we can see how the birth of Eve symbolically cuts an umbilicus, bringing man to adult stature and giving the man-child control over the woman-mother as it inverts the traditional relationship of mother to child. *Paradise Lost* at times offers this impression that women ruin everything for men, thus justifying the need for sons to be patriarchs from the moment they are born.

As a lower form of life and a representative of the created world below Adam, Eve must be ruled by Adam and through Adam by God. She must learn to "love" Adam as Adam loves God, through obedience. On the other hand, Adam must not reciprocate this "love," but, again like God, he ought only to enjoy her obedience and derive pleasure from it in the way that he derives pleasure and use from other aspects of nature, like flowers or sun or stars. Unlike flowers or sun or stars, however, Eve represents an aspect of Adam, so that in finding pleasure with her he enjoys this aspect of himself and so becomes excessive, loses the definitive shape of his masculinity. Neither Adam nor Eve can escape the erotic circle. Given the firm line to which Adam should adhere, this circle becomes unhealthy. Thus he is reproducing the sin of Eve, self-worship, excessive pleasure in one's own nature, in nature generally, turning away from God. This is amply illustrated by the echoes of Adam's speeches and reasoning in Eve's words and actions and by the re-echoes of those imitations in the speeches of Adam, so that Adam becomes at times an echo of an echo, an imitation of Eve imitating him.

All these tensions come to bear on Adam's birth, which illustrates the ideal position of men—its glory and pain (VIII.253ff.). From the beginning Adam is heaven-directed. He awakes in sun, rather than shade. And whereas the offices of Eve's birth are done by the feminine earth and thus she is led to look down for her answers, the offices of his birth are performed by the masculine sun-son and Adam looks upward.[45]

Eve observed creation from bottom upward, from an experience of the world with which her own self intermingled, like her reflected face mingled with the reflected image of sky; Adam looks "directly" at creation from the top down, with a glance that orders and limits the world. For Eve, each part overlaps the other, touches and interfuses, exceeds—sky in water, liquid singing in air. Although Eve's glance also orders the world, Adam's has authority behind it, God-given reason directing his eyes, telling him names, placing each piece of creation in its proper position and category, defining "reason" and Adam through its action (VIII.352–54). What Adam sees exists, discrete blocks of creations, labelled and in place. Yet having put the world in place, Adam is overwhelmed by a sense of isolation, a sense that he differs from all around him (VIII.389–92).[46] Unlike Eve's, Adam's glance leaves him terribly alone in the world.

What Adam desires he states: "Among unequals what society / Can sort, what harmony or true delight?" (VIII.383–84). This seems profoundly important to understanding Adam's problematic masculinity. We have already seen the disequilibrium of Adam's relationship to Eve, and yet here as elsewhere we see Adam's desire for equilibrium. Eve may be to Adam a "wish exactly to thy heart's desire," as God states (VIII. 449–451). But this important other self cannot become his equal. The ontological boundary between Adam and Eve and the definitions of masculinity and femininity preclude both romantic love and companionate love, which they both simultaneously idealize. Eve is, as the words say, only a "likeness" of him, one who can be fitted to help him, one who is his other (and imperfect) self who will need to be restrained. Milton wrote in *The Doctrine and Discipline of Divorce* that "the best duty of marriage" is "a cheerful and agreeable conversation,"[47] and we find much conversation between Adam and Eve. But in it each partner often strains to please or impress the other, in the halting starts of new love: Adam self-consciously lecturing Eve and Eve repeating his words to him in song.[48] In these relations, Adam becomes Eve's mentor, not the relationship to women or the world that Adam expressly desired, not the role that he finds comfortable. His Father misinterprets his words.

Throughout, while *Paradise Lost* presents intimacy with its pleasures as one important aspect of human longing, a sense of separation also haunts the relationship of Adam and Eve, as does danger. The uneasy and slightly skewed nature of this relationship is captured in the ideal portraits painted of the couple by the poet (IV.288–318) Adam and Eve are "Not equal, as thir sex not equal seem'd" (IV.296). The description of the ideal couple at the beginning of the passage, however, seems to apply virtue equally to Adam and Eve, yet the images clearly suggest masculinity and Adam alone:

> Lords of all,
> And worthy seem'd, for in thir looks Divine
> The image of thir glorious Maker shone,
> Truth, Wisdom, Sanctitude severe, and pure,
> Severe, but in true filial freedom plac't;
> Whence true autority in men.
>
> (IV.290–95)

The above words, meant for both man and woman, primarily describe man, implicitly suggesting the inequality and loneliness of Adam while apparently doing the opposite. Not only do "Lords" and "men" emphasize the masculinity of the traits, but the "head" words—"Truth, Wisdom"—also emphasize masculinity. And too the repeated word "severe," which the word "freedom" opposes, suggests both strictness and the type of boundedness that characterizes masculinity in this work. The descriptions that follow suggest that equality is specious and resemblance imposed on the woman by the man whose "Front and Eye sublime declar'd / Absolute rule" (IV.300–301). Moreover, the vine-like images of Eve "impli'd / Subjection" (IV.307–8) to her husband, while "vine," *vitis*, also offers a Latin pun on Eve's latent vice and the danger her intermingling with Adam poses.[49]

In this description too, Milton concentrates on the genitals of Adam and Eve, which evince shame ("those mysterious parts") and longing ("his happiest life"). Adam's situation, though unfallen, already encodes the masculine problem: the shame of and the desire for what the epic marks as feminine.[50] Clearly the masculinity here expressed does not offer an unequivocally happy state. The picture of the couple sheds light on the desire for intimacy that Adam has, his sense of the danger of intimacy, and his required distance, rectitude, and isolation. The person in control of the evasions of language in the scene apparently shares the ambivalence that Adam suffers.[51]

Against such a background of isolation from and longing for intimacy, it is perhaps not surprising that of all the senses, touch should be so central to the story of Adam and Eve, counterpoised against masculine reason.[52] In the work "touch" refers to sexual activity. In previous works touch has been only minimally present, but then they have also lacked man's naked desire for intimacy with women and with the common, temporal, earthly. Little wonder too that upon the issue of touch, which like intercourse stands for a wide range of intimate contacts, Adam's ambivalence towards the masculine ideal most fully emerges. The idea that some nonmasculine nature lies inside men and that men need to acknowledge that nature is strong in *Paradise Lost*. It becomes conspicuous through the absence of the penis, which the poet acknowledges that God created for no bad purpose and which the poem apparently longs to reclaim but which, allied as it is to touch, intimacy, origins, it cannot. The sensuous details of the poem also suggest longing for union with women, with the world, with growth. The poem both feeds on and undercuts this longing, echoing the precarious position of Adam between the masculine sun and the feminine bower. The poem's elaborate philosophical and intellectual system that tries to fly above the world cannot resolve this dissonance. It was present in the uneasy marriage of feminine meekness and masculine hardness, which like the ill-joined sons and daughters of Cain produced a monster. It is present here.

"Touch" and "feeling" are synonyms, and it is not accidental that the fruit is not only forbidden them to eat but "under ban to touch" (IX.925). Nor is it accidental that touching and tasting the fruit produces emotion and sensual appetite (IX.780–94). Nor is it accidental that in joining Eve in her fate, Adam displays, as some critics have argued, admirable feelings of love, compassion, and desire.[53] For it is feeling and touch, physical and emotional intimacy, banned by God, that the fruit represents and that are released by the sin of touching. Although "Reason" too may be synonymous with "sense," the one sense prohibited is "feeling." Emotion and reason cannot join. For whereas reason discerns and isolates, feeling joins and exceeds, as in Adam's "excessive" and "effeminate" compassion.

Milton's ideal presentation of intimacy—sexual union—pulls together all the aspects that Milton's masculine ideal threatens to overbalance. In particular it seems meant to show the intimacy that Adam desires, the breaking down of barriers, the release of emotion, the loss of controls. Adam's claims for "touch" are as excessive as they are new. Adam expresses his belief in the centrality of intimacy, emotion, and touch when he tells Raphael about his wedding night and calls his sexual union with Eve "the sum of earthly bliss":

> Thus I have told thee all my State, and brought
> My story to the sum of earthly bliss
> Which I enjoy, and must confess to find
> In all things else delight indeed, but such
> As us'd or not, works in the mind no change,
> Nor vehement desire, these delicacies
> I mean of Taste, Sight, Smell, Herbs, Fruits, and Flow'rs,
> Walks, and the melody of Birds; but here
> Far otherwise, transported I behold,
> Transported touch; here passion first I felt,
> Commotion strange, in all enjoyments else
> Superior and unmov'd, here only weak
> Against the charm of Beauty's powerful glance.
> Or Nature fail'd in mee, and left some part
> Not proof enough such Object to sustain.
>
> (VIII.522–35)

Adam goes on to say that at such times Eve's wisdom seems better and more complete than his. To Adam's words Raphael replies,

Accuse not Nature, she hath done her part;
Do thou but thine, and be not diffident
Of Wisdom, she deserts thee not, if thou
Dismiss not her, when most thou need'st her nigh,
By attributing overmuch to things
Less excellent, as thou thyself perceiv'st. . . .
But if the sense of touch whereby mankind
Is propagated seem such dear delight
Beyond all other, think the same voutsaf't
To Cattle and each Beast; which would not be
To them made common and divulg'd, if aught
Therein enjoy'd were worthy to subdue
The Soul of Man, or passion in him move.
What higher in her society thou find'st
Attractive, human, rational, love still;
In loving thou dost well, in passion not,
Wherein true Love consists not; Love refines
The thoughts, and heart enlarges, hath his seat
In Reason, and is judicious.

(VIII.561–92)

Raphael's concept of a rational sexual intercourse has a long church history; for instance, Augustine described intercourse in which the penis was controlled by reason.[54] Raphael's lecture, however, marks an ambivalence, for Milton had already written a paean to conjugal love in book IV that echoes the words for which Raphael rebukes Adam: "O yet happiest if ye seek / No happier state, and know to know no more" (IV.736–75). Puritan pamphleteers had often written of the particularly human enjoyment of sexual activity.[55] Yet Raphael's words throw a chilling caution on the distinctly "human," not only sexual pleasure, but all the things that the peculiar union of man and woman represent in the work—the joy possible in emotion, making mistakes, losing control, unrestrained growth, creativity, procreativity, nurture, locality, intimacy. Touch—the immense pleasure of proximity—stands for the whole world of nonreason that blurs the category between masculine and nonmasculine, whether beasts, women, or men.

Paradise Lost portrays conjugal love as the conduit through which men can reexperience nature and feeling, within a modest rational framework. Yet through touch, through breaking barriers, earthly love can lead to the fall. Thus the consequences of touching and tasting the mortal fruit, against reason, appear as concupiscence, then shame, then repression, the hiding of the genitals. Yet most of this existed before the fall, and this creates the central unremitting tension: men must repress what they imperfectly perceive to be their nature and nature generally, they reject origins, they become isolated at every moment in the theological history—before they are fallen, when they are fallen, when they are raised. The fall does not change the state of unfallen men.

The fall is fortunate. For while it cannot change the stringent checks placed on Adam's sensuality, while it cannot dissipate his intense desire for companionship or for the breaking of boundaries or for a world in which creation intermingles, it can allow Adam to travel through those experiences before his return to a new heaven and earth. The intensity of Adam's desires and their melancholy yet joyful fulfillment imparts the work's final glow. Rather than seeming dispossessed in their fate, Adam and Eve are beautified by possession of the world opening before them, a world that may ultimately drive them apart but which now, facing it anew, equally as strangers, equally moved, they find binds them. The closing simultaneously suggests intimacy lost in Paradise and gained now, the best aspects of nature and the worst that lie before them, the moving paradox of involuntary desire and circumstantial forbearance, emotional intimacy at the point when physical intimacy is no longer possible, the mixed and mangled world in which men find themselves always struggling to escape isolation:

> In either hand the hast'ning angel caught
> Our lingering Parents, and to th' Eastern Gate
> Led them direct, and down the Cliff as fast
> To the subjected Plain; then disappear'd.
> They looking back, all th' Eastern side beheld
> Of Paradise, so late thir happy seat,
> Wav'd over by that flaming Brand, the Gate
> With dreadful Faces throng'd and fiery Arms:
> Some natural tears they dropp'd, but wip'd them soon;
> The World was all before them, where to choose
> Thir place of rest, and Providence thir guide:

They hand in hand with wand'ring steps and slow,
Through Eden took thir solitary way.

(XII.637–49)

In these unfathomable lines that echo the whole work, the voice of
Milton becomes, significantly, the voice of Eve, an echo that parallels
the moving simplicity of her evening song. These lines transform elements of the poem to a human and earthly scale. From the vantage
point of humans, the divine appears "dreadful"—faces of angels, fire,
swords are the real destroyers of Paradise. The first human parents,
endowed finally with fellow feeling, as "lingering" and "slow" emphasize, have entered the world of nature and touch and intimacy that
each desired. Adam at last shares Eve's place. Their steps are "wand'r-
ing." Their tears are "natural." Hand and hand they share solitude
and seek rest, originate human history. They enter the world finally, a
world of excess, step over the boundary between themselves and
nature.

This passage may have the calm of Mulciber's fall, which arises
from the beauty of nature and simplicity of it, but the moral pointing
of that poetry becomes more complex here.[56] No dreadful voice, only
those dreadful faces, reminds us of Adam's and Eve's sin. Instead, the
lines free us to feel in their fall the loss and the possible repair in the
comforting pleasure of holding hands. Adam and Eve are transformed
from the Mother and Father of Mankind into "Our ling'ring Parents."
And in this context the reader is invited to share their feelings. This
moment of sadness and loss becomes a moment of beauty and harmony and unison, for this picture is "touching."

Paradise Lost, like so many ecstatic verses of the seventeenth century, ends when the poet loses contact with the divine vision and falls
to an earthly perspective. From juxtaposition of the two worlds of the
poem—divine and earthly—the poem asserts that men have lost their
dignity, their essence, their reason, but that men have gained feeling,
companionship, the world. In the end, when Eden is lost, Milton employs his powerful feminine voice to suggest men's current position,
paying homage to one of the fortunate aspects of the fall.[57] But in
empathizing the feminized man, he honors that which he also hopes
to quiet while he echoes the persistent longing his contemporaries
experienced within the ideal of masculinity, inside the patriarch,

struggling under the hard shell of masculinity, a longing felt throughout the poem.[58]

All the "marl" (I.296) lies not in Hell.[59] Earth fertilizes Milton's story: the sense of local origin, with which Milton in the act of denying suffuses the work, the sensual pleasures of simple connections, of rolling the particular names off the tongue. So too the desire to feel, to touch, to know the world through experience in all its particularity emerges through Adam's experience, just as in Adam we find struggling aspects of an ungendered self associated with the bower, with family, with feeling, with vulnerability, with companionship.

Milton, like Adam, is at the threshold, unable to lend his imagination to the construction of a perfect and perfectly happy prelapsarian Adam. His imagination struggles at the threshold of his own postlapsarian pleasures and pains, his Pisgah vision tensed by the tensions of his own masculinity. The previous masculine ideals of efficacious actions and heroic ordering now lie in the possession of the Heavenly Father. For earthly men, the way to rule out the pressures of change, growth, women, becomes reason, passivity, obduracy. And yet, as in Milton's story of Adam, men, even in these compromised ideals, have moved closer toward the world they had excluded as feminine— nature, sense, procreation, family. The rise of the man of reason, which we see in the Renaissance, and glimpse in Hamlet, and which continues into our century emerges side-by-side with the rise of the feminine man, which we see Hamlet struggling with and Adam in some ways incorporating. The nineteenth century, however, will secure his victory, as we will see in *Hard Times.*

Notes

1. All quotations from John Milton, *Paradise Lost,* ed. Merritt Y. Hughes (New York: Odyssey Press, 1962).

2. The echoes of Shakespeare's plays throughout *Paradise Lost* present an interesting problem in a work that tells the story of the first humans.

3. C. S. Lewis, *A Preface to "Paradise Lost"* (New York: Oxford University Press, 1961), 40–61; Christopher Ricks, *Milton's Grand Style* (Oxford: Oxford University Press, 1963). B. Rajan accepts that the style is not "natural" but tries to show that it is not univocal: see "*Paradise Lost:* The Providence of Style," *Milton Studies* 1 (1969): 1–14; and "The Language of *Paradise Lost,*" *Milton: "Paradise Lost,*" ed. Louis Martz (Englewood Cliffs, N.J.: Prentice-Hall, 1966), 56–60.

4. Thomas Nashe, *Pierce Penniless*, in *The Unfortunate Traveler*, ed. J. B. Steane (Baltimore: Penguin, 1972), 113.

5. Kay Stockholder, *Dream Works: Lovers and Families in Shakespeare's Plays* (Toronto: University of Toronto Press, 1987), 45.

6. James Andrew Clark, "Milton *Naturans*, Milton *Naturatus*: The Debate of Nature in *A Mask Presented at Ludlow*," *Milton Studies* 20 (1984): 3–27, finds that Milton seeks "the accommodation . . . of *natura naturans* [nature in itself, self-generating, moving, growing] and *natura naturata* [nature as made, stative, orderly]" (24).

7. Milton's ideas about kingship, reflected in *Paradise Lost* and his other writings, suggests he favored rule by the divine, a direct covenant between the fit few and God: see Stevie Davies, *Images of Kingship in "Paradise Lost"* (Columbia: University of Missouri Press, 1983).

8. Milton seems to suggest an equality of men and women at times, but always it retreats to inequality (Lewis, *Preface to "Paradise Lost*," 120; Helen Gardner, *A Reading of "Paradise Lost"* [Oxford: Clarendon Press, 1965], 87; John Halkett, *Milton and the Idea of Matrimony* [New Haven, Conn.: Yale University Press, 1970], 106ff.). Some have seen this as misogyny: see Sandra K. Gilbert, "Patriarchal Poetry and Women Readers: Reflections on Milton's Bogey," *PMLA* 93 (1978): 362–82. Some have argued that Eve is Adam's equal, as in Joan Mallory Webber's response to Gilbert, "The Politics of Poetry: Feminism and *Paradise Lost*," *Milton Studies* 14 (1980): 3–24; also see Dorothy Durkee Miller, "Eve," *JEGP* 61 (1962): 542–47; Marilyn R. Farwell, "Eve, the Separation Scene and the Renaissance Idea of Androgyny," *Milton Studies* 16 (1982): 3–20. A few even suggest Eve's superiority. Christine Froula, "When Eve Reads Milton: Undoing the Canonical Economy," *Critical Inquiry* 10 (1983): 321–47, for instance, argues that Eve submits to patriarchy, but there is a memory of a previous state.

9. Insemination is a motif in the creation of the world and its parturition. In fact, the metaphors suggest that Milton knew of Aristotelian embryology—perhaps Harvey's *Anatomical Exercises on the Generation of Animals*—and accepted epigenesis. Harvey's studies were primarily of birds, which may have made them suitable to Milton's purposes. The point is, however, that embryos exist only in the lower orders of nature; higher beings—Adam, Eve, Satan—are created, come into existence without an embryonic stage. J. B. Broadbent recognized the intrauterine waters of creation: see *Some Graver Subject: An Essay on "Paradise Lost"* (New York: Schocken Books, 1960), 239. He is wrong, however, about Milton's spermatics, for spermatozoa were not discovered until 1677.

10. Throughout, local origins are shown to be false and even evil: see the genealogy of idols, book II.

11. Marcia Landy writes that by identifying Satan with fatherhood and Sin with motherhood, reproduction is denied any value as creation. As a result, the Father-Son become the only creators: "Kinship and the Role of Women in *Paradise Lost*," *Milton Studies* 4 (1972): 11.

12. The eighteenth-century novel exhibits this pattern as well. Main characters who have been displaced from home look for their parents, but they often find surrogate parents who embody a divine ideal, or the divine parent Himself.

The family, which is the setting or backdrop for many of these works, exists not so much for familial purposes but for a model of human behavior. In Defoe's novels, like *Robinson Crusoe* or *Moll Flanders*, family is really secondary, since the protagonists keep rejecting their actual families in their search for ideal families. In *Pamela* desire is converted into discipline, and the family relations that culminate the book are embodied in a set of moral and religious precepts. In *Tom Jones* Mr. Allworthy is a surrogate parent who embodies a benign morality which is familial in nature, and it is important that he is not Tom's natural father but his spiritual father. Similar patterns can be found in *Humphry Clinker* and other novels.

In *Tristram Shandy,* however, an interesting reversal takes place. Because human emotion and temporal existence are valued, the family's role shifts; for the family—as it has been constituted in previous novels—cannot serve as a model of human behavior. The philosophical father crushes the reproductive life out of his son. The son and uncle in spite of their socially inflicted incapacities continue to feel, to yearn; and their seriocomic impulse becomes the center of the work.

13. This argument flies in the face of those who believe that Adam and Eve grow in the garden or that growth is good: see Joseph Summers, *The Muse's Method* (Cambridge, Mass.: Harvard University Press, 1962), 71–95; John Evans, *"Paradise Lost" and the Genesis Tradition* (Oxford: Clarendon Press, 1968), 250; Diana Kelsey McColley, "Free Will and Obedience in the Separation Scene of *Paradise Lost*," *Studies in English Literature* 12 (1972): 102–20; Barbara Kiefer Lewalski, "Innocence and Experience in Milton's Eden," *New Essays on "Paradise Lost,"* ed. Thomas Kranidas (Berkeley: University of California Press, 1974), 86–117. By and large their arguments that "in *Paradise Lost* the Edenic life is radical growth and process" (Lewalski, "Innocence and Experience," 88) rest almost exclusively on an analogy between the luxuriance of the garden and Adam and Eve as parts of that garden.

They do not point out, however, that Adam and Eve are told to stop the growth, to cut off limbs and lop off flowers, seeds, and fruit. Their actions in the garden suggests that their task is anti-growth.

J. B. Broadbent argues against growth. In "The Nativity Ode," *The Living Milton*, ed. Frank Kermode (London: Routledge and Kegan Paul, 1960), 12–31, he argues that very little of the "human" event of birth is described, for Milton is not interested in the human and natural dimension, only the "idea" of the birth. He suggests this is typical of Milton's work in general.

14. Those who believe that Adam and Eve grow regularly cite this image as central: see Lewalski, "Innocence and Experience," 103–5.

15. Much has been argued on the pre- and post-lapsarian uses of language in Milton. Among the necessary works are these: Arnold Stein, *Answerable Style* (Minneapolis: University of Minnesota Press, 1953), 66–67; Anne Davidson Ferry, *Milton's Epic Voice* (Cambridge, Mass.: Harvard University Press, 1963), 111–15; Ricks, *Milton's Grand Style*, 109–17; Stanley Fish, *Surprised by Sin* (New York: St. Martin's Press, 1967), 107–57.

16. Of course, the whole of the poem is presented as being inspired by contact with the spiritual, so that Milton gains perfect control by giving up control, so that the purity of the language could be viewed as God's doing, its impurity as Milton's fault. The result is, however, not the erasure of earthly origins, but a justification for confusion and ignorance about them.

Wellek's and Warren's comments on the creation of *Paradise Lost* in response to C. S. Lewis seem amusing in this light: "*Paradise Lost* is, first of all, about Satan and Adam and Eve and hundreds and thousands of different ideas, representations, and concepts, rather than about Milton's state of mind during creation. That the whole content of the poem was once in contact with the conscious and subconscious mind of Milton is perfectly true; but this state of mind is inaccessible . . ." (Rene Wellek and Austin Warren, *Theory of Literature* [New York: Harcourt, Brace, Jovanovich, 1942], 138). Wellek and Warren simply reify Milton's own version of the poem. The poem has no personal origins. The poem is simply a series of ideas and themes that were "once in contact with the . . . mind of Milton." That it was still possible to write this in 1948 shows the tenacity of the idea that Milton promulgated, although for Wellek and Warren social history, not God, is the great inspiriting force.

17. See Halkett, *Milton and the Idea of Matrimony*, 13. In "Kinship and the Role of Women," Marcia Landy argues that the priority of men over women is kept in place by privileging the married household as the ideal "state." Without really disputing Landy's central points, Barbara Kiefer Lewalski argues that marriage stresses the human companionship of Adam and Eve and their roles as partners of equivalent, not identical, status, in her unfortunately titled "Milton on Women—Yet Once More,"

Milton Studies 6 (1974): 3–20; see Landy's reply in "'A Free and Open Encounter': Milton and the Modern Reader," *Milton Studies* 9 (1976): 3–36.

18. Milton makes this argument about verse form in his preface to the poem. Lana Cable argues that the typical Miltonic tactic to lend credence to an ad hoc argument is to invoke obscured, divine origin: see "Coupling Logic and Milton's Doctrine of Divorce," *Milton Studies* 15 (1981), 143–59.

19. That Milton records the contemporary in his picture of the primeval is widely recognized, as in the discussion of edenic sexuality. See, for instance, Roland M. Frye, "The Teachings of Classical Puritanism on Conjugal Love," *Studies in the Renaissance* 2 (1955): 148–59. Critics rarely perceive the problems this creates for a poem that purports to be divinely communicated.

20. Arnold Stein pointed this out to me. Anthony Low regards this as a moment of domestic bliss and high housewifery: see "Angels and Food in *Paradise Lost*," *Milton Studies* 1 (1969): 136.

21. *The First Treatise of Government*, ed. Thomas I. Cook (New York: Hafner, 1947). Feminists have rightly been troubled by Locke's "foundation in nature." For excellent criticism see Susan Moller Okin, *Women in Western Political Thought* (Princeton: Princeton University Press, 1979); Jean Grimshaw, *Philosophy and Feminist Thinking* (Minneapolis: University of Minnesota Press, 1986), 49. Locke is primarily interested in arguing against absolute monarchy, and so he uses answers to antifeminist arguments that he did not originate and that had been around for two hundred years: see Linda Woodbridge, *Women and the English Renaissance: Literature and the Nature of Womankind, 1540–1620* (Urbana: University of Illinois Press, 1984). I use Locke here because he argues against "patriarchy," as such. He argues against the right of fathers or husbands to rule, except for that granted them by custom, law and contract.

22. In his *Patriarchia* (ed. Thomas Cook [New York: Hafner, 1947]) Filmer makes all men "fathers" and thus entitles them to power. However, Locke points out that "fathers" refers specifically to having children; i.e., the authority, if there is any, of fathers only occurs after offspring. Fatherhood grants no inherent rights of men over women or husbands over wives. And yet this usurpation of a procreative role by a socially prescribed nonprocreative role is typical, as we have observed, of male strategies for dealing with women and fertility. We can see it too in the Nashe quotation on "degenerate effeminate days" (Thomas Nashe, *Pierce Penniless his Supplication to the Devil*, in *The Unfortunate Traveller and Other Works*, ed. J. B. Steane [Baltimore, Md.: Penguin, 1972],

113). For a man to be perceived as feminine is somehow to have degenerated. What is a birth term has become a moral category for being itself. The term "degenerate" has nothing to do here or elsewhere with any entitlement that birth confers on a human. In fact, it is a term that, in co-opting the entitlement of humanity by birth, denies birth any status or value. These types of replacements are constant features of masculine vocabulary here and throughout.

23. Don Parry Norford has been the most persistent commentator on this. In "The Sacred Head: Milton's Solar Mysticism," *Milton Studies* 9 (1976): 37–75, he comments on the "phallic" sun-Son who inspires masculine virtue by maiming—particularly by castration: "The Miltonic solar hero can attain transcendence only through destruction, through . . . 'patriarchal castration,' the mortification of the lower masculinity in the interests of the higher, through enfeebling of the feminine side of the psyche, to which the lower masculinity belongs" (68). Milton's blindness and Samson's are such "castrations." Yet Adam in paradise lives with his eyes closed, as we are told in books XI and XII. He does not appear to welcome the "castration" of transcendence. In "The Separation of the World Parents in *Paradise Lost*," *Milton Studies* 12 (1978): 3–24, Norford also points out static "mindlessness" of Adam, as opposed to the dynamic creativity of Eve (20). More recently, Anne Ferry, in trying to lay feminist arguments of misogyny to rest once and for all, argues not only that Adam and Eve are equal, but that here imagination, sensation, and feeling make Eve in some respects superior: "Milton's Creation of Eve," *Studies in English Literature* 28 (1988): 113–32.

24. "*Paradise Lost*: The Pattern at the Center," *Milton's Epic Poetry*, ed. C. A. Patrides (Baltimore: Penguin, 1969), 179–214.

25. Hugh MacCallum, *Milton and the Sons of God: The Divine Image in Milton's Epic Poetry* (Toronto: Toronto University Press, 1986), 111–12, 121–34.

26. Of course, some are sure to object that Adam does question God in his demand for a companion and in his reply to Raphael. Leaving the ambiguity of the response to Raphael to one side, we might observe that Adam's question to God corresponds to what God wished to hear. But Adam could not have asked any other question, since that is the one the story dictates he ask. Being written from Genesis, the story is already inscribed in obedience to the word of God; Milton and his characters accept the confines of that hermeneutic circle.

27. Ferry ("Milton's Creation of Eve," 120) and Cable ("Coupling Logic," 158–59), among others, argue that disequilibrium creates the possibility of real union. In their insightful article, "'Rational Burning': Milton on Sex and Marriage," *Milton Studies* 13 (1979): 3–33, David

Aers and Bob Hodge show that Adam is separated, isolated, and alienated from Eve, even as the intimacy of marriage seems meant to overcome solitude. This paradox is seen to be a manifestation of "contradictions that [Milton] never fully resolved" (4). Although Milton "struggled to find in marriage the complete solution to the psychic consequences of bourgeois individualism and isolation, fragmentation of the personality, crippling frustration," he never gives up the structures that bring this about (7–8).

28. See Richard S. Ide, "On Begetting of the Son in *Paradise Lost*," *Studies in English Literature* 24 (1984): 141–55.

29. Hugh MacCallum writes that "natural wisdom . . . [is] the consequence of the image of God in man." The knowledge is not innate, just the mechanism for acquiring it (*Milton and the Sons of God*, 134).

30. Halkett finds that Milton thinks of sex without procreation (*Milton and the Idea of Matrimony*, 13). Turner remarks in the Divorce Tracts how Milton shows "remarkable indifference to the question of children." This "seems to correspond to [his] noxious-excremental vision of the human seed." In the tracts, "the human is defined in such a way as to exclude the physiological completely. . . . Growth, fertility, reproduction, and nurture are barely mentioned" (James Grantham Turner, *One Flesh: Paradisal Marriage and Sexual Relations in the Age of Milton* [Oxford: Clarendon Press, 1987], 199).

31. "The way out of the prison of egotistic individualism is through . . . extreme individualism" (Aers and Hodge, "'Rational Burning,'" 18–19).

32. Milton warns the reader that free will is debated only in "Hell." Despite that warning, the debate is a staple of Milton criticism. Writing against is notably William Empson in *Milton's God* (London: Chatto & Windus, 1961); see more recently K. W. Gransden, "Milton, Dryden and the Comedy of the Fall," *Essays in Criticism* 26 (1976): 116–37. Writing for is Dennis Richard Danielson, *Milton's Good God: A Study in Literary Theodicy* (Cambridge: Cambridge University Press), 92ff.; and J. B. Savage, "Freedom and Necessity in *Paradise Lost*," *ELH* 44 (1977): 286–311.

33. "Human parents restrain and discipline their children in preparation for their growing up, whereas God, it seems, wanted Adam and Eve to remain children forever, punishing them for their efforts to grow. . . . Whatever growth comes about does so against the (overt) will of God" (Norford, "Separation of the World Parents," 7). "Innocence is ignorance" (ibid., 8). Thomas Wheeler coined this famous phrase: "Adam can please God only by doing nothing" (*"Paradise Lost" and the Modern Reader* [Athens: University of Georgia Press, 1974], 67). Al-

though there is free choice, Wheeler points out that it "emphasizes restraint and the maintenance of a static condition" (69).

34. *The Tempest, or The Enchanted Island* in *After the Tempest,* ed. George Robert Guffey (Los Angeles: William Andrews Clark Memorial Library, 1969), 58.

35. The child takes a long time to come into literature. Literature is rarely up to this point about growth and education. It is significant that in *Lyrical Ballads* Wordsworth devotes so much time to childhood, and even more significant that what may be conceived of as his reply to Milton, *The Prelude,* that nonheroic, domestic epic, is about human development and subtitled *The Growth of the Poet's Mind.* The late eighteenth- and early nineteenth-century bildungsroman represents a new and antithetical vision to Milton's view and, to some extent, to all previous literature that had been interested in guiding adult behavior, in adult states, in the rules to organize mature life.

36. Farwell, "Eve," 11.

37. This fiction of the patriarch does not correspond to the way men of the time experienced fatherhood in many cases. See, for instance, Alan McFarlane, *The Family of Ralph Josselin: A Seventeenth-Century Clergyman* (New York: W. W. Norton, 1977). For a brief account of the various readings of Josselin's diaries, see Nancy Armstrong and Leonard Tennenhouse, "The Interior Difference: A Brief Genealogy of Dreams, 1650–1717," *Eighteenth-Century Studies* 23 (1990): 461–65.

38. Splitting of these traits between Adam and Eve is discussed by Farwell, who states that Adam embodies reason and Eve emotion, nature or body ("Eve," 11); see also Ferry, "Milton's Creation of Eve," 129–30.

39. On Eve's egotism see Wheeler, *"Paradise Lost" and the Modern Reader,* 93; W. B. C. Watkins, *An Anatomy of Milton's Verse* (Hamden, Conn.: Archon Books, 1965), 37–39. Citing Marcuse, Norford finds in Eve's narcissism "'a fundamental relatedness to reality which may generate a comprehensive existential order.' . . . That is to say, narcissism may become the source of a new relatedness to the world, not one based on work, domination, and repression, but one that will 'release the powers of Eros now bound in the repressed and petrified form of man and nature'" ("Separation of the World Parents," 12); See also Lee A. Jacobus, "Self-knowledge in *Paradise Lost,*" *Milton Studies* 3 (1971): 103–18.

40. Ferry links her with the powers of poetry: see "Milton's Creation of Eve," 129–30.

41. Jacobus argues a similar point ("Self-knowledge," 103–18).

42. Milton's uneasy relationship with the poetic and artful has been explored in Peter Berek, "'Plain' and 'Ornate' Styles and the Structure of

Paradise Lost," PMLA 85 (1970): 237–46; Christopher Groze, *Milton's Epic Process* (New Haven, Conn.: Yale University Press, 1973), 7.

43. Froula makes a similar point about the repression of the mother ("When Eve Reads Milton," 333). As part of an ingenious argument, she writes that Adam sees Eve as complete: "The 'completeness' he fears in Eve and lacks in himself attaches to the function Adam associates with his rib: the power to create a human being." What she calls "archetypal womb envy" she finds "constitutive of male identity" (331–32). One could argue that if the rib were a penis, his spiritual power comes from ceding exclusive procreative power to her, the castration connected with the solar myth. Whatever the specific nuances, *Paradise Lost* at times suggests that reproduction and male sexuality produce a residue of shame that puts tension on the poem's attempts to allay the fears of sexual self-loathing that we saw in *Hamlet* and to integrate sexuality into the higher order (*natura naturans* and *natura naturata* joined).

44. It was not an uncommon view of breast-feeding at this time that children would suck all the life from their mothers: see David Hunt, *Parents & Children in History: The Psychology of Early Modern France* (New York: Basic Books, 1970), 119–23. That mothers will be raped by their children appears a Freudian caution but one that flows from the idea of the mother-feminine aspect directing the children to do what comes "naturally."

45. See, for instance, Geoffrey Hartman, "Adam on the Grass with Balsam," *ELH* 36 (1969): 168–92.

46. Regina Shwartz has commented that for Milton "the violation of categories is not simply abhorrent; it is dangerous": "Milton's Hostile Chaos," *ELH* 52 (1985), 347. She shows the numerous boundaries and the extraordinary boundedness of *Paradise Lost.*

47. Book I, chapter iii. In John Milton, *Prose Works,* ed. Kathleen Burton (London: Dent, 1958), 262.

48. Aers and Hodge have suggested that what Puritan authors meant by "conversation" was a one-way lecture ("'Rational Burning,'" 6). They cite Dod and Cleaver, *A Godly Forme of Household Gov't* (1630) and William Gouge, *Of Domestical Duties* (1622).

49. Throughout *Paradise Lost* Milton plays elaborate games with the etymological possibilities of his words, in an effort to sing "the meaning, not the name" (VII.5). In this description of Eve in particular, Milton activates the latent resonances of his words. Eve's ringlets are "wanton," not trained (IV.306), suggesting her need to have her potentially errant nature guided by Adam's straightness. The image of the trained vine does not eradicate the image of Eve's subversive twisting, reinforced, as it is, by the resonace of *vitis* and *vitium,* as of "vice," indicating something twisted, and "vice," meaning defect.

50. Much has been written on prelapsarian sexuality and its connection with Milton's and contemporary thought. Besides Frye, "Teachings of Classical Puritanism," see Peter Lindebaum, "Lovemaking in Milton's Paradise," *Milton Studies* 6 (1974): 277–306; Kathleen M. Davies, "Continuity and Change in Literary Advice on Marriage," *Marriage and Society*, ed. R. B. Outhwaite (London: Europa Publications, 1981), 58–80; Maureen Quilligan, *Milton's Spenser: The Politics of Reading* (Ithaca, N.Y.: Cornell University Press, 1983), 237; Theodore de Welles, "Sex and Sexual Attitudes in Seventeenth-Century England: The Evidence from Puritan Diaries," *Renaissance and Reformation* 24, no. 1 (1988): 45–64.

51. Many writers see that Milton is deeply divided, not only on the issue of sexuality and intimacy in marriage, but also on the issue of feminine companionship. He seems both to desire and to fear it: see Douglas Anderson, "Unfallen Marriage and the Fallen Imagination in *Paradise Lost*," *Studies in English Literature* 26 (1986): 125–44. Aers and Hodge ("'Rational Burning'") speculate that Milton could not rise above what he considered the givens of his world; similarly, Turner suggests that two competing models of love exist in *Paradise Lost,* one from experience and "the other from the hierarchical arrangement of the universe, and the craving for supremacy" (*One Flesh,* 183). Rather than a "craving," in Adam it appears as a habit.

52. Aers and Hodge point out that "touch" and "taste" are equivocal ideas for Milton, sometimes good, sometimes bad ("'Rational Burning'"). In the Divorce Tracts Milton uses the term "intimate" and suggests that intimacy is needed to overcome solitude.

53. A. J. A. Waldock, *"Paradise Lost" and Its Critics* (Cambridge: Cambridge University Press, 1962), 52.

54. Augustine wrote on prelapsarian sex: "Those parts, like all the rest, would be set in motion at the command of the will; and without the seductive stimulus of passion, with calmness of mind and with no corrupting of the body, the husband would lie upon the bosom of his wife" (qtd. in Lindebaum, "Lovemaking in Milton's Paradise," 280). This, of course, does not fit Adam's description. "Aquinas ascribed intense erotic pleasure to the prelapsarian state" (Turner, *One Flesh,* 195).

55. Similar points are made about German and French family relations during the Reformation by Stephen Ozment, *When Fathers Ruled* (Cambridge, Mass.: Harvard University Press, 1983) and Jean Louis Flandrin, *Families in Former Times: Kinship, Household and Sexuality,* trans. Richard Southern (New York: Cambridge University Press, 1979).

56. See Geoffrey Hartman, "Milton's Counterplot," *Critical Essays on Milton from ELH* (Baltimore: Johns Hopkins University Press, 1969), 151–62.

57. Ferry rightly points out that for Milton true poetry, like Eve, was "simple, sensuous, and passionate": "Milton's Creation of Eve," 130.

58. Harold Tolliver locates this new man in the Puritan antiheroic domestic values: "Milton's Household Epic," *Milton Studies* 9 (1976): 105–20.

59. The "burning Marl" may be the lime one throws into the hole of the outhouse after a bowel movement, or it may simply be the fertile clay-lime mixture that is metonymic for "earth" generally. Yet the two cases are really the same. Throughout *Paradise Lost* Satan is associated with fertility and with excrement—his expulsion for instance employs submerged motifs of defecation and ejaculation. That plants grow from and grow better in decomposed excrement and fertilizer causes Milton to associate both fertility and excrement with Satan, thus once again suppressing growth and denying it value; equating, as did Hamlet, defecation and insemination; proscribing intercourse and defecation as ignoble aspects of humanity; denying them not only value for humans, but denying them part in the definition of "human."

5

Blurring Gender Lines: *Hard Times* and Dismembering Masculinity

[Dickens] was a *hearty* man, a large-hearted man . . . , perhaps the largest-hearted man I ever knew. . . . His benevolence, his active, energizing desire for good to all God's creatures, and restless anxiety to be in some way active for the achieving of it, were unceasing and busy in his heart ever and always.

—Thomas Adolphus Trollope,
What I Remember, 1887

My poor mother was afraid of my father. She was never allowed to express an opinion—never allowed to say what she felt.

—Kate Dickens

FROM THE Renaissance on, the development of masculinity seemed to take two different lines that supplanted the earlier warrior code. On one hand, experience previously marked as feminine seems to have been more generally accepted as human and therefore masculine. For instance, men acknowledged their senses, their sexual desires, their familial relationships. At the same time, reason, rather than force, had appeared as a supervenient masculine virtue. From Alberti, who proposed the geometrization and rationalization of space, to Descartes, who mechanized the inner workings of humans, men seized reason to refigure and control what was now acknowledged as a recalcitrant and inherently changeable world. This shift, which we have marked through *Hamlet* and *Paradise Lost*, created two opposing possibilities for masculinity, possibilities that Charles Dickens saw culminating in the mid-nineteenth century with the conflict between a mechanical culture, abstract reasoning, and callous calculation, on one hand, and sensual particularity, selfless sympathy, and rich imagination, on the other.

Written in 1854, *Hard Times* reflects Charles Dickens's growing concern that industry was mutilating the imagination and the human spirit. The idea of progress, dividing the world between the heroically mechanical and the redemptively human, seemed to Dickens to split men and women apart and to split human beings down the middle. In *Hard Times*, Dickens examines these divisions, including the gender divisions that reinforce a dichotomy that does not seem to him inevitable, healthy, or desirable.[1] Dickens's analysis of the complicity of a particular masculinity in what he sees as the alienation of the human spirit and of the human community will interest us here, for in discussing the public social problems the book focuses primarily on the personal and domestic—men, women, and families—and particularly on the role of masculinity in producing dissensions and discomforts to which men also fall victim. The many interwoven stories in *Hard Times* all concern families—what unifies them, what divides them.

The central plot focuses on the family of Thomas Gradgrind, a member of Parliament representing the interests of industry. His philosophy of abstract reason over particular circumstances and emotions unfortunately promotes the destruction of his family. Gradgrind arranges a logical marriage between his daughter Louisa and a pompous self-made magnate, Josiah Bounderby. When Louisa finds herself disgusted by her husband, she flirts momentarily with a dashing and callous profligate named Harthouse.

A second plot involves Tom, Louisa's beloved brother. Tom gains employment in Bounderby's bank because he has helped promote his sister's marriage. Tom, however, becomes an embezzler and covers his dishonesty by framing a kind and long-suffering factory worker named Stephen. In the end Louisa returns home to her father and collapses physically and mentally, while Tom, discovered as the thief, flees retribution and dies repentant in exile.

These experiences chasten Mr. Gradgrind. He decides that calculation needs the mollification of human love, a conclusion arrived at through the help of Sissy, a circus performer's child whom Gradgrind had adopted, and Rachael, the faithful companion of Stephen, the worker falsely accused by Tom. The force of unpremeditated love seems overwhelmingly to motivate the women of the novel—Sissy and Rachael being the most perfect exemplars, Louisa latently sharing their impulses; on the other side, cold, methodical calculations of gain and power appear to precipitate male action, as illustrated by Gradgrind *père* and *fils*, Bounderby, Harthouse, and Bitzer.

But if Dickens's analysis stopped there, it would reproduce the simplistic dichotomies that it seeks to bridge. *Hard Times* offers men masculine roles that appear mostly negative: the pedant (Thomas Gradgrind), the whelp (Tom Gradgrind), the blowhard (Josiah Bounderby of Coketown), the rake (Jem Harthouse), the opportunist (Bitzer). In the failure of gender roles to make the world a better place, men are not simply the selfish producers of a masculinity that wreaks havoc upon the world; they are also products of that masculinity and its victims. Dickens's work implies, moreover, that these types of masculinity could be altered for the better not by being joined to a feminine activity or by being feminized *per se* but by leaping across the boundaries of gender altogether. The novel, although trapped in the language of duality and opposition, attempts to define the problem as not one of an innate masculinity or femininity but of an artificial division of male and female and the labelling of certain activities as unmanly or feminine.

Dickens, in other words, appears to activate one line of thought that we have seen emerging but repressed in Milton. Dickens believes that divisions imposed on the outside world are also divisions imposed within the fabric of the human character. He believes that such divisions lead inevitably to hatred, violence, and self-loathing. For Dickens, society's organization has alienated men and women from aspects of themselves, from their companions, and from their activities. Division results in insurmountable injuries to one's self and insurmountable barriers to mutual understanding. Division creates frustrations for which it provides no mechanism of release.[2] Thus Dickens turns from examining the costs of the male role to questioning the idea of a male role altogether. In *Hard Times* divisions drive people together in unstable arrangements and force men to inflict injury upon themselves and on others. The men of this novel, with few exceptions, have these common characteristics among others—they lead lives of desperate unhappiness, lives both destructive and self-destructive.[3]

The powers of taxonomic division are exploited by the male characters of the book. "Now, what I want is facts!" Thomas Gradgrind exhorts Mr. McChoakumchild in the book's opening line. Fact represents a product of taxonomy that can be used to control others. The pernicious nature of facts and the equivocal meaning of the word "fact" in the book seems demonstrated when we find Gradgrind and McChoakumchild browbeating the class with facts. Dickens appears to use this beginning to undermine the seemingly fixed divisions created by fact in order to demonstrate fact's fiction, power, and danger. When Gradgrind comes to address girl number twenty—a particularly slow student and an emblem of the nonfactual, nonmasculine world—he transmutes a select few of the facts she tells him into new facts with which he constructs his own fictional world.[4] Sissy tells him that her father "belongs to the horse-riding." "We don't want to know anything about that here," Gradgrind retorts. "He doctors sick horses, I dare say? . . . Very well, then. He is a veterinary surgeon" (13).[5] This "fact" is hardly factual, though not fanciful either, a term Dickens reserves for something childishly innocent and feminine.[6] Similarly, when girl number twenty introduces herself as "Sissy," Gradgrind objects: "Sissy is not a name. . . . Call yourself Cecilia" (13). In other words, a "fact" for Dickens apparently refers to a conventional locution or discourse by which a group has seized control of other people and situations.[7] A fact indicates an authoritative trick of the voice, a way of browbeating an unequal into submission, not truth. In *Hard Times* to be a fact the language must be hard, someone must be its victim, men must be its custodians.

That "fact" raises issues of control, not of truth, is illustrated further in the same scene. For instance, one might infer that because her father had called her Sissy and because she preferred that name, those who loved her most would use that name. When, for instance, Gradgrind grows kinder and gentler, he immediately begins calling her Sissy. Yet Mr. Sleary, the owner of the circus where Sissy's father worked and one whom the book characterizes as Sissy's surrogate father, calls her "Thethelia," the name Gradgrind conferred on her in the classroom scene. Thus the book suggests that the name holds less importance than the speaker's attitude. If Mr. Gradgrind cared for Sissy he might have called her "Sissy," "Cecilia," "Jupe" or "girl number twenty" or he might have called her by some other name, just as her father had. By the same token, Bounderby's insistence on calling his "good" friend "Tom" Gradgrind does not suggest affection; it represents a calculated attempt to control the other person or the situation.[8]

Facts, then, are slippery, equivocal, in themselves neither good nor bad. But they have been regulated and then seized on as weapons in the struggle for control, as they are, for example, by a government official who states: "People are to be in all things regulated and governed," and adds: "by fact" (16). The particular brand of factualism by which control is exercised is generalization.[9] Blue-books, tables, and calculations quantify experience, allowing the grouping of items, lumping apples and oranges under the name of fruit. Generalization also allows authority to repress what might otherwise seem peculiar to particular situations. In the book this powerful machine for manufacturing facts belongs exclusively to men, Gradgrind and Bounderby in particular.

Mr. Gradgrind's system, for instance, makes no adjustments for individuals, as is clear in the case of Jupe's failure: "Mr. Gradgrind . . . had no need to cast an eye upon the teeming myriads of human beings around him, but could settle all their destinies on a slate, and wipe out all their tears with one dirty little bit of sponge" (101).[10] Mr. Gradgrind's generalization and abstraction give him control over the destinies of countless beings, even as his system erases the characteristics that individuate those beings and make their lives particular and human. Mr. Gradgrind's response to Louisa's problems about the "proposed" marriage to Bounderby is to exhort her to think of the statistics on marriage, not on her peculiar condition or her disposition towards that union. The marriage, according to Bounderby, is a contract without regard to individual circumstances, such as incompatibility or the number of rooms in a person's house (80). To Gradgrind, marriage is a business "proposal" that includes the "offer" of a hand (102).

Indeed, according to the much-abused Tom, his son, Gradgrind had not paid any special attention to him, but had formed him as he formed all others—according to the system (139). As a father, Gradgrind was always "drawing a line and tying [Tom] to it from a baby, neck to heels" (177). Gradgrind is seen as an ogre, "taking childhood captive, and dragging it into gloomy statistical dens by the hair" (18). Tom views the "parental home" as a "jail" (57). The regulating of Tom's behavior by his "governor," as Tom calls his father, produces an attempt to adhere to masculine rule that first brings unhappiness and later tragedy. Trying to get along in the world, Tom finds himself "stuck into a bank" where he would always "get in scrapes" (159). Ultimately the generalizing power of abstraction, repressing parts of experience, creates a serious abrasion for those confined to its categories.

Finally, even the workers in their Union are asked to, and do, disregard "private feeling" for the "common cause" (151). When he is cast out, Stephen is treated not as a particular person with particular problems and particular reasons, but as a species of traitor, a type to which his role as a worker in relationship to the Union reduces him. As will be seen, although Stephen is himself aware of his own integrity, the action of his fellow men disgraces and shames him to himself because of the importance that he himself attaches to his role as a worker and class member. This is an insightful point in Dickens. The self-esteem men gather from their roles puts them in the bind of needing to tolerate that which is ultimately reductionist and stressful. Because of the benefits of work and of his roles, a man not only endures the stresses but blames himself for those stresses, feeling shame when he cannot perform up to others' expectations which he has incorporated as expectations of himself. So, for instance, Stephen feels shame at his wife's behavior. Men are, in this work by Dickens, victims of the systems, generalities, and abstractions that they create for themselves.

Dickens shows how deeply control and regulation have worked their way into the fabric of male existence. Stephen has internalized the system to the extent that he reviles himself with guilt and shame for having a private life, just as he seeks to become part of the machine and feels unhappy when he no longer feels harmony in what has been a condition of alienation.

For Dickens, training in abstraction has defined masculinity, which itself is an abstraction; moreover, the metaphoric violence of abstraction has also made men actually or potentially violent. This inculcation of a brutalizing masculinity occurs in part because, according to Dickens, to make matter homogeneous, abstraction violently suppresses and excises particular differences. Thus abstraction figures and participates in a kind of violence and brutality. Learning to abstract becomes conflated with other masculine training and violent modes of behavior. What *Hard Times* lacks in actual physical violence it more than makes up for in the general violence that pervades the actions, lives, and language of its men. Dickens's description of the government gentleman offers the type:

> A mighty man at cutting and drying he was; a government officer; in his way (and in most other people's too), a professed pugilist; always in training, always with a system to force down the general throat like a bolus, . . . ready to fight all England. To continue in fistic phraseology, he had a genius for coming up to the scratch, wherever and whatever it was, and proving himself an ugly customer. He would go in and damage any subject whatever with his right, follow up with his left, stop, exchange, counter, bore his opponent (he always fought All England) to the ropes, and fall upon him neatly. He was certain to knock the wind out of common sense, and render that unlucky adversary deaf to the call of time. And he had it in charge from high authority to bring about the great public-office Millennium, when Commissioners should reign upon earth. (15)

This lies little distance from Bounderby's own system of education: "Education! I'll tell you what education is—to be tumbled out of doors, neck and crop, and put upon the shortest allowance of everything except blows. That's what I call education" (238). Both his system and the way in which he declares for it are violent. Education, even in the relatively benign Gradgrind system is viewed as "cramming" (52) and "grinding in the mill of knowledge" (63). In politics, Gradgrind's party devoutly wishes to "cut the throats of the graces" (128). The production of educated citizens is based on a masculine model that suggests competition, struggle, violence, and selfishness— a model of masculinity that seems to have incorporated in an exaggerated fashion the rhetoric of the warrior code. Based on the mechanical systems of machine and factory, this masculine ideal suggests that reason and aggression are synonymous, that men have not changed by trading might of arms for the logic of the blue-books. In the attempt to incorporate past models of masculinity, reason becomes hard.

According to the myth of masculinity as Dickens sees it, life is supposed to be hard and men are hard enough to take it—a myth that Dickens tries to dispel. If Bounderby, a Smilean confabulation of "hard" work and self-creation, represents "fine bluff English independence" (174), he also stands for the model male. His hard life, in which he "fought through" (25), exemplifies the hardness and violence of the male approach.[11] He contrasts his "hard" life to the "soft" life of the ladies, like Mrs. Sparsit and Louisa Bounderby. His house knows no "feminine touch" to alloy its unabashed masculinity:

> There was no mute sign of a woman in the room. No graceful little adornment, no fanciful little device, however trivial, anywhere expressed her influence. Cheerless and comfortless, boastfully and doggedly rich, there the room stared at its present occupants, unsoftened and unrelieved by the least trace of any womanly occupation. As Mr. Bounderby stood in the midst of his household gods, so those unrelenting divinities occupied their places around Mr. Bounderby, and they were worthy of one another and well matched. (132)

In this passage Dickens appears to treat as feminine all that men do not consider masculine.[12] And while, as an image of its owner, the passage suggests that men should incorporate the feminine, that masculinity should therefore be redefined, Bounderby's castle projects what Dickens sees as the dominant beliefs about men and their hardness. Bounderby is a suppressor and fighter of anything that he considers to smack of the unmanly—from "fancy" to "mother." Having been treated in a hard and violent fashion in his childhood, according to his description, Bounderby reproduces his father's image, the expectations of him as a male in a world structured by this violent masculinity. Of course, Bounderby has fabricated the story of this father and this youth. Rather than being a product of a personal history, Bounderby has constructed his personal history to conform with an ideal masculinity that he conceives of as "hard-headed, solid-fisted" (26). As a result, he has become the "Bully of humility."[13] The violence of his ideal is implicit in the furnishings of his rooms.

So too when Tom Gradgrind, Jr., walks through the woods, the world of nature, he beats branches, rips up moss, picks buds to pieces (175), simply reexpressing the ideals of his father and the men of his circle.[14] And yet, part of the reproduction of this violence depends, as in the case of Tom, on discomforts and repressions that express themselves in a cruelty that then becomes defined as masculine and even virtuous. So in the image of Tom picking buds to pieces we see the image of both the scientist and the male who despises nature, as well as, given the tradition of the bud as a symbol, of an aggressive hostility towards the female genitals. But we also see the torment of the young boy who has had a restraint imposed upon him and whom the restraint has not straightened but deformed emotionally.

Thus men have either chosen to define themselves or been beaten into circumscribing themselves in a bellicose, selfish, and mechanical masculinity. In either case, division, the product of education and instrument of control, becomes an expression of masculinity's sublimated passions in a socially acceptable form of violence. Men are not the villains; an ill-defined masculinity is.

In producing artificial harmony, division has produced dismemberment. Dismemberment is the result of abstraction's violence. Dismemberment may come as "cutting and drying," maiming and distorting, or repressing and suppressing. For example, take Bitzer's well-known "definition" of a horse: "Quadruped. Graminivorous. Forty teeth, namely twenty-four grinders, four eye-teeth, and twelve incisive. Sheds coat in spring," and so forth (14). Such general classification not only kills the living distinction of individual horses but also dismembers the beast.[15] Piecemeal, without order, Bitzer gives the description not of a horse but of "horse" in shards of information. The definition draws limits that exclude by cutting and drying. Education, generally, is seen as splitting up. McChoakumchild cannot "kill outright" the fancy that lurks in each child; sometimes he can "only maim him and distort him" (18). McChoakumchild's own education was "head-breaking" (17). No wonder. For the "ologies," emblematic of the subject of education, are figured as "bits of stone and ore" that seem to have been "broken from the parent substances by those tremendously hard instruments their own names" (20).

The dismemberments resulting from divisions are figured in the details of community life as well. For instance, the architecture of Coketown and the lives of its workers are maimed, distorted, and dismembered, as in this passage that introduces Stephen Blackpool:

> In the hardest working part of Coketown; in the innermost fortifications of that ugly citadel, where Nature was as strongly

bricked out as killing airs and gases were bricked in; at the heart of the labyrinth of narrow courts upon courts, and close streets upon streets, which had come into existence piecemeal, every piece in a violent hurry for some one man's purpose, and the whole an unnatural family, shouldering, and trampling, and pressing one another to death; in the last close nook of this great exhausted receiver, where chimneys, for want of air to make a draught, were built in an immense variety of stunted and crooked shapes, as though every house put out a sign of the kind of people who might be expected to be born in it; among the multitude of Coketown, generally called "the Hands"—a race who would have found more favour with some people if Providence had seen fit to make them only hands, or, like the lower creatures of the seashore, only hands and stomachs . . . (70)

The twisting labyrinth of the sentence, which still has not arrived at its destination, reproduces the environs of Stephen Blackpool.[16] In the twisted heart of the city, we find the same "piecemeal" that we found in the definition. We find, too, stunted and twisted chimneys representing maimed lives, the healing home or hearth turned into "unnatural family," healthy expression distorted by repressed desires. Finally we come to the Hands, "generally called," whose roles and identities are confined to that one part of themselves, as if the rest did not exist. In the context of this dismemberment the healing wholeness often represented by hands (small *h*) and homes takes on its most important meanings.[17]

So too we may see other types of more figurative dismemberments: the casting off of family members, from the Gradgrinds to the Bounderbys to the Jupes and the Bitzers; the ostracism of Stephen, his body broken at the end, his right arm and hand, significantly, doubled under him, the arm and hand that Rachael holds; the repression of affection, love, passion that typifies such characters as Louisa, but also Harthouse, who has a "cavity where his heart should have been" (236).[18]

Overall the story involves a series of divisions and disunions between family members, between workers and employers, people and their government, as well as within people themselves. As has been suggested, one of the most important divisions, bearing importantly on the rest, is that between men and women. The story's opening introduces us to the arbitrariness of gender divisions: "The boys and girls sat on the face of the inclined plane in two compact bodies, divided up the centre by a narrow interval; and Sissy, being at the corner of a row on the sunny side, came in for the beginning of a sunbeam, of which Bitzer, being at the corner of a row on the other side, a few rows in advance, caught the end" (14). This artificial division of female and male, of soft and hard, of caring and controlling—of which the sunbeam seems naturally ignorant—is echoed throughout the work.[19]

Over and over, Dickens illustrates the lines of division that have been drawn between masculine and feminine. For instance, Sissy, who can't acquire "facts," is told to be happy in her "relations" (97). The antithesis between a masculine order of seeking control and a feminine one of seeking relationships becomes a major theme in the work and is exemplified by Sissy's account of her difficulty with generalities: "'And I find (Mr. McChoakumchild said) that in a given time a hundred thousand persons went to sea on long voyages, and only five hundred of them were drowned or burnt to death. What is the percentage? And I said . . . it was nothing. . . . Nothing . . . to the relations and friends of the people who were killed. I shall never learn,' said Sissy" (65).

The province of men in *Hard Times* may be abstraction and generality, but of women it is the particular and individual. Louisa, when she visits Rachael and Stephen, finds herself unprepared for the particular workers she has had so much general information about from her father and her husband: "for the first time in her life she was face to face with anything like individuality in connection with them. She knew of their existence only by hundreds and by thousands" (160). When Stephen appears before Bounderby for the second time, he addresses himself to Louisa, just as Louisa addresses herself to Rachael, and Rachael to Sissy. In each instance, the speaker trusts the most feminine member to be the most understanding about his or her particular problem. So one indication of the falsity of the so-called workers' union is that the "brotherhood" excludes women. And when men try to constitute a separate family it is, as we would expect, exclusionary, generalized, and arbitrary.[20]

Yet the configurations of gender and their associated values are never absolute. For instance, Louisa's thoughts center on the house, a symbol of the nurturing world that for her possesses the power to heal and to draw people into relationships.[21] Particularly, Louisa wishes to use the house's power to aid her brother Tom. Tom, however, seeks to escape the house. In part the house epitomizes for him a universal but impersonal paternal authority that restrains him; yet in part for him the house also represents threatening feminine nurture. That is, Tom decides to escape the pain caused by a masculine-feminine division. His reactions show the dangers of such a division, the perversion of each category by the other. Tom has so often been restrained by masculine authority that he also rejects the restraints of feminine authority (58). To him Louisa's proffered relationship seems like a further control upon him. Thus for Tom, masculine and feminine prove equally coercive, equally destructive. Rather than one being the solution for the other, each calls the other into being.

Moreover, although Tom's character incorporates what are marked by the world of *Hard Times* as feminine traits—desire for relationship, for particularity, for nurture—restraint has driven Tom's secret life inward where, according to Dickens, it has become perverted. Tom, feeling guilty about what lies within him, would not care to share what he has repressed, partially because such sharing would require a renunciation of masculinity which would, regardless of his personal renunciation, still occupy a powerful cultural position that would create immense discomforts for him.[22] Yet Tom notes that, given their common social situation, restraint still harms men more than women: women can give pleasure to themselves and others, when men cannot. The divisions that masculinity enforces make men, at least in Dickens's book, the most difficult group to recuperate.

Moreover, men become losers in many ways. Women, because of their ability to understand and sympathize with individual problems, differences in lives and in conditions, are able to sustain intimate relationships; men are not. Dickens does not show, however, how this ability arises in women. That Louisa has a revelation of it seems to suggest that he views it as something innate, not learned, while his treatment of Tom, as seen above, argues that men's incapacity to appreciate nurture is learned. Dickens seems to imply that all people have feminine qualities, but because the expectations for men and women differ, the effects of masculinization on both differ. Regardless of the ultimate source of the problem, men cannot enjoy intimacy. Rather men seek distance and control.

Yet if the story depicts the evils of control, generality, hardness, and division, if it depicts the male-centeredness of these evils, it also depicts solace in the form of losing control, of crossing lines, of intimacy, of the union of male and female. Union is necessary in all aspects of Coketown life, private and institutional. As Stephen Blackpool tells Bounderby, "drawin' nigh to fo'k" is important, otherwise, "they will be as one, and yo will be as anoother, wi' a black unpassable world betwixt yo, just as long or short a time as sitch-like misery can last" (154). The novel advocates the union of those aspects considered the separate domain of each gender and considered valuable by each. Head (male) should join heart (female); fact (male) should join fancy (female).

The solutions involve personal choices, rather than institutional ones; however, the book also suggests that institutions will become more perfect the more they can be brought to resemble a whole and healthy individual human nature.[23] The primary image of this healthful union is, of course, the home. So the book closes, "Dear reader! It rests with you and me whether, in our two fields of action, similar things shall be or not. Let them be! We shall sit with lighter bosoms on the hearth, to see the ashes of our fires turn grey and cold" (292). At the hearth, in the family, reconciliation takes place. We may also note that with writing (masculine) and reading (feminine) working together the reader and writer become joined like husband and wife sharing the hearth after their equally satisfying activities.[24] But we should keep in mind that the reader may be male or female, as may the writer; moreover, the writer is always and also a reader. Although the terms of the reconciliation are gendered, the metaphor pushes in the final analysis beyond that gendering.

Union is figured in several important motifs and symbols in the work. Sleary's company, the moral center of the work, represents caring family relationships that replicate themselves in all social relationships.[25] For instance, in their performances the riders depict family histories of symbolic significance, like the Babes in the Woods performance.[26] One of the main riders, Mr. E. W. B. Childers, crosses all boundaries, with a name like "child" and long hair like a woman. In this context, the horse-riding's "Ring" takes on an important symbolism. The final scene between Gradgrind and Tom, which takes place in the ring, with Tom moving from the back of the audience to the peripheries of the ring to its center, draws on that symbolism. The teamwork in the rescue of Stephen takes place in a ring, at the center of which the main actors are drawn together into healthy relationships. The images of people being encircled by arms or of the men joining both their hands to Sissy's creates and reproduces rings. Finally, the arm encircling the neck, an image of nurture and comfort, is the most repeated and perfect image of this circle. These circles stand in contrast to the "rows" of classroom desks, blue-book tables, factory smokestacks, and in contrast to Gradgrind's "square forefinger" (11). Other circles also exist—the family circle and hearth being primary among them, as the family represents union.[27] While in the book men do cross boundaries regularly, the book also suggests that it is men who most need to change, who are taught, forced, or psychologically compelled to absent themselves from home or from the homely even when they are at home, who have been divided, who stand outside the circle.

In the world governed by the masculine ideal of division and its resulting hardness, control, violence, excision, abstraction, dismemberment, victims are numerous. Mrs. Gradgrind, for instance, "whenever she showed a symptom of coming to life, was invariably stunned by some weighty piece of fact tumbling on her" (23). When we first meet her she is entertaining Bounderby, who "took up a commanding position, from which to subdue Mrs. Gradgrind" (23). She is afraid to speak because she is continually browbeaten into submission, never hearing the last of anything. The few times she exerts herself, "Mr. Gradgrind's eye would fall upon her, and under the influence of that wintry piece of fact she would become torpid again" (69).

Certainly, Louisa is a primary victim. Her relationships, almost exclusively with men, have taught her control, denial, excision, repression. When Stephen tells Bounderby not to mistake quiet for peace (154), he warns about a general social malaise that Louisa participates in and represents: "There was an air of jaded sullenness in . . . the girl; yet, struggling through the dissatisfaction of her face, there was a light with nothing to rest upon, a fire with nothing to burn, a starved imagination keeping life in itself somehow, which brightened its expression. Not with the brightness natural to cheerful youth, but with uncertain, eager, doubtful flashes, which had something painful in them, analogous to the changes on a blind face groping its way" (22). Over and over again we are told that her nature is "locked up" (131–32), that she has been "chained down" (168), that something lies within her to blaze out. When, unable to repress herself any longer, Louisa returns to her father's house to demand his help, her speech becomes violent and her actions self-destructive (214–18). They suggest that because she knows only the violence of the masculine world Louisa must, even in discovering her subjection to the masculine, inflict violence on herself.

We see the way that the lessons of restraint and division create domestic victims even more clearly in Louisa's speech concerning her failed marriage: "When I was irrevocably married, there rose up into rebellion against the tie the old strife, made fiercer by all those causes of disparity which arise out of our two individual natures, and which no general laws shall ever rule or state for me, Father, until they shall be able to direct the anatomist where to strike his knife into the secrets of my soul" (217). "Tie" takes on a sinister color from the book's prevalent imagery of bondage; so too "general law" with its opposition to "our two individual natures" resonates with the tone of the previous pages. But also striking is the asperity of the language, its violence, its suggestion of a hard nature in conflict with other hard natures. Louisa, emphasizing the personal consequences of impersonal forces, claims that the controlling powers of the world will seek to tie her down and dissect her.[28] She sees herself clearly as the victim of latent and not-so-latent violence of the controlling men who surround her. Yet her defiance in matching that violence shows how, learning to wield the knife, the victim makes herself her own victim. Dickens comments that "all closely imprisoned forces rend and destroy" (223). But Louisa, on the verge of destruction, survives to discover what had long lay repressed, though there are scars and disabilities left.

Although Louisa's struggle replicates the struggles of many of the male characters—Stephen, Tom, Gradgrind—that Louisa survives differentiates her from most of those characters. Tom states three times that Louisa is well-off being a girl, because girls survive. Except for Mrs. Gradgrind most of the women do survive. Certainly Sissy, Rachael, Louisa, and even Stephen's unnameable wife do. Yet, except for Gradgrind, the main male characters die or are exiled: Tom is exiled and dies before reaching home; Harthouse is exiled; Stephen literally and figuratively falls into the pit that the masters have created for him and dies before reaching home; Bounderby falls dead in the street in mid-life. While this may seem a fit punishment for the villains of the piece, except for Stephen their victim, it should be noted that of the three deaths connected with Sleary's, all are of men: Jupe; Emma Gordon's first husband; Mrs. Kidderminster's first husband. Moreover, two passages are devoted to the deaths of workingmen. To add to this, Mr. Gradgrind suffers a kind of mutilation.

Men, therefore, have most to gain by change, so *Hard Times* suggests. For, as we have seen, men are their own chief victims, suffering most from the violence and hardness that they have created. Most people recognize that domestically men kill women, but overall men oppress and kill men much more frequently and in greater numbers, in the workplace, in the streets, and on the battlefields. Men suffer higher mortality rates than women at every stage from conception on. The heritage of being a man is vulnerability. In Dickens, masculinity make everyone's life miserable, but men also suffer most from their adopted behaviors.[29]

Dickens shows that, in order to survive, men must change—change themselves, their education, their livelihood, their minds, their world. For men, change involves, as implied by Stephen's lines, becoming softer, becoming, in effect, more like what they conceive women to be; it involves acknowledging and acting on, in themselves and in others, what they have so long excluded from their characters by dividing the world between masculine and feminine:

> The strong hand will never do 't. . . . Agreeing fur to mak' one side, unnat'rally awlus and forever right, and toother side unnat'rally awlus and forever wrong will never, never do 't. . . . Not drawin' nigh to fo'k, wi' kindness and patience an' cheery ways, that so draws nigh to one another in their monny troubles, and so cherishes one another in their distresses wi' what they need themseln . . . will never do 't till th' sun turns t' ice. Most o' aw, rating 'em as so much Power, and reg'latin' 'em as if they was figures in a soom, or machines: wi'out loves and likens, wi'out memories and inclinations, wi'out souls to weary and souls to hope . . . this will never do 't, sir, till God's work is onmade. (154)

His "dyin' prayer [is] that aw th' world may on'y coom together more, an' get a better unnerstan'in' o' one another, than when I were in 't my own weak seln" (268).

Dying, Stephen calls for breaking down barriers that facts, hardness, and regulations have erected. Thus, hardness itself will be breached and softened. Breaking down barriers will give men access to the intimacy and understanding—"kindness and patience an' cheery ways, that so draws nigh to one another in their monny troubles, and so cherishes one another in their distresses wi' what they need themseln," the "loves and likens," "memories and inclinations"—that they have considered the province of women. Breaking down gender barriers, men may accept in themselves qualities they have defined as "feminine." According to Dickens's analysis, mouthed by Stephen, men suffer because they have been separated from and by those around them and from and by themselves, for they have never learned to value themselves and their affections, so they have never learned to know themselves or to be watchful of others.[30]

We have seen that the workers are dismembered and separated by their conditions of life.[31] At the same time, those with power are also portrayed as hardened and separated from each other and from aspects of themselves. Thus those relationships that seem most to promise intimacy only parody that intimacy when practiced among men imbued with the normative code of masculinity. The relationship between Bounderby and Gradgrind exemplifies this: "Why, Mr. Bounderby was as near being Mr. Gradgrind's bosom friend as a man perfectly devoid of sentiment can approach that spiritual relationship towards another man perfectly devoid of sentiment. So near was Mr. Bounderby—or, if the reader should prefer, so far off" (23). The "near" of intimacy is "far off." When the softened Gradgrind calls Bounderby "My dear Bounderby," this epitome of masculinity replies "Now, you'll excuse me . . . but I don't want to be too dear. That, to start with. When I begin to be dear to a man, I generally find that his intention is to come over me" (237), that is, take advantage of him. Bounderby sees intimacy as a form of control. In *Hard Times*, Bounderby's assessment of intimacy seems accurate when applied to most of the men. But more, as in the case of Tom's aversion to home, all intimacy seems to include aspects of control; yet intimacy becomes coercive partially because masculine training has made men and women very concerned with restraint, one's own and others'. Thus the issues of intimacy are complicated in the book.

The book's handling of the figure of "hands" suggests the complications to intimacy in a world of control. In the book, hands as de-

vices of control and production are contrasted with hands as means
of contact and intimacy. The intimacy of Rachael and Stephen is exemplified by her touch: "'Always a muddle?' said Rachael, with another gentle touch upon his arm, as if to recall him out of the thought-
fulness in which he was biting the long ends of his loose neckerchief
as he walked along. The touch had its instantaneous effect. He let
them fall, turned a smiling face upon her" (73). Although Stephen is
a man in much pain, Rachael's touch "could calm the wild waters of
his soul, as the uplifted hand of the sublimest love and patience could
abate the raging of the sea" (83). "To [Rachael] alone he had opened
his closed heart all this time on the subject of his miseries" (87). Although in some sense Rachael does control Stephen, the touch opens,
rather than closes; it allows one safely to lose control.

In contrast to this picture of intimacy is the touch of Tom when he
visits Stephen: Tom "wormed a finger, in the darkness, through a but-
ton hole of Stephen's coat, and was screwing that corner of the garment tight around and around in an extraordinary manner" (63).
Harthouse practices a similar deceptive bonhomie upon Tom in an
interview in which he repeatedly addresses Tom as "my dear": "Harthouse clapp[ed] him on the shoulder again, with an air which left him
at liberty to infer—as he did, poor fool—that this condition [to be
kind to his sister] was imposed upon him in mere careless good nature
to lessen his sense of obligation" (179). It is perhaps worth pointing
out that some recent studies have shown that men touch men more
frequently than women touch women. However, control, not intimacy, most often motivates masculine touch—the pat on the back,
the firm handshake. Clearly both Stephen and Tom succumb so easily
to the deceptions of intimacy because they desire it.[32]

We are not surprised, then, that Gradgrind never knew Louisa was
unhappy (23, 198). To see his daughter's unhappiness, Gradgrind
"must have overleaped at a bound the artificial barriers he had for
many years been erecting between himself and all those subtle es-
sences of humanity" (104–5). During her interview about the marriage proposal she seems "impelled to throw herself upon his breast,
and give him the pent-up confidence of her heart" (105), but he moves
away, cut off from her, unable to see her because of the barriers he
has erected. This is in sharp contrast with Sissy's reaction: "When
Mr. Gradgrind had presented Mrs. Bounderby, Sissy had suddenly
turned her head and looked, in wonder, in pity, in sorrow, in doubt,

in a multitude of emotions towards Louisa. Louisa had known it, and seen it, without looking at her" (108). Sissy and Louisa see into each other "without looking." Yet Gradgrind seems unaware of his own disabilities: "He was an affectionate father, after his manner; but he would probably have described himself (if he had been put, like Sissy Jupe, upon a definition) as 'an eminently practical' father. He had a particular pride in the phrase eminently practical" (20).

Gradgrind's failures as a parent flow from his following his role too closely, a role on which he has grounded his pride and his identity. Like Stephen, for whom leaving work and his co-workers becomes painful, most men seem to find that roles, even when producing frictions and discomfort, confer power, identity, community. In Gradgrind's case affection is distorted by manner. This manner, unfortunately, precludes him from understanding his affection, precludes him from observing carefully the affections of others, creates stresses in those relationships from which he expects to derive emotional solace.[33] This manner, which controls himself and others, opposes the intimacy that tears down barriers, just as the tearing down of barriers would oppose a masculinity devoted to erecting barriers.

By imprisoning others in their system, men like Gradgrind have also imprisoned themselves. The allusion to the Englishman's home as a castle, repeated in several places, reminds us of the way the book labels "citadels," "fortifications," and "barriers," traditional symbols of masculinity, as "unnatural" (70). Stone Lodge is Mr. Gradgrind's particular castle, and he is viewed as an ogre in it. The castle may remind one of Heorot in *Beowulf,* an important bulwark against the overwhelming passions inside and outside of men, forces connected with nature. Moreover, Louisa herself is described in ways that suggest Grendel: "'Did your father love her?' [Louisa asks Sissy of the relationship between her father and mother.] Louisa asked these questions with a strong, wild, wandering interest peculiar to her; an interest gone astray like a banished creature . . . hiding in solitary places" (65). Louisa has been turned into a beast by her exclusion from the relationships described in Sissy's tale. And as in *Beowulf,* Louisa's predicament represents the exclusion of some emotions from the masculine society in which she lives, and thus the placing of certain peoples and behaviors outside that society. That the book describes Gradgrind as the ogre who has usurped the castle suggests, however, that the repression of emotions creates a bestiality in men as well. The divisions create deformations that occur on both sides of the divide, thus questioning division.

That division creates bestiality seems ironic in a world in which, as in previous fictions of masculinity, the taming of beasts becomes the metaphor for socialization. *Hard Times* differs from previous fictions, however, in the self-conscious way in which it insists that order creates the monstrosity by which it justifies itself. It also differs through Dickens's insistence that the beasts, rather than being external threats to society or masculinity, are instead the members of society, both male and female. These wild animals must be domesticated by harsh measures or, to use Dickens's metaphor of dismemberment, they must be "broken," like horses. McChoakumchild, like a horse, has been "trained" by being "put through a variety of paces" (17). Jupe, such another horse, needs rigid "training" (55). Obviously, such training has use in promoting control and productivity, but such training also suggests a fear of the bestial that the training emphasizes rather than obliterates.

Throughout the book, violent sexuality arises from the distance between people, not from intimacy. The dominant image of male sexual energy has an odd propriety: the horse. From the *Iliad* to *Equus*, mastery over nature, riches, station, military prowess, sexual potency have been symbolized by the horse, a horse that men control. Yet, given the book's association of the horse with a genderless human nature, the appropriation of the horse, the desire to own and control that energy, becomes a particularly masculine disposition, one associated with a perversion and repression of that energy. Some men, like Bounderby and McChoakumchild, are "conventional hacks in harness" who discharge their sexual energy and passion through their work. The horse between Harthouse's legs is a matter of aristocratic display. After being jilted by Louisa, he, like the warriors after the death of Grendel's dam, rides furiously up and down the streets (225). In contrast, in Sleary's company horses integrate all aspects of the community's life: people get married on horseback, rear children on horseback, teach on horseback. As many studies have shown, intimacy integrates sexuality with comfort and affection.[34] Intimate relations, regardless of the connotations given to that phrase in our age, preclude violence and sexual aggression. In fact, the more nurturing the touch that occurs in a relationship, the higher the level of emotional intimacy and more tender the sexual encounters. Most of the derangements of emotional energy come from divisions, distance, repression, dismemberment. The title *Hard Times* clearly connects the social and the sexual for men. Men have it hard, in the many senses of the word, when they cannot maintain intimacy. As Rachael says, "'Tis better not to walk too much together. 'Times, yes! 'Twould be hard, indeed, if 'twas not to be at all." To which Stephen replies, "'Tis hard anyways, Rachael" (72). Rachael and Stephen, because of Stephen's previous marriage, find themselves unable to consummate their relationship sexually—because of what is for them an insurmountable civil law. And to save themselves from the scandalous talk of their neighbors as well as from their overpowering physical longing they find it necessary to separate, although, as Stephen points out, society has already placed a distance between them. Nor is it coincidental that Stephen trembles and will not have Rachael touch him when he sees his wife and thinks of murdering her, for the impulse to murder his wife and his sexual impulse lie close together.

For Stephen, who seems to represent the other men of the book in this, repression of emotion results in an unbridgeable isolation and a haunting guilt, disquiet, and anger. Clearly Stephen's unnamed wife is a victim of the society in which women are oppressed and made peripheral. She too shares with Louisa a description echoing Grendel's "wandering," her "woeful eyes, so haggard and wild, so heavy and large" (89, 90, 93). Her life tells the story of thousands of mid-century women.[35] Yet this unnamed woman, an artifact of a social realism, also represents much that Bertha Mason does in *Jane Eyre:* a male passion repressed because it has gone wrong and gone wrong because it has been repressed. Stephen's wife represents a part of him, what Dickens calls (in the case of Tom) "grovelling sensualities":

It was very remarkable that a young gentleman who had been brought up under one continuous system of unnatural restraint should be a hypocrite—but it was certainly the case with Tom. It was very strange that a young gentleman who had never been left to his own guidance for five consecutive minutes should be incapable at last of governing himself—but so it was with Tom. It was altogether unaccountable that a young gentleman whose

imagination had been strangled in his cradle should be still in-
convenienced by its ghost in the form of grovelling sensualities—but such a monster, beyond all doubt, was Tom. (136)

The monstrous perversion of emotion results from distance, restraint,
violence, hardness, lack of intimacy. The wife, its figure, remains both
unnamed and unnameable.

Stephen's dream elaborates his confusion of violence and sexuality.
In that dream he feels an impending doom and a general condemnation because of some unnameable shape: "If he led them out of rooms
where it was, if he shut up drawers and closets where it stood, if he
drew the curious from places where he knew it to be secreted, and got
them into the streets, the very chimneys of the mills assumed that
shape, and round them was the printed word" (92). The shape, on
one level, represents his wife, who shames him and whom he has
secretly desired to murder. The unnameable shape is also the instrument for that murder—the poison. The unnameable shape is also the
cause of this desire to kill his wife—Rachael, whose association with
him brings scandal to both. Finally, the unnameable shape is the general guilt and dread that all these thoughts bring. In this dream, then,
shame, guilt, desire, women, poison, and murder are fused.[36]

Yet this analysis leaves out the other unnameable shape that underlies all the others—Stephen's hard, unnameable, alienated penis. In all
its aspects this dream comes from Stephen's unfulfillable desire for
Rachael: the alienation and shame of his condition which hang over
him. The hardness of the times leaves Stephen with anger, violence,
aggressive sexuality, and shame seething in him. Not only can Stephen
not acknowledge his body and his sexual desires, but the shame, guilt,
and violence of those restrained desires make them an obstacle to
intimacy. The desire to murder his wife is only one unspeakable thing
about which Stephen cannot tell Rachael. He is ashamed of all his
unspeakable feelings, and so his refusal to allow her to touch him is
also here a rejection of the calming effects of intimacy which her
touch has always represented. Here again, in the context of that repressed rage, intimacy seems a type of coercion.

In this devastating picture of the male condition, Stephen is portrayed sympathetically, but he provides no example of a cure. Stephen's solution to this distance is to transform Rachael into a saint
and passionately abase himself before her (94–95): the elevation of

women to a pedestal where intimacy is imitated and where distance is deified is clearly the result of the inability to integrate intimacy and sexuality. Rather than being a real solution to the problem, it is simply a way of perpetuating the problem—severing romantic-spiritual passion from the physical need that apparently gives rise to it. Spirituality, violence, distorted sexual energy can exist side by side in a character like Stephen. *Hard Times* suggests that in a society in which dismemberment is an important feature, the cutting and drying of the male member is not the least of men's problems. Restraint, then, according to Dickens, not only cannot promote intimacy but cannot cure violence or curb sexual energy, converting them into something benign, as it claims to. In fact, restraint and distance are shown to be sources of male violence.

Masculine barriers to intimate relationships clearly hurt men. All the "hard" men of Dickens's book desire intimacy, affection, tenderness. For instance, although Bounderby's marriage to Louisa is neither sexual nor intimate, and although he wishes his wife to treat him "dutifully" and "submissively" (237), what he really desires is intimacy. He has spent his life disavowing what he calls "connections": "So far from having high connections I have no connections at all" (54, 27). He denies the existence of his loving mother and supplants her with a fictional mother who by beating him and abandoning him gives him what his real mother could not, a "hard," "factual" beginning that confers power, control, and masculinity upon him.[37] His parents had only wanted him to get ahead in the world, so that regardless of whether or not his case is one of bad nurture, whether or not Bounderby felt a distance from his parents that he punishes them for by killing them and having them beat him, Bounderby knows that getting ahead in the world, achieving his parents' objectives, means conforming to the world's notion of the fine, bluff, independent Englishman.

Yet for all that, Bounderby can be sensitive to a slight. He is scared of Mrs. Sparsit and finicky about how she will take any news. Moreover, seeing that Louisa slights him, Bounderby, like Stephen, cannot be brought to name what it is that is troubling him—partially because such confession would be odious and antithetical to his nature, partially because society has provided him no name for it. Or if it has, he has never learned it or has forgotten it. Yet he knows that—contrary to "fact"—this unnameable want exists. His reply, however, when pressed, is that if he wanted to have something, he would have it (195). This response, with its cleverly evasive wording, seems to suggest that his desires are tangible, that if he needs to claim his woman's affections, he would do so by violence if necessary. Yet his words imply the opposite: a violent sexual encounter is not what Bounderby desires, but it is the closest thing he can name, when pushed. And when pushed, he must fall back upon his adopted masculine behavior towards desire generally—if I want a thing, I'll have it. So too Bounderby's response, with contradictions, reveals his repressed rage and stress at not being able to name what he desires or act upon what he desires. Thus the violence of his reaction is also an expression of the distance between his real desire and what his masculine persona authorizes him to know.

Of course, even more than Stephen, Bounderby is incapable of resolving his confusion, much less confessing it. Yet he does suffer. After years of puffing himself up in front of fireplaces—which are symbols of home, passion, intimacy that he is drawn to, yet blocks like a dog in the manger—he finally explodes in the street one day: he dies from a fit.[38] Once again the image is of repressed explosive forces. Yet Bounderby's desire to reproduce himself somehow, while bypassing the normal ways, is testified in his ludicrous will in which twenty-five fifty-five-year-old men are to assume his name and character. Only at one point is he allowed a view into what is missing: "Mr. Bounderby went to bed, with a maudlin persuasion that he had been crossed in something tender, though he could not for his life have mentioned what it was" (188). Mr. Bounderby, who has been "crossed in something tender," is not a farfetched masculine character. That his hardness and inability to soften to himself and others creates misery in the lives of others is clear; equally clear, however, is the painful and self-destructive life that he leads in his attempts to retain control of himself and others.

Of course, outside of Sleary's charmed company, and aside from Stephen who is "saved" by his intimate relationship with Rachael but crushed by a hard society that dismembers and separates, that digs "rings" that are voids, that turns "promises" into "pro-messes" (as Stephen calls them), Gradgrind is the exemplary male of the story. If the hardness that Gradgrind has instilled in life around him rebounds to crush him, his ability to know himself, to feel affection, to establish an intimate relationship with his natural daughter, Louisa, and his adopted daughter, Sissy, a relationship that allows him to become intimate with all the other members of his circle, saves him. The series of disclosures to which he is subjected by Louisa, Stephen, and Tom lead to the disclosure of much of himself. He finds himself unsettled (220–23, 271). In losing control of himself, he also loosens his control of others.

The elements of his transformation are turned into dramatic images in the final scene of the second book, in which Louisa confronts him: "He tightened his hold in time to prevent her sinking on the floor, but she cried out in a terrible voice, 'I shall die if you hold me!' " (218). For once, he grants Louisa's wish, but the result is to see "the triumph of his system lying, an insensible heap, at his feet" (218). The next day we find him by her bed. He speaks "in a subdued and troubled voice, very different from his usual dictatorial manner; and was often at a loss for words." He confesses that "the ground on which I stand has ceased to be solid under my feet" (220). Hardness, system, division, control are dissolving in and around Gradgrind. Louisa, who represents his system, becomes "insensible," loses her "sense" (reason) and her "sense" (feeling). The collapse of his daughter is also the "triumph of his system"—its ability to crush the individual, to triumph over the heart.

In its triumph, the dangerous unreasoning and unfeeling of the system is exposed. Thus its triumph is also its collapse, for as the system triumphs in its monstrous, human-destroying insensibility, it leaves Louisa insensible, incomprehensible. That is, the system will not let Gradgrind understand her. Deprived of the hard ground of theory, of fact, of language, of existence, he is speechless.[39] His loss of words shows him groping to try to express what before—under the power of the system—had been nearly impossible to experience, much less express. He is going into that nameless place of the senses and into that other nameless "super-sensational" realm where for Dickens affection dwells. He confesses to her. He takes "her outstretched hand, and retained it in his." Finally "he softly moved her scattered hair from her forehead with his hand" (220–21).

The reconciliation of Gradgrind and Louisa involves both father and daughter in recovering the feminine traits that masculine upbringing had hardened over. For Gradgrind the price he pays is harrowing, and the effects on him are impressive: "Aged and bent he looked, and quite bowed down"; yet, as Dickens states, "he is a better man" (271).

Indeed this is Dickens's view, not that Gradgrind becomes a better human being, which he does, but that by crossing the ground of masculine/feminine, he becomes a better *man*. Physically Gradgrind in his transformation grows to resemble the one man who approached that indeterminate border state of masculinity/femininity—Stephen: "a rather stooping man, with a knitted brow, a pondering expression of face, and a hard-looking head sufficiently capacious on which his iron-grey hair lay long and thin" (71). Stephen's long hair on his hard-looking head is an interesting blurring touch.

As both Stephen and Mr. Gradgrind show, the hard world that masculinity has created exacts a heavy price from the hard. Yet it exacts a heavier one from those who transgress its boundaries. To enter Sissy's world is to be perceived as a "sissy." To be open is to be vulnerable. Gradgrind, returning to his work after his revelatory experiences, finds himself scorned and taunted "five nights a week until the small hours of the morning" (291). On the whole it is easier in a hard world of men to be hard. As always, the hard thing for men (the *difficult* thing) is to transgress the norms of masculine behavior. But as Stephen and Mr. Gradgrind also show, while the hard world exacts a heavier price from those who resist its divisions, the "unified" man can remain cheerful and tender towards others, who return cheer and tenderness to him.[40]

Ultimately, Dickens cannot scuttle the notion of a masculinity. Instead, he reshapes it to include elements that he feels have been falsely marked as feminine, but which instead are shared among all people. He articulates his ideal masculinity in Stephen's glowing description of workingmen: they are faithful, affectionate, tender, gentle, comfortable to the poor, sick, and grieved; they are patient and want to do right; they are never better than when they are moved to tears. Dickens praises Tom for his tears (178); smudging his letters home, they are tokens of his reformation (292). So Stephen, a "plain," "steady" man weeps before Louisa, who, unused to seeing men weep, is incredulous, frightened, but finally sympathetic (162). Tears are good, but it would be difficult for many men to be confronted by a reaction even as ultimately understanding as Louisa's. So patience and submission, too, are important traits that men are to share with women. But although Stephen learns to overcome his anger, which is the typical and practically the only expressed male emotion, his patience and submission do not lead to his success in the hard world.

What then are the rewards for men who abandon masculine and feminine divisions and share a common ground with women? Dickens's answer is clear and rather good: although being "mixed" or "unified" may cause men to suffer, being "hard" or "divided" not only causes men to suffer, but causes others to suffer as well. Moreover, being "mixed" allows men to experience private moments and feelings of joy and pleasure, whereas being hard does not allow such opportunities. Being hard, in fact, perverts all emotional discharge into acts of anger and violence; makes men parody intimacy in ways that may achieve conquest but never union; induces a form of self-control that becomes more and more necessary to exert in order not to become violent to oneself and others; creates stresses that lead to ill health; leads to poor relations within the family—including abuse; leads to loneliness and the desire to escape. Dickens does see the terrible power of public life to shape private life, but he also sees the justifications the public side takes from the distortions of private life it has induced. He therefore advocates the liberation of the private, believing, as his model for familial and social interaction demonstrates, that private affection will reproduce itself in public institutions.

Of course, even in Dickens the solution is not as simple as saying let's all be nice to one another. Even were men to transform themselves and society through the release of feeling and the discovery of intimacy within their circle, the work men do in the world would need to be transformed radically. In the world Dickens represents in *Hard Times*, men gain an identity only through their work. Work, even the most lowly, confers status. This is true for Bounderby and Gradgrind, as well as for the workingmen. It binds men together in a way, making their problem a common one. Stephen's only source of self-worth is his work (71). Sissy's father is shamed and disgraced when he fails (40), and so wants Sissy to be the opposite to himself, for he is a "poor, weak, ignorant, helpless man" (66). Ultimately, it is lucky for Sissy that he is, but that can be no comfort to him. Men, working under the pressures of needing to provide for a wife and children, die (88), and the image of Old Hell Shaft attests that it is work that kills them. As Stephen says, "I ha' fell into th' pit, my dear, as have cost, wi'in the knowledge o' old fo'k now livin', hundreds and hundreds o' men's lives—fathers, sons, brothers, dear to thousands an' thousands, an keeping 'em fro' want and hunger. . . . They ha' pray'n and pray'n the lawmakers for Christ's sake not to let their work be murder to 'em, but to spare 'em for th' wives and children that they loves as well as gentlefo'k loves theirs. When it were in work, it killed wi'out need; when 'tis let alone, it kills wi'out need" (267).

Dickens finds men's lot a hard one. Men have the source of their self-esteem as well as their wages from their work, and yet their work kills them. Dickens looks soberly at the difficulties in reconciling the good derived from human endeavors and the evils that attend them. When Stephen is about to begin life again, he is like a boy set free in the world, and yet, as unsatisfactory as his life has been in Coketown, he yearns for it again, knowing full-well that it will be better nowhere else.

Dickens is not about to say that attending to one's private life and affections will cure the evils that accompany the lot of men. The implicit conditions of labor, the stresses on men to achieve and perform, the stature gained through public performance, the problems inherent in any relationship will not go away. He does suggest that a benign public policy, one in which masculine and feminine mingle, head and heart, will do much to mitigate what at any time will remain a difficult, precarious, and often sorrowful world for human beings. The start at changing the lot of humans must be made, not by changing who has power per se, but by changing those with power—by changing men. If men would soften, if they would cross lines, take the risks of being weak, of meeting others halfway, life would improve. Dickens is not messianic in his message, nor does he call for heroic gestures—heroism with its horses, castles, and hardness is scorned.

What Dickens expresses through *Hard Times* is certainly in keeping with what has often been described as the tendencies of the Victorian age. One may demean its themes by calling them bourgeois and "Biedermier"; they undoubtedly are so.[41] Or one may see the book as part of the reaction to industrialization that led to the cult of emotion and the development of a culture that nurtured the human parts overlooked by laissez-faire economics, industry, and science.[42] But to have said these things is not to exhaust the value of Dickens's work either as literature or as a reflection of the times.

Men found themselves, both by past standards and to the contemporary eye, becoming more feminine and women becoming more independent. Gradgrind's new-found ideal of education, to "encourage [better nature] to develop itself by tenderness and consideration" (238), was the watchword in magazines of the day such as *The En-*

glishwoman's Domestic Magazine and *Family Friend.* The following advice appears in *British Mother Magazine,* June 1849:

> When children touch objects that they should not, it's natural, the child should be taught to yield up what would be injurious. . . . In order to facilitate the acquisition, never allow anything to be taken from it without immediately supplying its place with some other attractive object; but as prevention is better than cure, you must avoid placing within its reach what it ought not to have. Try to make compliance with your wish pleasant to its feeling, by often requiring it to do what you know will provide pleasure.[43]

Anyone will recognize the beginnings of the code of middle-class permissiveness here. In fact, ideally childrearing was to involve as little discipline and as much love as possible; parents were to become intimate with their children, communicating openly with them.[44] Indeed, one contemporary reviewer of *Hard Times* mourned that such a system as Gradgrind's factory did not exist in English schools. English schools were much too permissive, the reviewer complained, and offered too much for the imagination and too little of the hard practical matters needed in the world.[45]

So too among the growing middle classes, men and women were becoming more intimate in their relationship of husband and wife. Marriages were becoming, as had been true in most middle-class families, "joint role relationships," in which men and women shared— with great imbalances, of course—responsibilities and roles in the household. In their work middle-class men were called upon to develop what are now called "interpersonal" or "affiliative" skills. The expansion of the service sector, the transformation of the household from a unit of production to a unit of consumption, meant that being "cheery" was incumbent on the man who hoped to get ahead. Middle-class education and childrearing practices necessarily tried to inculcate those affiliative skills.

In general the trend in Victorian life was towards what at the turn of the century was called "the feminization of men." Although throughout the Victorian era many reacted unfavorably against the growing "softness," within fifty years of *Hard Times* masculine culture was to experience a tremendous identity crisis and there was to be a major reaction against feminism—a reaction typified by the growth of "muscular Christianity" and the founding of the Boy Scouts. In the last quarter of the nineteenth and early twentieth centuries, men from all walks of life, including the ministry, wanted to see men become hard again, wanted to reclaim the category of masculinity as something unique, natural, and moral for men. *Sons and Lovers* embroils its hero in the problems that arise for this next generation.

Notes

1. "Like all Dickens's fiction, it is concerned essentially with the moral dilemmas of opposition between mechanical rigidity and vital fluidity, scientific learning and intuitive knowledge, self-propelling masculine aggressiveness and nurturing, feminine receptivity. Dickens polarizes these values in various characters and institutions of the novel": Sylvia Manning, *Dickens as Satirist* (New Haven, Conn.: Yale University Press, 1971), 133.

2. The theme of maiming and dismemberment was first noted by Carl Dennis, "Dickens' Moral Vision," *Texas Studies in Language and Literature* 11 (1969): 237–46.

3. For Nina Auerbach, one of Dickens's most important themes is the "tragic awareness" and "lacerations" that men feel through the triumph of patriarchy and the schism between the sexes: "Dickens and Dombey," *Romantic Imprisonment: Women and Other Glorified Outcasts* (New York: Columbia University Press, 1986), 128.

4. The intrusion of fancy into the world of Sparsit and Bounderby is noted by John Butt and Kathleen Tillotson, *Dickens at Work* (London: Methuen, 1957); a similar point is made by Steven Connor in *Charles Dickens* (Oxford: Basil Blackwell, 1985), when he notes that by presenting "fancy" and "fact" in binary opposition, "fancy" ceases to be fanciful and becomes factual.

5. Page numbers refer to *Hard Times* (New York: New American Library, 1961).

6. There have been many discussions on the meaning of fancy. For Manning, for instance, "fancy" simply means "all the values embodied in Sissy Jupe, not only wonder and fairy tales but charity and love" (*Dickens as Satirist*, 142). Recently Robert Newsome has suggested that "fancy" means the "authentic," whereas "fact" is "artificial": "'To Scatter Dust': Fancy and Authenticity in *Our Mutual Friend*," *Dickens Studies Annual* 8 (1980): 39–60. Stefanie Meier associates "fancy" with "empathy which is the source of animism as well as human sympathy": *Animation and Mechanization in the Novels of Charles Dickens* (Bern:

Francke, 1982), 136. Generally she believes that "fancy" is *biophilus* and "fact" *necrophilus* (139).

7. Steven R. Rounds, "Naming People: Dickens' Technique in *Hard Times,*" *Dickens Study Newsletter* 8 (1977): 36–40; Janet Kartsen Larson, "Identity's Fictions: Naming and Renaming in *Hard Times,*" *Dickens Study Newsletter* 10 (1979): 14–19.

8. Of course, the giving of names seems to suggest the exchange of a benevolent for a malevolent paternalism—the coercion of affection versus the coercion of command. Yet Dickens implies that while people do not name themselves, they agree on the names given them in each situation.

9. Larson, "Identity's Fictions," 17.

10. See Joseph Gould, *Charles Dickens: Radical Moralist* (Minneapolis: University of Minnesota Press, 1972), 201.

11. In a series of books with titles such as *Self-help* (1859), *Thrift* (1875), and *Duty* (1880), author Samuel Smiles advocated the type of self-improvement for the uneducated and working poor that Bounderby seems to embody.

12. The sexism of the male/female division in Dickens has been widely discussed. See, e.g., Kate Millet, *Sexual Politics* (New York: Ballantine, 1970), 126; Donna Cassid, "Dickens: A Feminist View," *Women* 2 (1970): 21–22.

13. According to Bruce Haley, *The Healthy Body and Victorian Culture* (Cambridge, Mass.: Harvard University Press, 1978), by mid-century the "manly ideal" was becoming equated with hardness and the pugilistic, promoted by industrial alienation on one hand and middle-class "softening" on the other; by and large, however, writers, artists, and many others rejected this "ideal" (261).

14. Robert Barnard sees Tom's tearing the flowers as "the wanton sacrifice of Louisa's virginity": *Imagery and Theme in the Novels of Dickens* (New York: Humanities Press, 1974), 89. He connects it generally with the suppression of the irrational forces of passion, affection, and sex that he finds in the novel and that are expressed in the "dangerous and destructive," symbolized particularly by water, fire, confinement, and bursting out.

15. Myron Magnet, *Dickens and the Social Order* (Philadelphia: University of Pennsylvania Press, 1985), agrees with many others that Bitzer's "definition blows into atoms the complicated living reality of the horse," yet he believe that definition is part "of what is incontestably a noble project" (18). Overall, in examining aggression in *Nicholas Nickleby,* Magnet comes to the conclusion that for Dickens art has the social and communal function of helping to create a social order that keeps

nature from erupting. Like many others, e.g., John Carey, *The Violent Effigy* (London: Faber and Faber, 1973), Magnet finds a tension between Dickens's love for that which cannot be reduced to order and his perception of the incipient social chaos that only authority (the newly established police, for instance) can keep in order (e.g., 43).

16. Most critics see in the descriptions of Coketown a contrast between nature and town: see A. O. J. Cockshut, *The Imagination of Charles Dickens* (New York: New York University Press, 1962), 132; Manning, *Dickens as Satirist*, 138, 151. F. S. Schwarzbach, *Dickens and the City* (London: The Athelone Press, 1979), makes the point that "nature" may be suggested through the comparisons, but it is largely absent from the book (145). A good instance is Rachael and Sissy's walk in a country maimed by industry (260–62).

17. The reduction of people to "Hands" is "actual violence as well as a quirk of language" (Connor, *Charles Dickens*, 92). The presentation of the metaphoric as metonymic constitutes, according to Connor's deconstructive reading, a linguistic violence. He does not notice the metonymic "hands."

18. Ellen Moers argues that Dickens is secretly in sympathy with men like Harthouse, so that his analysis and punishment of them is lenient: *The Dandy: Beau Brummel to Beerbohm* (New York: Viking, 1960), 215ff.

19. Windows are used in *Hard Times* to suggest facts. The window provides Dickens with a powerful image of his notion of language. Windows provide people with an attitude, a point of view, in the sense that, like Mrs. Sparsit, one can frame life by looking through them. Like Mrs. Sparsit, one can also hide behind them, seeing without being seen. Finally, however, every word, like every window, has the possibility of letting in and letting out more than might have been intended. Wind, rain, sun, dark can intrude to break apart boundaries and distinctions, just as one can let oneself out a window or pitch someone headlong through a window. In a sense, the window is a Foucaultian interstice through which the nineteenth-century world falls in and out in much of its literature.

20. Manning, *Dickens as Satirist*, 140.

21. Catherine Gallagher believes that the final retreat into the metaphorical family is a retreat into a paternalism that offers no solution to social ills: "*Hard Times* and *North and South*: The Family and Society in Two Industrial Novels," *Arizona Quarterly* 36 (1980): 70–96.

22. The brother-sister relationship has been the study of several essays. In them the sexual repression brought about by the society (personified by Gradgrind-father) leads to a confusion of sensual and familial

emotions. The affect in the relationship of brother and sister, then, becomes primarily sexual and, therefore, guilty and repressed or expressed in the masquerade of familial affections, as in the bedroom scene between Tom and Louisa: see Daniel P. Deneau, "The Brother-Sister Relationship in *Hard Times*," *Dickensian* 60 (1964): 173–77; Russell M. Goldfarb, *Sexual Repression and Victorian Literature* (Lewisburg, Penn.: Bucknell University Press, 1970), 128, 137; Richard Fabrizio, "Wonderful No-Meaning: Language and the Psychopathology of the Family in Dickens' *Hard Times*," *Dickens Studies Annual* 16 (1987): 61–94.

23. Manning's insights have been followed up in Nina Auerbach, "Dickens and Dombey: A Daughter After All": "Each [male and female] can generate life, but untempered by the other, each becomes the reaper of its own kind of death" (116).

24. In the end, Dickens "matches heartless rationality with rational warmth": Barbara Hardy, *The Moral Art of Charles Dickens: Essays* (New York: Oxford University Press, 1970), 15–16. On the contrary, Richard Dunn believes that Dickens does not see himself at the hearth: "Far, Far Better Things: Dickens' Later Endings," *Dickens Study Annual* 7 (1978): 229.

25. The circus as the moral center has long been noticed: see, e.g., Wendell Harris, "Fiction and Metaphysics in the Nineteenth Century," *Mosaic* 4, no. 3 (1971): 53–61; Joseph Gold, *Charles Dickens: The Radical Moralist* (Minneapolis: University of Minnesota Press, 1972), 203. Philip Collins in "Dickens and the Popular Amusements," *Dickensian* 61 (1965): 7–19, is among those who view the circus as an inadequate answer to social ills.

26. Fabrizio finds the circus an extended family outside the distorting mores of society ("Wonderful No-Meaning," 85). A similar point is made by Sena Jeter Naslund in "Mr. Sleary's Lisp," *Dickens Study Newsletter* 12 (1981): 42–46. In his lisped line "*kith* me" Sleary shows that an organic society is built on a familial model that crosses blood lines (44).

27. The symbolism of the "ring" has been pointed out by Manning (*Dickens as Satirist*, 148). Naslund has, however, given it the most complete definition: "The ring stands for a kind of brotherhood, a circle of responsiveness to the needs and pain of individuals" ("Mr. Sleary's Lisp," 44).

28. Her line about the anatomist resonates with a passage in "Signs of the Times" in which Carlyle chides a Dr. Cabanis who in *Rapports du Physique et du Morale de l'Homme* published the scientific discovery that brains secrete thought (rpt. in *The World of the Victorians*, ed. E. D. H. Johnson [New York: Scribners, 1964], 37–61, see 45–47). *Hard Times* is dedicated to Carlyle and supposedly influenced directly by "Signs of

the Times." On the Carlyle-Dickens connection see Michael Goldberg, *Carlyle and Dickens* (Athens: University of Georgia Press, 1972), 78–99.

29. It cannot be stressed enough that in the place where most "murders" occur—the home—women are the primary victims and men the murderers.

30. See Manning, *Dickens as Satirist*, 140, 146.

31. Fabrizio points out that "the space that holds a precious wife and children . . . is punctured by the ladder that separates them" ("Wonderful No-Meaning," 79).

32. That men desire intimacy (or the feminine) has been remarked on in Dickens criticism, e.g., Auerbach, "Dickens and Dombey," 107. Manning in "Families in Dickens," *Changing Images of the Family*, ed. Virginia Tufte and Barbara Myerhoff (New Haven, Conn.: Yale University Press, 1979), 141–53, writes that although few happy families exist in Dickens, the characters aspire to "being embosomed in the stereotypical family. . . . The happy family represents a number of desiderata: protection, nurture, emotional security, physical warmth and food, children's laughter, and above all the endless flow of love to satisfy an endless thirst" (150).

33. "Gradgrind's manner in relation to females displays the silent truth beyond the surface of his words; his innate affection suffers from public image" (Fabrizio, "Wonderful No-Meaning," 69). Marianna Torgovnik finds that in the case of the Gradgrind family "twisted social values impede and distort private life": *Closure in the Novel* (Princeton: Princeton University Press, 1981), 49; also see Manning, *Dickens as Satirist*, 146.

34. On the relationship among sex, intimacy, and violence, see Alan E. Gross, "The Male Role and Heterosexual Behavior," *Journal of Social Issues* 34 (1978): 87–107.

35. See Patricia Branca, *The Silent Sisterhood: Middle-Class Women in the Victorian Home* (London: Croom Helm, 1975); Asa Briggs, *Victorian People: A Reassessment of Persons and Themes, 1851–67* (New York: Penguin, 1965); G. Clark Kitson, *The Making of Victorian England* (Cambridge, Mass.: Harvard University Press, 1962); E. J. Hobsbawm, *Industry and Empire* (New York: Penguin, 1968); John D. Baird, "'Divorce and Matrimonial Causes': An Aspect of *Hard Times*," *Victorian Studies* 20 (1977): 401–12.

36. Warrington Winters, "Dickens' *Hard Times*: The Lost Childhood," *Dickens Studies Annual* 2 (1972): 217–36, argues that the shape is the poison (230). Fabrizio argues that the shape is woman who is absence and becomes death ("Wonderful No-Meaning," 81–83). Edward Hurley, "A Missing Childhood in *Hard Times*," *Victorian Newsletter* 42

(1972): 11–16, argues that as a dream of incest the shape is Rachael, who is a displacement of Stephen's mother.

37. Howard W. Fulweiler views the parent-child relationship this way: "Josiah Bounderby's rejection of his mother in *Hard Times* is another emblem of a widely shared anxiety about the collapse of the family in the face of the Industrial Revolution": "'Here a Captive Heart Busted': From Victorian Sentimentality to Modern Sexuality," *Sexuality and Victorian Literature,* ed. Don Richard Cox (Knoxville: University of Tennessee Press, 1984), 239. On parents and children see Arthur Adrian, *Dickens and the Parent-Child Relationship* (Athens: Ohio University Press, 1984).

38. Bounderby's obstruction of the fireplace is like Sparsit's obstruction of the table; although she is "non-nurturing" she spends more time than any other character around food: Diane Dewhurst Belcher, "Dickens' Mrs. Sparsit and the Politics of Service," *Dickens Quarterly* 2 (1985): 92–97.

39. A similar point is made by Naslund in speaking of Sleary's lisp. One must continually read through the nonsense of Sleary's speech, such as his assertion that "Tharp'th the word" when "'tharp' is not the word." In Sleary's association with this playful signification he is allied both to "fancy" and to the greater "reality" of feeling (as opposed to *logos*) that Dickens seems to value in the work ("Mr. Sleary's Lisp," 45). Fabrizio proposed a similar, although antithetical, Lacanian reading ("Wonderful No-Meaning").

40. One could compare Gradgrind's emasculation to that of Rochester. See Adrienne Rich, "*Jane Eyre:* The Temptations of a Motherless Child," *On Lies, Secrets, and Silences: Selected Prose 1966–1978* (New York: W. W. Norton, 1976); see also Dianne F. Sadoff, *Monsters of Affection: Dickens, Eliot, and Brontë* (Baltimore: Johns Hopkins University Press, 1982).

41. See Mario Praz, *The Hero in Eclipse in Victorian Fiction* (London: Oxford University Press, 1969).

42. See Raymond Williams, *Culture and Society, 1780–1950* (New York: Penguin, 1963).

43. Quoted in Branca, *The Silent Sisterhood,* 110.

44. Ibid., 109.

45. Similar complaints were lodged in the 1950s, Dr. Spock years, by literary critics. See K. J. Fielding, "Charles Dickens and the Department of Practical Arts," *Modern Language Review* 48 (1953): 270–77.

6

Inventing Primal Masculinity: Beyond Sons and Lovers

[The] ideal is a man who fears God and can walk
a 1000 miles in a 100 hours—who, in the language which Mr. Kingsley has made popular,
breathes God's free air on God's rich earth, and at
the same time can hit a woodcock, doctor a horse,
and twist a poker around his fingers.
                           —T. C. Sandars, *Saturday Review,*
                           21 February 1857

D. H. LAWRENCE was born in 1895, the year the Boys' Brigade was
founded in England. He came to manhood and began writing in a
period of widespread male concern about the changing shape of masculinity. As sociologist Jeffrey Hantover observes, "Men in the period
1880 to World War I believed that opportunities for the development
and expression of masculinity were being limited. They saw forces of
feminization in the world of adults and adolescents."[1] In both
America and England the growth of an urban middle class that required traits different from those needed in pit, farm, or factory, the
sanctification of motherhood, the changing status of women in school
and workplace—all created new or exacerbated old conflicts between
expectations of what a man should be and current realities of what a
man could be, would be, and was.

The nineteenth-century masculinity that sought to do away with
the stark and artificial lines between male/female was in many ways
an odd and new construction. First, the idea of "reason" that was so
central to masculinity seems not to have been powerfully present in

English male fictions before the early seventeenth century. Therefore, it seems not to have achieved the same high masculine value as physical endurance had, for instance. Second, while domesticity had been recognized as the province of women, the particular kind of domesticity outlined by Dickens—highly affective, imaginative, and civilized—was also of recent origin. Previously, images of women showed them as wild or suffocating. Therefore, when masculinity sought to bridge the gap between the rational and the domestic, the two promontories on either side of the bridge were fairly new and fairly ambiguous in terms of their gender associations. The rational, for instance, might seem effete or feminine. In fact, to battle the idea of the warrior for the masculine mantle, sometimes, as we have seen, the rational borrowed the warrior's rhetoric.

The issue of the femininity of nineteenth-century masculinity might never have surfaced, however, except for a shift in class structure and the formation of new subgroups—most importantly the urban laboring class. With the emergence of a working-class subgroup into the public political arena, different concepts of gender contested dominant middle-class ones, as was already suggested in *Hard Times*. Thus middle-class men found their masculinity susceptible to attacks from those embodying alternate masculine ideologies, attacks that often left middle-class males feeling uncertain.

Ironically, however, while moral custodianship of civilization had been part of the semiotic of masculinity for centuries, modern masculinity constructing itself in opposition to Victorian versions of manhood identified the civilized with the feminine. At the same time, it identified the wild and natural, previously the province of the feminine, with the masculine. Thus not only had the lines between the masculine and feminine blurred, but masculinity had become feminine and the feminine had become masculine. The modern reaction that attempted to recuperate, refashion, and reimagine traditional masculinity was, therefore, caught in a peculiar area of gender ambiguity.

In the forty years prior to World War I, men apparently suffered psychic conflict from the softening of gender lines under the influence of urban middle-class domestication and from the concomitant construction of a more rugged, natural, rural masculine identity that became identified with a primitive past and that people felt society had eroded.[2] Suburban games replaced aristocratic sports, like shooting, as typical English pastimes. Lawn tennis (patented in 1874), golf, and cycling were each mild enough that both men and women could play. At the same time, however, rugged games, often identified with primitive, rural, folk and under-class culture, such as rugby, football, baseball, and cricket, were becoming widespread professionally and in colleges, grade schools, and towns.[3] Attesting to the victory of liberal, urban middle-class Victorian values, "Home, Sweet Home" was the most popular English song for a decade and seems to have been listened to with sincere and heartfelt emotion by urban householders.[4] And yet only a few years later, the most popular slogan was "Back to the Land" as singers of "Home, Sweet Home" fled the urban prison, at least for the weekend.[5]

In religion, too, liberal English evangelical philanthropy, with its cosy humanitarian philosophy, found its authority increasingly challenged by a popular church that was invigorated with a new ideal of virility as preachers espoused "muscular Christianity" from street corner, pulpit, newspaper, and pamphlet, in works with names like R. W. Conant's *The Virility of Christ,* which was published in 1915, two years after *Sons and Lovers.*[6] Christ, who had become the middle-class model for submissive, passive, charitable, loving males, was represented as "the supremely manly man" who was attractive to women, individualistic, athletic, self-controlled, and aggressive.[7]

Organizations in the United States and Great Britain, like the Boy Scouts, arose to deal with male fears of emasculation. In the United States, positions of Scout Leader were filled primarily by urban clerks who in their applications expressed a desire to reclaim their masculinity. In England this movement appears part of a larger desire to escape to a "simple life," a life both purer and more natural, one which actually had little to do with either purity or nature but instead created a fiction necessary for a male populace eager to reject adult urban life:

Another . . . escape [was] back to childhood, catered for by Kenneth Grahame's *Golden Age* (1895) and still more by Barrie's play *Peter Pan* (1904), the 'boy who never grew up'. *Peter Pan* and a host of boy's books exemplify yet another escape—that to the wild, to the life of the scout and the frontiersman, and the primitive sensations that civilization, in proportion as it holds sway, eliminates. Based on this was Sir R. S. S. (afterwards Lord) Baden-Powell's enormously successful invention, the Boy Scout movement. Baden-Powell's starting-point was the Boys' Brigade, in which he became interested about 1905, when it was already twenty-one years old and numbered 54,000 boys. The Brigade satisfied boys' taste for drilling and playing at soldiers; but he saw that for providing an 'escape' . . . the scout was a much better model than the drilled soldier.[8]

This masculinity that looked to a wild and primitive male spirit, violent and rugged behavior, had little to do with traditional norms of masculinity which, although they had taken violent and even stoic forms, had tried to repress the wild and primitive which had been identified with the feminine. The new masculinity, however, rather than advocating social maturity, instead founded itself on the rejection of adult masculine roles, of urbanization, and of the middle-class experience. It rejected this in the name of masculinity by constructing a new femininity and accusing men of becoming "feminized." In its avoidance of adult responsibility, the new masculinity sought to delay adulthood and prolong childhood. This suggests that men may have reached adulthood without having clearly resolved the issues of sexual identity. The problem may have been too many models of masculine behavior, too many divergent expectations.

In the period of D. H. Lawrence's youth, England was experiencing the so-called death agonies of the liberal spirit, as described by George Dangerfield in *The Strange Death of Liberal England*, written in 1936. According to Dangerfield, Sir Henry Campbell-Bannerman typified that spirit: he "believed in those amiable deities who presided so complacently over large portions of the Victorian era, inspiring their worshipers with so many generous sentiments and protecting them from so many of the coarser realities." The peace-loving liberal spirit was the spirit of the "feminized" man, as Dangerfield typifies Campbell-Bannerman, "whose three passions in life were his wife, the French nation, and his collection of walking sticks." Dangerfield, himself a product of the era of reaction, cannot restrain a guffaw at the expense of those poor men who loved their wives and seemed unaware that reality was really "coarser"—more brutal, more violent, more deadly, more truly masculine.[9]

So too Dangerfield describes the "unreality" of Georgian culture on the eve of World War I, which he characterizes as a view of the world "gone soft at the heart."[10] Dangerfield senses that these poets and artists were so suffocated by this softness that "when War came they welcomed it with a cry of eagerness, as if they had been rescued from the lavender-scented, the nightmare-haunted embrace of a large feather bed"[11] Dangerfield, like many other men of his generation, believed that this softness was unreal, that it masked a coarser, truer life that was ready to spring out, and that men, being men, were yearning for.

Dangerfield is struck by these lines of Rupert Brooke's, that effete representative of the turn-of-the-century spirit:

> White plates and cups, clean-gleaming,
> Ringed with blue lines; and feathery, faery dust;
> Wet roofs, beneath the lamp-light; the strong crust
> Of friendly bread; and many-tasting food;
> Rainbow; and the blue bitter smoke of wood;
> And radiant raindrops crouching in cool flowers.[12]

In their appreciation of the small, common, and domestic, these lines echo sentiments of Lawrence's autobiographical hero Paul Morel. Dangerfield's comments are instructive:

> These are pleasing lines—rather more than pleasing, in a quiet way. Only one is shocked to realize that both poet and public thought them not inconsistent with their title ["The Great Lover"], and that the sentiment at the heart of them was much admired. Yet anything could happen in those days. Harold Monro . . . was able to write some verses in which he berated man for not being more grateful to his furniture and kitchen utensils. . . . And nobody thought this at all odd. Was it the poet who was to blame? or was it that haunted and bewildered and inexplicable and rather sorry phenomenon—the soul of Liberal England?[13]

If men felt themselves becoming domesticated, this feeling did not bring unalloyed joy, as Dangerfield's own reaction demonstrates. Men, including Rupert Brooke, reacted with misgiving and self-doubt. They needed to find ways to reaffirm a manhood that they felt the age had destroyed. That this masculinity was not precisely what Beowulf or Gawain, Shakespeare or Milton would have recognized as masculinity made little difference. "Masculinity"—anyone must know (so it was thought)—is and has always been (so it was said) the opposite of "femininity." Thus masculinity was a natural, essential quality of men, which was antithetical to the petty, peaceful, materialistic, rational, citified culture of Victorian and Edwardian England which had come to be represented as feminine. Moreover, because men considered masculinity as the essential part of men, that which conferred manhood, they thought it so ingrained in their very nature and spirit that it was recoverable and reclaimable—if one dug deep enough.

D. H. Lawrence was one of many crusaders who set out to save what was seen as a crippled manhood and reclaim what was believed to be the essential, buried, primitive man.[14] Lawrence, who felt himself emasculated by the forces of feminization afoot in England, saw in himself the lot of all English men. In "Nottingham and the Mining Countryside" he lamented that "the English may be mentally or spiritually developed. But as citizens of splendid cities they are more ignominious than rabbits. And they nag, nag, nag all the time about politics and wages and all that, like mean, narrow housewives."[15] In describing *Sons and Lovers* to Edward Garnett in 1912, Lawrence saw men as split down the middle between the demands of femininity and masculinity, represented by mothers and fathers, by middle class and working class. "It is a great tragedy," he writes. "It's the tragedy of thousands of young men in England."[16]

Sons and Lovers conveys Lawrence's ideas about masculinity, but it also tells the story of competing masculine norms and of the "role stress" that they produce. In the novel, Paul Morel, the semiautobiographical protagonist, grows up in a household split by antagonisms between his middle-class, educated mother Gertrude and his working-class, coal-mining father Walter. Paul tries both to fulfill his mother's aspirations for respectability and to escape her suffocating attentions. In order to escape he attempts relationships with two women. Each fails. Miriam Leivers is a childhood friend, an introverted intellectual who wishes to share an artistic-spiritual companionship but whose repressed sexuality and resemblance to Paul's mother leave him frigid and distrustful. Clara Dawes, a factory girl estranged from her husband, is both strongly sexual and strongly feminist. Yet when Paul's mother dies, Paul helps reconcile Clara and her husband, Baxter Dawes. In the end, Paul, companionless, seems to be preparing to move beyond the small world that had contained him up to this point. Because *Sons and Lovers* has been analyzed from the perspective of Lawrentian philosophy, it has often been viewed as an expression of Lawrence's ideal of masculinity. Rather than viewing *Sons and Lovers* as an exposition of the problematic situation of masculinity and hence the stress and confusion experienced by men of his age, early appreciations of the novel, as well as many later readings, saw it as the solution to problems experienced by men. Such reading of the novel has led to a skewed notion of what actually happens in the book and what actually happens, according to Lawrence, to men.

Dorothy Van Ghent's essay is typical of the early critical appreciations in that it reaches out tentatively to accept Lawrence's later themes and ideas as means of understanding the earlier book.[17] For instance, Van Ghent speaks of Walter Morel, the rarely seen father, as the book's sole representative of the "life force."[18] For Van Ghent "integrity is . . . associated with the man [Walter] Morel and his own integrity of warm and absolute maleness."[19] One could easily raise many objections to this view: that the notion of absolute maleness that Van Ghent invokes has little relevance to the views either of men or of masculinity expressed in the book; that warmth has rarely been associated with masculinity, and that in the book warmth occurs in those scenes when Morel is made most vulnerable, discloses most, or acts in some way feminine, for instance in giving Paul his dinner (461, 492);[20] that Morel's behavior is brutal much of the time, and that this activity of aggressive domination is much more in keeping with age's emerging idea of masculinity, as well as those internally authorized by the book as constituting masculinity:[21] "[Paul] was staring back at her, unswerving. She met his eyes for a moment, then took off her glasses. He was white. The male was up in him, dominant. She did not want to see him too clearly" (363).

The deeper problem with Van Ghent's description of the novel lies in making beloved, large characters, like the mother, become small and making small characters, like the father, become large: "Morel, the father, the irrational life principle . . . is equally embattled against the death principle in the mother, the rational and idealizing principle working rhythmlessly, greedily, presumptuously, and possessively."[22] This analysis shows the fear of feminization at work, at least in the critic's mind. One may also notice that the latter "death principles," here identified with the feminine, were in the previous two centuries identified with the masculine; and the "life principle," here masculine, was identified with the feminine. But although Lawrence employs these inversions in his later works, he does not do so in *Sons and Lovers*. The book, which characterizes everyone in many and contradictory ways, rarely if ever characterizes Mrs. Morel as rhythmless, greedy, or presumptuous.[23] Regardless, Van Ghent's account suggests that Lawrence could impute some clear value to his mother, which it is doubtful he does in this book.

No matter how reductive his own views of the book may appear in his correspondence, Lawrence also admits in those letters that the book was not written like a spiritual autobiography, after the resolution of the problem, but was itself an attempt to resolve the problems of sons and mothers, masculinity and femininity, by writing about them. Therefore, instead of the mother's being reduced to a figure of good or evil, ambivalence dominates, an ambivalence predominated by admiration and love. This would seem to be the experience of most readers and not far from even the author's intent: "The son loves the mother—all the sons hate and are jealous of the father."[24]

And yet even this view is misleading. As he was writing *Paul Morel,* the original drafts of which were to become *Sons and Lovers,* Lawrence repeatedly remarked that Paul chooses his mother's view.[25] In fact, Jessie Chambers, the original for Miriam, denounced Lawrence in disgust when, on viewing his manuscript, she realized that he had depicted her through the eyes of his mother.[26] This is all very interesting, especially since Chambers believed that Lawrence had not seen her as the narrator depicts her. Although some commentators felt that the narrator, like young Paul himself, sides with the mother against the father, neither the narrator's nor Paul's point of view appears self-evident.

For instance, one critic cites the following lines to support his contention that "the novel as a whole . . . assumes Mrs. Morel's purposes and standards":[27] "The pity was, she [Mrs. Morel] was too much his [Mr. Morel's] opposite. She could not be content with the little he might be; she would have him the much that he ought to be. So, in seeking to make him nobler than he could be, she destroyed him. She injured and hurt and scarred herself, but lost none of her worth. She also had the children" (21–22). This passage is not clearly on Mrs. Morel's side; in fact, a distaste and hatred of the mother lurks very close to its surface. She "*would* have him" such and such a way. She destroyed the father, but she was only slightly injured. This hardly seems like unambiguous praise. Rather, like so much of the novel, no clear authorial voice intervenes to direct our ideas positively to mother or father. Rather, the narrator often looks uneasily at what the boy saw positively. And even when Paul himself assumes his mother's point of view, he does not do so unambiguously, and, moreover, he is often self-deceived about his views and motives.

Lawrence's ambiguous attitude towards his mother and father also appears to suggest ambiguity about his own gender identity. In this light, it is not unimportant that Walter Morel became the prototype of later Lawrentian heroes and that Mrs. Morel evolved into a death principle. The strains in identity, the "role strains," uncovered in *Sons and Lovers* required such a solution.

"Role strain" has been defined as "felt or latent difficulty in role fulfillment or the experience of low rewards for role conformity."[28] Basically, "role strain" involves interpersonal and intrapsychic conflicts that arise from dissonances or ambiguities among behavior, expectations, codes of behavior, beliefs, values.[29] The title of the book identifies roles that make competing demands on the book's main character, Paul. Yet "role strain" is a feature in the lives of all the characters in *Sons and Lovers,* particularly the male characters. Walter Morel and Baxter Dawes find that since gender roles are relational and since social expectations are shifting, their particular type of masculinity, which a middle-class woman like Gertrude may find attractive, creates problems for them within their relationships and, moreover, creates crippling personal stress. Paul Morel's problem arises in part because he embodies what people were beginning to identify as a "feminized" masculinity, which made dealing with what was defined as "traditional" role expectations difficult.

Ambiguity, conflict, stress, and (ultimately) formlessness of contemporary masculinity is reflected in the structure of *Sons and Lovers.* Despite Lawrence's passionate assurances that the book "has got form—*form,*" early critics were taken aback by what they perceived as the book's formlessness and failure to resolve itself into any clear meaning.[30] More recently they have been struck by the book's "openness."[31] This openness can be attributed to Lawrence's exploration of the conflicts among the expectations that make resolution problematic. Lawrence recreates the conflicting viewpoints that surrounded each event in his life and never seems to take a clearly moral (or even

Morel) point of view. The Morel-moral viewpoint seems precisely what the book questions. For instance, one evening when Paul and Miriam go to see a "certain wild-rose bush she had discovered" in the middle of a woods, the tension between Paul's feeling of obligation to be home with his mother and Miriam's need to commune with him and his desire to fulfill both women's expectations leads to an open-ended scene in which the shifting import of the moment is colored by different meanings for Miriam, Paul, and Mother, and in which the meaning shifts for some of them and often seems to cover a deeper meaning that the vibration of words suggests:[32]

> Paul looked into Miriam's eyes. She was pale and expectant with wonder, her lips were parted, and her dark eyes lay open to him. His look seemed to travel down into her. Her soul quivered. It was the communion she wanted. He turned aside, as if pained. He turned to the bush. . . .
> She looked at her roses. They were white, some incurved and holy, others expanded in an ecstasy. The tree was dark as a shadow. She lifted her hand impulsively to the flowers; she went forward and touched them in worship.
> "Let us go," he said.
> There was a cool scent of ivory roses—a white, virgin scent. Something made him feel anxious and imprisoned. . . .
> She walked home slowly, feeling her soul satisfied with the holiness of the night. He stumbled down the path. And as soon as he was out of the wood, in the free open meadow, where he could breathe, he started to run as fast as he could. It was a delicious delirium in his veins.
> Always when he went with Miriam, and it grew rather late, he knew his mother was fretting and getting angry about him—why, he could not understand. She could feel Paul being drawn away by this girl. And she did not care for Miriam. "She is one of those who will want to suck a man's soul out till he has none of his own left," she said to herself; "and he is just such a baby as to let himself be absorbed. She will never let him become a man; she never will." . . .
> She glanced at the clock and said, coldly and rather tired:

"You have been far enough to-night."
His soul, warm and exposed from contact with the girl, shrank back. (198–99)

In the first paragraph of this passage, the "communion" is not defined for the reader. The idea seems partially religious in that the roses "kindle something in their souls" (198). Yet the same words that underscore the religious and mystical nature of this moment— "soul," "communion," "holy," "ecstasy," "worship," "virgin"—are combined with words and phrases like "dark eyes lay open to him," "travel down into her," "quivered," "white," "incurved," "touched," "impulsively," "scent" that underscore the sensual, musky, sexual moment for the pair. The two reactions of the "lovers" are interesting: Miriam is satisfied with "the holiness" of it all, whereas for Paul there is a feeling of imprisonment—which may be caused by her possessive absorption of him or by her sense of holiness or by her desire for a religious-sensual communion that goes no further than the penetration of her eyes by his or by the raw desire that is evoked in the whole scene and that, for whatever reason, Paul cannot act upon.[33]

When Paul flees, the narrator tells us that "It" was like "a delicious delirium in his veins." But is "it" the open space, the escape, or the experience itself, which Paul can enjoy better once he has escaped? If the episode has been so negatively suffocating, why is Paul's soul later described as "warm and exposed from contact with the girl?" The ambiguous "it" leaves the reader in doubt about what Paul is finding delicious, just as "it" suggests that Paul himself is in doubt. Is Miriam too holy or is she too sensual? Does she expect too much or does he feel too much? Is he imprisoned or is he overwhelmed and nervous? Throughout *Sons and Lovers* when the narrator represents Paul's thoughts, "it" often appears without any clear referent, in a way that reminds one of the governess's thoughts in *Turn of the Screw*, where "it" masks the subjective erotic truth that underlies the governess's romantic fable.

Consider the heavy and shifting use of "it" in Paul's thoughts about intercourse: "In the morning he had considerable peace, and was happy in himself. *It* seemed almost as if he had known the baptism of fire in passion, and *it* left him at rest. But *it* was not Clara. *It* was something that happened because of her, but *it* was not her. They were scarcely any nearer each other. *It* was as if they had been blind agents of a great force" (436–37; my emphasis). The second "it" is certainly "baptism," but what about the first? And yet "it" and "baptism" both seem to refer to sexual gratification, which they equally evade. But then *what* wasn't Clara? A "baptism"? And the last "it"? Of course this passage can be translated sensibly; the point is that it cannot be translated definitively. And a further point is that this reminiscence of passionate lovemaking is much like the view of the rosebush. It is filled with a religious metaphor which, in this case, is definitely not Miriam's or even Clara's, but Paul's. The disappearing act he performs through the holes of his "its" distances him from the cause of his passion, fights intimacy with his own body and with the women before him. He is running away again and shifting the blame. Just three paragraphs later in this scene he is irritated with Clara: "He felt as if she were helpless, almost a burden to him, and it irritated him" (437). But what is "it" that irritates him—that she is a burden or that he *feels* she is a burden?[34]

With similar unresolved questions the reader and Paul arrive home from the rosebush to Mother, from whom one expects some illumination. We are told that Paul does not understand why his mother is angry with him. But the narrator is suddenly in the mind of the mother at a moment when Paul the child is not. She is angry because Miriam will "want to suck a man's soul out till he has none of his own left." Paul's sense of imprisonment, his penetration of Miriam's quivering soul, his fascination in her, all seem to justify this explanation. But is that what has happened? Paul's soul has not been imprisoned; it has been "exposed from contact with the girl." Moreover, the sense of imprisonment may just have been the reaction of the boy to the type of trespass of desire that the moment seemed to invite. Is the mother's sense of the situation accurate or simply the rationalization of her own desire to cling to her son, her jealousy of a rival? Is the mother's own situation different from the one she projects onto Miriam, for is not "his soul in his mother's hands,"[35] to use Lawrence's own words?

And, finally, what does it mean that Miriam "will never let him become a man?" Gertrude Morel often invokes the idea of manliness, but she never explains it to us or herself, nor is it clear in her relationship to men that she particularly prizes any part that is distinctly "manly" above any other aspects of human nature. It would appear that Gertrude Morel is searching for a word to describe what she fears and hits on "man"—which is in all probability the exact opposite of what she means, for her dread is that her son will become independent of her, wrapped up in an adult relationship with a woman, which, indeed, would make him a "man"—or at least reveal to her that he was an adult male.[36] On the other hand, Gertrude's later acceptance of Clara suggests that Miriam threatens the mother because Miriam fills roles that the mother fills. Gertrude might be less concerned about a frivolous, sexual attachment. But we do not know. We cannot trust any of the characters' views. They do not say what they mean, even to themselves. Or they do not know the exact source of their pain.

What Lawrence records, then, is a series of experiences and views of the same situation by three different people, none of whom can make his or her experience and view cohere exactly with the situation, and none of whose views or experiences helps validate or authorize any one of the views above the others. This "open" technique, while not explicating a particular philosophy, does suggest and delineate the discomfort, the interpersonal and intrapsychic conflicts that each of the characters experiences. Paul's relationship to Gertrude and Miriam—to his roles as son and lover—in particular brings out this conflict.

One other ambiguity of view operates in this passage, and that ambiguity arises from Lawrence's image of the rosebush. In his letter of 17 January 1913 to Ernest Collings, Lawrence describes "a man's body as a kind of flame."[37] The description of the flame in that letter echoes in its images the description of the bush. He also states in that letter that his "great religion is a belief in the blood, the flesh, as being wiser than the intellect." For Lawrence this flame that represented the male body also engendered in him a religious awe for primal being itself. Likewise for Lawrence the rosebush that Miriam and Paul visit is primal being, the male body, and the religion they share is an epiphany of the flesh and blood.[38] But at least two interesting points may also be raised in connection with this reading. First, why does Paul dread Miriam's touching the bush?[39] Is he afraid of someone touching the primal male body or is he afraid that she will take a rose from the bush, thus trying to possess it and thus destroying it? Lawrence would certainly later decide upon the latter possibility. But here he is uncertain. Also in both the descriptions of the rosebush and of the flame the images are male and female, and of course the rose is traditionally female with its "incurved"-ness. That Lawrence does not acknowledge this implicit blurring of his masculine ideal helps one understand why Paul is in such desperate straits about his masculinity.

The diverse views of experience that leave the work open-ended derive from Paul's intrapsychic and interpersonal conflicts, from ambiguities in Paul's masculine roles and from the masculine norms and stereotypes emerging at the time, represented by Paul's father. First and clearly, Paul's upbringing, disposition, occupation, and social associations make him an example of what James Joyce called in *Ulysses* the "new womanly man."[40] This brings him into conflict with the emerging Anglo-American masculinity of the twentieth century that has been given the following colorful attributes: (1) "no sissy stuff"— the avoidance of everything feminine; (2) "the big wheel"—success in the public sphere, high status, competence; (3) "the sturdy oak"— self-reliance, independence, inner and outer strength, self-confidence; (4) "give 'em hell"—dominance, aggression, violence, risk-taking.[41]

Paul Morel conforms to but also violates many of these stereotypes, and Lawrence is very aware that Paul exemplifies a more "feminine" species of man: "Paul she [Miriam] eyed rather wistfully. On the whole, she scorned the male sex. But here was a new specimen, quick, light, graceful, who could be gentle and who could be sad, and who was clever, and who knew a lot, and who had a death in the family" (178). Miriam does not scorn Paul's being a "new specimen." The attributes "light, graceful . . . gentle" and "sad" are not unattractive; in fact, they confer high heterosexual value—they attract women. On the other hand, they are not those traits that are typically associated with the book's "manly" men like Walter Morel or Baxter Dawes, nor would one likely find these traits, even today, in most adjective checklists for masculinity. The fact is that Lawrence has gone out of his way to give us an effusive Paul who admires gardens and china with cornflower designs, who exclaims that stiff egg-whites are "lovely" or that a swing is a "treat," who paints, who bakes bread, who usually prefers the company of women to men, who is a clerk and a pacifist, and who sells designs for ornaments, cloth, and cups.

Paul's sense of his own masculine identity is ambiguous. Part of himself, what he would regard as his mother's part, creates problems for what he regards as his manhood, as Lawrence writes in his letter to Garnett: "But when they [sons] come to manhood, they can't love, because their mother is the strongest power in their lives, and holds them." As a result, they are "split."[42] Writing of Lawrence after his death, Jessie Chambers saw the writer himself as split and living in unhappiness because he could never accept his "softer" side, a side that Chambers does not regard as uniquely feminine: "He looked in woman only for the animal—female—qualities. It made his dilemma a cruel one, because it compelled him to deny what was best in himself. Consequently his prison was also a terrible battleground where his two selves were constantly fighting each other."[43]

In spite of or even because of the gentle, domestic aspects of his personality, Lawrence himself denies that the soft is feminine by alternately viewing the feminine as animalistic.[44] Again, however, this creates discomfort, for when women become animalistic they intrude into what he has marked as a "masculine" domain and hence they become threatening. At the same time, therefore, he tried to distinguish between his important "masculine" animal nature and the possessive, acquisitive, repressed "feminine" nature that endangered the masculine spirit. Henry Miller, who felt a "passionate appreciation" for Lawrence, also complained of him as "a little runt. . . . I despise his workingman's (no, it was bourgeois) attitude—scrubbing floors, cooking, laundering, etc. . . . There is something feeble about him despite his glorious language." "The poor genius is half a woman anyway. He's pissing in his pants all the time—for fear of one thing or another. Mostly for fear they'll [women will] castrate him."[45] Miller's own confusion is instructive in that he posits a domesticity that is not feminine and a fear of castration that is. Yet Miller's phrases seem both peculiar and peculiarly appropriate, at least for Paul. Paul is confused about what a man or woman should be. Like Beowulf, Gawain, and Hamlet, Paul fears women. Although he and they each conceive of women differently, their fear is also in part a fear of being womanlike. Given the loop of Miller's argument—the fear of being womanlike *is* womanlike—extricating one's self would be difficult.

Paul feels strains in his role as lover particularly when, as in the cases of Clara and Miriam, women seek emotional intimacy with him. Sociologist Robert Lewis defines "emotional intimacy" as "mutual self-disclosure and other kinds of verbal sharing, as declarations of liking or loving the other, and as demonstrations of affection such as hugging and nongenital caressing."[46] Many men, Lewis finds, fear emotional intimacy. Particularly difficult for them is self-disclosure, both receiving and giving intimate details, perhaps because of the emphasis placed upon manly traits that include "aggression, competitiveness, task orientation, unsentimentality, and emotional control."[47] The result of this emotional control is the "inexpressive male."[48]

Although, in Lawrence's terms and the terms of modern sociologists who lack a historical perspective, Paul has been "feminized," he believes in the masculinity of the behaviors listed above, which resemble the "sturdy oak" stereotype. He is uncomfortable disclosing, as he confides to his mother: "I feel sometimes as if I wronged my women, mother. . . . I even love Clara, and I did Miriam, but to give myself to them in marriage, I couldn't. I couldn't belong to them. They seem to want me, and I can't ever give it them" (432). Here, apparently, is one of the manifold contradictions of the book. Previously Paul has felt that Miriam wants to take and take and take; now he states it as his own problem: he can't give (which implies that she *does* give). But from the standpoint of the type of emotional intimacy that Miriam had demanded, he must have felt that her desire to know him was exorbitant, regardless of whether or not she "gave" to the relationship. Moreover, he sees marriage as a covenant of emotional intimacy, though viewing his own parents' relative lack of intimacy he might have felt otherwise. The types of demands that "his women," including his mother, make of him fundamentally alter the idea of marriage: that is, not only does he know that "his women" want disclosure, but being himself like them to an extent, he believes that disclosure is desirable, even though it is uncomfortable.

That emotional intimacy is a problem for Paul, and for the men of the book in general, and that it is desirable, even from Paul's standpoint, is affirmed in a later exchange between Paul and Clara:

"About me you know nothing," she said bitterly—"about me!" . . .

He felt puzzled, and helpless, and angry. There she walked, unknown to him, though they had been through such an experience together.

"But you know me pretty well," he said.

She did not answer. . . .

"And haven't I let you know me?"

"It's what men won't let you do. They won't let you get really near to them," she said.

"And haven't I let you?"

"Yes," she answered slowly; "but you never come near to me.
You can't come out of yourself, you can't." (446)

Here Paul thinks that he and Clara have intimately known each other.
Yet her "disclosure" shows not only that he has not disclosed to her
but that he has not welcomed her disclosures to him. She is "unknown" to him. Although he thinks he has "let" her "get really near"
him, he has not been open to receive whatever she had revealed.

It is also important that this is a postcoital discussion. Recent critics have frequently pointed out Lawrence's belief in the importance of
the individual and at the same time have shown that Paul's relationships in *Sons and Lovers* are basically impersonal.[49] Yet Lawrence
makes a distinction: Miriam and Clara can know Paul individually,
but not personally, for the individual is the essential person, and the
personal is the social confluence: "for the whole of his life he could
not reconcile an intimate knowledge of a woman's mind with sexual
attraction towards her."[50]

It is important to note, however, that the problem of disclosing is
complicated by the dread that what is disclosed will not meet with
approval. For while Paul recognizes that both Miriam and Clara wish
to know the *real* Paul, he fears that they will not like what they find.
Miriam he knows would be unhappy to find a nonfeminine, less-than-
spiritual Paul: "he was nearly a religion to her. He could not bear to
fail her" (344). On the other hand, he senses that Clara really desires
a manly man: "Clara could not stand for him to hold on to. She
wanted him, but not to understand him. He felt she wanted the man
on top, not the real him that was in trouble" (501). In other words,
Paul's fear of intimacy comes in part from a feeling that being honest
will violate the expectations of his partners.

Here Paul's two "liberated" companions cling to two notions of
masculinity—the "manly"-heroic man of the newly invented remote
past and the feminine-"spiritual" man of the recent liberal Victorian
past. Paul conforms to neither. And although he seems closer to Miriam's vision of him, he cannot come to grips with a sense of gender or
find a conceptual framework for gender that is presentable. He is
ashamed. Partially because of the stress that competing gender expectations place upon Paul, he seeks to redefine masculinity through the
sexual experience, and at the same time he seeks to use sexual inter-

course as a common, overwhelming, humbling experience that will somehow cut through every hindrance to disclosure, that will replace disclosure altogether.

As implied above, Paul may believe that emotional intimacy is important, but he confuses sex with intimacy, sexual longings with a longing for complete disclosure. Although he tells Miriam that "there is between . . . us all these years of intimacy. I feel naked enough before you" (347), he goes on to ask "why," considering this, "should n't we belong to each other altogether?" (349). Paul declares that he and she are intimate, but even before his "Test *on* Miriam" (i.e., on top of her), Paul states that without physical intimacy—which he likewise equates with sexual intimacy—"real" intimacy is impossible. "There was some obstacle; and what was the obstacle? It lay in physical bondage. . . . With her he felt bound up inside himself. He could not go out to her. Something struggled in him, but he could not get to her" (343). Paul realizes that he is not disclosing himself, and yet he wishes to. Throughout chapter 11, as in the passages above, the idea of disclosing, of "going out" to someone, is based on a penile image. In that sense, he is not naked without being naked; he cannot penetrate her without penetrating her physically; she cannot know him without knowing him sexually.

Miriam, however, fails the test on her, because during sexual intercourse Paul cannot really let go; he feels he needs to be concerned with her feelings. Here the two meanings of "going out" conflict. He cannot escape into sexual oblivion if he goes out of himself to understand her; he cannot go out of himself to understand her if he escapes into sexual oblivion. As he describes it: "He had always, almost willfully, to put her out of count, and act from the brute strength of his own feelings. And he could not do it often, and there remained afterwards always the sense of failure and death. If he were really with her, he had to put aside himself and his desire. If he would have her, he had to put her aside" (358). To Paul's mind, when he was forced to pay attention to her needs during the intercourse (her disclosure), he felt he had to repress his own physical need and his own desire (his disclosure). Although Paul rationalizes his sexual encounters as a form of intimacy, he enjoys sex only by denying the intimate personal level. If he wants to gratify himself, he has to ignore her, as he does the first time by shutting his eyes. Then "his blood beat back again"

(357). Miriam must become "woman" for him; it is her "woman-being" that he believes he can be intimate with.

Although Paul uses a rhetoric that sounds like that of intimacy, for him desire is "great hunger" and "impersonal":

> Often, when he grew hot, she put his face from her, held it between her hands, and looked in his eyes. He could not meet her gaze. Her dark eyes, full of love, earnest and searching, made him turn away. Not for an instant would she let him forget. . . . Never any relaxing, never any leaving himself to the great hunger and impersonality of passion; he must be brought back to a deliberate, reflective creature. As if from a swoon of passion she called him back to the littleness, the personal relationship. (351)

Paul may conceive of sexual intercourse as the ultimate intimacy, but intimacy is precisely what sex allows Paul to escape. Intimacy is feminine; escape is masculine. Holding and gazing is feminine; sexual passion is masculine. Sacrificing oneself to another's needs is feminine; taking what one wants is masculine. The so-called "littleness, the personal relationship" is feminine; the large, impersonal, individual force is masculine.

Lawrence has been criticized for focusing too much attention on the individual, rather than on the larger forces that determine individual behavior—social and economic forces that determine his father's and mother's behaviors, for instance. But by "individual" Lawrence means something totally distinct from and independent of the "personal." In fact, containing aspects he fears are feminine, Paul tries to construct the idea of a "person" who is immune to the forces of the "personal." Hence, he constructs the idea of the "individual"—a chimera that, like earlier masculine ideals, separates men from society and from women.[51]

The individual is not a knight who is the exemplar and embodiment of the social ideal. The individual is, as Rousseau formulated it, resolutely antisocial. Yet as individual, rather than knight, the twentieth-century masculine ideal enfolds several aspects that older forms of masculinity kept out. First, it makes central sexual desire and desire generally and makes men responsible for their desires. As individuals men for the first time acknowledge the importance of their bodies; they escape the former social expectations of how desire is supposed to behave, even though they may simply be constructing new expectations. Second, the ideal acknowledges that men have particular existences that cannot perfectly embody the social ideal. In this sense, for Paul exposing his sexual side to others *is* a disclosure.

On the other hand, because the individual is an abstraction, the new masculine ideal simultaneously denies the very incorporations it makes. That is, desire, rather than being a personal force, becomes an impersonal, instinctive, Dionysiac force that simply works through the bodies of individual men. It is clear, however, in the sexual scenes that this "impersonality"—like "baptism" and "it"—is just an evasion. Going out of himself in sexual terms means paying attention only to himself, leaving the social dimension, escaping the "intercourse" of intercourse, and literally enjoying himself. Also, as I have argued, the individual while deriving from the sense that particular people exist, with particular histories, needs, and problems, is firmly entrenched in its antipathy to the sociopersonal forces that give what we call "individuality" being but that also weaken the notion of individuality.

Paul's sense of conflict with the forces that give him being is the heart of his problem. For Paul, as for Lawrence, as for many males who saw themselves as feminized, maturity meant achieving manhood—a social and spiritual category as well as a biological one. For the "feminized" male struggling against "feminization," manhood did not simply mean the ability to inseminate, but meant claiming or "reclaiming" a version of one's self that was masculine. This meant the symbolic death of the feminine within one, as it meant freeing oneself from external feminine forces that threaten to "possess" one. Thus men like Paul find themselves in a strange position: their own identities, which they need to prove are masculine, in many cases include aspects that they regard as feminine. This leads them simultaneously to affirm and deny a feminine trait, usually, as we have seen, by transforming it.

Personal intimacy, for instance, may be important to Lawrence's men, but those men reconstitute intimacy as giving oneself to impersonal forces so that women will be excluded. As a result, a man often desires "personal" intimacy with a woman but has constructed the rules in such a way that such intimacy is impossible. This is the gist of the teachings of Otto Gross, under whose influence Lawrence supposedly fell at the time of his revisions of *Sons and Lovers:* "To love erotically is not to feel identified with the other person, but with a third being, the relationship itself. Erotic love alone can finally overcome man's loneliness. Relationship understood is that third thing, that worshipped as a supreme value, will allow the lover to combine an erotic union with an uncompromised drive to individuality."[52]

As one recent critic writes: "The novel gives the deeper sense of the very life flow of the individual, the deep yearning for spontaneous expression of one's possibilities, and the deep psychic injury that results from the thwarting or clogging of life energies by industrialism, by poverty, by middle-class expectations, and by repressive spirituality."[53] For Lawrence and many others this "life energy" which is the essence of individuality becomes identified with the "sexual instinct," which when "repressed . . . comes out either in aggressive action or in its opposite, pathological cowardice."[54]

With this transformation of the feminine personal into masculine individual, and emotional intimacy into erotic intimacy, men can reject the origins of their feelings and behaviors, the "world of women" which in many cases had molded them—mothers, lovers, wives. For these reasons, Paul desires to kill his mother, as well as his father; and he does so symbolically. Yet he also literally kills his mother so that he might free himself from her influence. That he kills her at the point of his most intimate contact with her, under the guise of understanding and caring for her, during passages of extraordinary intimacy, by poisoning the milk with which he now feeds her, demonstrates and expresses the deadly perversion needed both to claim and to free himself from his supposed feminine nature.

Of course, the resemblance between Miriam and Paul's mother makes Miriam particularly threatening. Although Paul is drawn towards Miriam and she appears his alter ego at times, her virtues of understanding are also her sins. For in this understanding, she is too much like his mother (344). For this reason intimacy makes Paul feel guilty of replacing his mother with Miriam, makes sexual congress with Miriam distasteful, and makes contact of any kind seem incestuously suffocating.[55] But even later when Paul seems to connect with Clara, who is in no sense like his mother, he has the same problems in achieving intimacy.

The conflicting demands of sexuality (the lover) and of emotional intimacy (the son) seem unresolvable. Like Miriam, Clara asks him: "Do you think it's worth it—the—sex part?"

"The act of loving, itself?"

"Yes; is it worth anything to you?"

"But how can you separate it?" he said. "It's the culmination of everything. All our intimacy culminates then." (447)

The view of sex as "loving" is a tremendous shift from previous views of love. To accept fully this notion, that "intimacy culminates then," creates, as we have seen, tremendous stress on sexual partners to slake their own passions, as Paul wishes, and yet be sensitive to the specific needs of a partner, as Miriam demands. In so far as it looks to non-sexual love as the justification of sexual union, this conception places tremendous restraint on what men at that time, like Paul, felt to be an impersonal force "strong and blind and ruthless in its primitiveness" (435), the essence of "man-being."

Even though Paul may believe he accepts this association of erotic and emotional intimacy, he finds their association distasteful. What seem to be the radically different natures of emotional and erotic intimacy and the conflict between them are brought out in the remainder of the dialogue:

"All our intimacy culminates then."

"Not for me," she said.

He was silent. A flash of hate for her came up. After all, she was dissatisfied with him, even there, where he thought they fulfilled each other. But he believed her too implicitly.

"I feel," she continued slowly, "as if I had n't got you, as if all of you were n't there, and as if it were n't me you were taking—"

"Who, then?"

"Something just for yourself. It has been fine, so that I dare n't think of it. But is it me you want, or is it It?"

He again felt guilty. Did he leave Clara out of count, and take simply woman? But he thought that was splitting a hair. (447)

The problem here, however, is not sex itself as the culminating act of intimacy, but rather Paul's performance: his ability to be sexual and personal. Yet he has admitted to himself that it is "woman" he copulates with, or, as he puts it here, "if I start to make love to you, . . . I just go like a leaf down the wind." And yet immediately after he believed that during sex he was aware of the "wonderful stillness of each thing in itself" (448). Paul is aware of the impersonality of desire and of himself as the vehicle and the woman as the object, yet at the same time he seems to be aware of the being of things in themselves, their most particular existence. Characteristically, however, that awareness is never focused on his partner. The two idealized states of inter-course—abstracting desire and intimating awareness—operate side by side, rather than each within the other. Only when another human being is on the other end of the process and so becomes the object of these parallel phenomena simultaneously do conflicts arise within Paul, within his partners, and between them as well.

Moreover, lying within the divisions of love that Lawrence makes is a conflict that seems philosophically unresolvable. The erotic is characterized as desire that remains only until satisfaction takes place. Love, on the other hand, implies satisfaction. One could think of *eros* as being a pathway to love, as Plato does in the *Symposium,* for in-stance, but the two states could not exist simultaneously. One would need to give up love in order to have desire and give up desire in order to have love. Paul, who begins to see his desire and his love as being disengaged, has no problem with the impersonality of passion and the temporary nature of satisfaction. On the other hand, the women in the book do not seem to regard either the division or the conflict as real. To take Clara's point of view, we see that the women seek to prolong passion through emotional intimacy—through making sex "intercourse," a personal sharing (compare Miriam and the rose, which metaphorically could stand for this pattern) rather than an "impersonal" orgasm.[56]

After Paul finds that he can neither deny emotional intimacy nor successfully join it with sexual intimacy, he tries separating emotional intimacy, sexual intimacy, and work and labelling them: work is work; intimacy is intimacy; sex is sex. Only by redividing his roles and finding what are appropriate boundaries for each can he make a relationship to the world.

> [Clara] invariably waited for him at dinner-time for him to em-brace her before she went. He felt as if she were helpless, almost a burden to him, and it irritated him.
> "But what do you always want to be kissing and embracing for?" he said. "Surely there's a time for everything."
> She looked up at him, and the hate came into her eyes.

"Do I always want to be kissing you?" she said.

"Always, even if I come to ask you about work. I don't want anything to do with love when I'm at work. Work's work—"

"And what's love?" she asked. "Has it to have special hours?"

"Yes, out of work hours."

"And you'll regulate it according to Mr. Jordan's closing time?"

"Yes; and according to the freedom from business of any sort."

"It is only to exist in spare time?"

"That's all, and not always then—not the kissing sort of love." (437–38)

Here Paul withdraws behind certain barriers he had not before erected in his relationships. In the earlier phases of his courtship of Clara, when he had given her candy at work, flirted with her, and waited breathlessly for her arrival, Paul had not felt this way. Moreover, the rejection here is fundamentally a rejection of emotional intimacy—"the kissing sort of love." And yet a few lines later we find that "he was uneasy until she had forgiven him again" (438). That is, Paul in this primary emotional relationship, which he needs, finds that he is unable to meet the expectations of his partner—he is unable to achieve an intimate relationship with her. And yet the assertion of "role boundaries"—as when he tried to assert his affiliation with the working class—works no better to alleviate the stress. Although the construction of boundaries may allow him to deal with some of the intrapsychic pain, it creates new pain as well as a good deal of interpersonal conflict.

Throughout the book, as we have seen, we find Paul trying to come to grips with his uncertain sexual identity. Now towards the end, he moves to a notion of adult masculinity that takes him out of his "lover" stage, which had preoccupied his thoughts about masculinity, and that helps him escape the pressures of sexually and emotionally intimate performance. He hopes that this form of masculinity will carry him beyond the role of son (which he conceives as childish and feminine) or lover (which he conceives as adult and mixed), that it will carry him beyond roles altogether, past the petty social confluence to a primal masculine self that will resolve the ambiguities, stresses, conflicts created by the rub of feminization against a sense of masculine stereotype and norm that he finds embodied in his father Walter Morel.

In the closing episodes Paul is trying to align himself with "man" more fully by coming into relationship with Baxter Dawes, who in his working-class identity, his brutality, his drinking, resembles Paul's father.[57] Paul tests in this relationship whether he and Baxter are not alike and in the process learns about masculinity from Dawes, even though ultimately Paul, as always, needs to prove that he is superior. In the battle with Dawes, Paul feels himself rend the dainty clothing of society and claim as part of himself that which is "without reason or feeling" (451), without the previous formulations of masculine and feminine, claim what he considers manly, pure brutal instinct that allows him to out-Dawes Dawes:

> Pure instinct brought his hands to the man's neck, and before Dawes, in frenzy and agony, could wrench him free, he had got his fists twisted in the scarf and his knuckles dug in the throat of the other man. He was a pure instinct, without reason or feeling. His body, hard and wonderful in itself, cleaved against the struggling body of the other man; not a muscle in him relaxed. He was quite unconscious, only his body had taken upon itself to kill this other man. For himself he had neither feeling nor reason. He lay pressed hard against his adversary, his body adjusting itself to its one pure purpose of choking the other man, resisting exactly at the right moments, with exactly the right amount of strength, the struggles of the other, silent, intent, unchanging, gradually pressing its knuckles deeper, feeling the struggles of the other body become wilder and more frenzied. Tighter and tighter grew his body, gradually increasing in pressure, till something breaks. (451)

The glow of the words in this passage awes: the repetitions of "pure" and "right," the words "wonderful" and "instinct." Man to man, Paul and Dawes mirror each other as they "cleave" and lie upon each other feeling each other, the wildness, the frenzy. Many critics have remarked the same orgasmic loss of self in this passage as in the sexual passages.[58] The resonant phrases like "hard and wonderful in itself" remind us how closely this passage parallels the passages of lovemaking: "As a rule, when he started love-making, the emotion was strong enough to carry with it everything—reason, soul, blood"

(448). If anything, in fact, the passage with Dawes and Paul is a more graphic physical representation than the ones of sex: a feature of the novel that has less to do with taboos, one feels, than with the underlying dread of women and the proximity of hate and violence to Paul's physical approach to women: poking the stick in the ground as he tries to be honest with Miriam on the two occasions that he breaks off, the constant reminder that he "almost hated her" (whoever "her" was at the moment). Sex and violence, eros and hate are thus joined in the masculine persona, as the descriptors of blind, primitive instinct clearly suggest.

This is neither a homoerotic roll in the hay with Dawes that Paul enjoys, nor a glorification of violence per se or as a form of bonding, as we find in Lionel Tiger's work or in the cinematic epic fistfights that John Ford or Howard Hawkes used to cement male relationships, although that is there: "They had met in a naked extremity of hate, and it was a bond. At any rate, the elemental man in each had met" (468).[59] Instead, the violence seems the expression of a real frustration, a sense of impotence, of inability to cope with manhood on the terms he has inherited: born to the working class, but educated to the middle class; drawn to women of education and independence; drawn to occupations and interests that an emerging masculine ideal finds feminine; driven by desires that are strongly heterosexual and physical; admiring and even giving his cognitive endorsement to views of masculinity that he does not fit, based as they are partially on working-class-centered models, partially on traditional models, partially on the inversion of his own self. The scene could be symbolic not just of the desire of the manly son to slay the manly father, but of the feminized son to kill simultaneously the "manhood" and the "feminine" which keep threatening him. That is, in jumping at Dawes, Paul's hatred is powered by his outrage at the masculine expectations that Dawes represents. Yet it is just in that passion of hatred that he becomes "masculine" so that he meets Dawes as if in a mirror. Paul has transformed himself into the image that he has both sought and hated.

At first one might think that Paul had in this battle escaped into manhood, that he had created an unambiguous situation that can be used as a way to release his frustrations. But it is the very ambiguity that floods in upon him. Even here, we find the obstacle of background: "Then suddenly he relaxed, full of wonder and misgiving"

(451). One might say that a moral sense intervenes.[60] Alternatively, one might say that personal discomfort with the situation intervenes. Had he really been Dawes, his situation would have been less ambiguous. So too, had he been able to acknowledge the person he feels himself to be, his situation would have been less ambiguous. Because he is neither one person nor the other, his actions are always impromptu, skewed to the situation at every step.[61]

This is not to say that Baxter Dawes is not of intense interest or importance to Paul. Paul feels, as he states, that Clara had screwed up Dawes as she was screwing up him: "I consider you treated Baxter rottenly" is the accusation Paul raises more than once—an odd thing to say to a lover (443). But in his own discomfort with women and his own discomfort in his role, Paul finds it easy to see his situation and Baxter's similarly—women want something from men that men cannot give them. In Baxter Dawes he sees a man who, because he could not conform to the demands of workplace obeisance nor to the demands of a "changed" woman, felt role stress and rage. In Baxter's relationship to Clara, Paul also sees a picture of his father's relationship to his mother, a relationship that here he can fix. And yet for Baxter and Clara to have a strong relationship, Baxter must do what Walter Morel cannot do and what Paul cannot do—change: he must renounce part of his masculinity. Like Rochester in *Jane Eyre* and like Gradgrind in *Hard Times,* Baxter Dawes must become a weakened man.

In the end, no real resolution of the forces that are pulling Paul apart takes place. We find man isolated as we often find him, in fear of intimacy that is often a fear, uncertainty, or shame of one's self. Here the forces of social change are pulling the idea of masculinity in new directions that are threatening and violent in their force. Unlike the knight who may cling to the past when faced with newfangledness, Paul is a new creature, without a past and without any clear sense of a future. He is going to make his own ethic, invent his inheritance, and thus forge a new story for his ancestors. Paul, it seems to me, is the new man, the rugged, post-liberal, middle-class feminized individualist. He represents the difficult amalgam that modern man became, and that postmodern man struggles with, the bundle of unresolved contradictions that make him the center of distress, frustration, conflict, and potential violence. Paul is the modern man who knows what a "real man" is—brutal, instinctive, natural, inexpressive, unsociable—because he has invented him; and because he has invented him he knows, somewhere in himself, that he can never be a "real" man—that "real" men do not exist, never have, never will.

Notes

1. "The Boy Scouts and the Validation of Masculinity," *Journal of Social Issues: Male Roles and Male Experience* 34 (1978): 186.
2. See Bruce Haley, *The Healthy Body and Victorian Culture* (Cambridge, Mass.: Harvard University Press, 1978).
3. R. C. K. Ensor, *England 1870–1914* (Oxford: Clarendon Press, 1936), 164–66.
4. Ibid., 169.
5. Ibid., 553
6. The phrase "muscular Christianity" was first used to describe Thomas Hughes's *Tom Brown's Schooldays* (1857). In 1879 Hughes published *The Manliness of Christ*, which was reprinted in the United States. Although this work seems to have fueled the muscular movement, George J. Worth's analysis suggests that Hughes's Christ was still primarily passive, tender, and dutiful: "Of Muscles and Manliness: Some Reflections on Thomas Hughes," *Victorian Literature and Society: Essays Presented to Richard D. Altick* (Athens: Ohio State University Press, 1983), 300–314.
7. Hantover, "Boy Scouts," 186.
8. Ensor, *England 1870–1914,* 554
9. George Dangerfield, *The Strange Death of Liberal England* (London: Constable, 1936), 16–17.
10. Ibid., 432.
11. Ibid., 433.
12. Rupert Brooke, "The Great Lover," *Poems of Rupert Brooke,* ed. Geoffrey Keynes (London: Thomas Nelson, 1952).
13. Dangerfield, *Strange Death,* 435. Rupert Brooke wrote "The Great Lover" in 1914, commenting that "we have taught the world to die," so that for love of the world he will commemorate all those things he loved. Brooke goes on to list "the rough male kiss / Of blankets" and "Unpassioned beauty of a great machine," among other less "effeminate" ideas. Brooke's poems often evoke an intense sexuality and just as often seem to loathe it: "If earth had seen Earth's lordliest wild limbs tamed, / Shaked, and trapped, and shivering, for *my* touch—/ Myself should I have slain? or that foul you?" ("Success"). One finds similar examples in "Lust," "Beauty and Beauty," and "Jealousy." *Poems of Rupert Brooke,* ed. Geoffrey Keynes (London: Thomas Nelson, 1952).

14. Lawrence's belief that manhood was an essential quality of men is well-established in his writings and in the critical commentary. For instance, in his letter to Arthur McLeod, 2 June 1914, he writes about "man-life and woman-life, man-knowledge and woman-knowledge, man-being and woman-being": Letter no. 731 in *The Letters of D. H. Lawrence*, vol. II, June 1913-Oct 1916, Ed. George J. Zytaruk and James T. Boulton (Cambridge: Cambridge University Press, 1987). See also Diane S. Bonds, *Language and the Self in D. H. Lawrence* (Ann Arbor, Mich.: UMI Research Press, 1987), 29.

15. *The Portable D. H. Lawrence*, ed. Diana Trilling (New York: Viking, 1947), 623.

16. Ibid., 559–60.

17. Dorothy Van Ghent, "On *Sons and Lovers*," *The English Novel: Form and Function* (New York: Rinehart, 1953). Similar ideas can be found expressed or implied in such diverse accounts as Mark Spilka, *The Love Ethic of D. H. Lawrence* (Bloomington: Indiana University Press, 1955), and Gavriel Ben-Ephrain, *The Moon's Dominion: Narrative Dichotomy and Female Dominance in Lawrence's Earlier Novels* (Rutherford, N.J.: Fairleigh Dickinson University Press, 1981), esp. 107–8. Some, like Carol Dix, *D. H. Lawrence and Women* (Totowa, N.J.: Rowman and Littlefield, 1978), and Declan Kiberd, *Men and Feminism in Modern Literature* (London: Macmillan, 1985), feel that Lawrence and Paul reconcile masculine and feminine in androgynous unity.

18. Van Ghent, "On *Sons and Lovers*," 252.

19. Ibid., 256.

20. Page numbers refer to *Sons and Lovers* (1913; New York: Modern Library, n.d.). Several critics have noted this side of Walter Morel, e.g., T. H. Adamowski, "The Father of All Things: The Oral and the Oedipal in *Sons and Lovers*," *Mosaic* 14, no. 4 (1981): 70–71.

21. According to Daniel A. Weiss, Walter Morel represents the phallus that disgusts Paul and that he nonetheless desires. Through his father, Paul comes to equate violence and sex: *Oedipus in Nottingham: D. H. Lawrence* (Seattle: University of Washington Press, 1962), 20–23.

22. Van Ghent, "On *Sons and Lovers*," 253.

23. This is Louis Martz's point of view in his otherwise illuminating essay, "Portrait of Miriam: A Study in the Design of *Sons and Lovers*," *Imagined Worlds: Essays on Some English Novels and Novelists in Honour of John Butt,* ed. Maynard Mack and Ian Gregor (London: Methuen, 1968), 360. According to Keith Sagar, *D. H. Lawrence: Life into Art* (Athens: University of Georgia Press, 1985), Lawrence seems to have intended the mother to be "a stable centre, pivot, source of vitality and standard of normality and wholeness" (89).

24. Letter to Edward Garnett, 14 November 1912, *Portable,* 560.

25. I am leaving aside the transposition of the Oedipal theme onto earlier drafts, the impact of his relationship with Frieda, etc., as discussed by Sagar (*D. H. Lawrence: Life into Art,* 90–91). Lawrence refers to the writing of the book as a process of working out his relationships; his various approaches to the book's original material simply illustrate that point, for none of them provides an exhaustive view.

26. Helen Corke, *D. H. Lawrence: The Croydon Years* (Austin: University of Texas Press, 1965), 33.

27. Scott Sander, *D. H. Lawrence: The World of the Five Major Novels* (New York: Viking, 1973), 35.

28. Mirra Komarovsky, *Dilemmas of Masculinity: A Study of College Youth* (New York: W. W. Norton, 1976), 225.

29. Ibid., 225.

30. Mark Shorer, "Technique as Discovery," *Hudson Review* 1 (1948): 67–87. Shorer sees the book as a kind of psychotherapy that does not make successful fiction because the distance between the patient and his tale is not complete.

31. Alan Friedman, *The Turn of the Novel* (New York: Oxford University Press, 1966), 130–39. There is something new in a writer using a public, artistic, and professional form to explore an idea rather than explain an idea—even, if not especially, in autobiography. The ambiguous and almost formless (though formal) nature of the work constitutes a new class of writing. This is close to the type of writing for therapeutic purposes so beautifully imitated and subverted into a meticulously formal art by Italo Svevo in *Confessions of Zeno.* This absolute betrayal of the private to public scrutiny is partially a feature of both the bildungsroman and the "Notebooks," but in its less artificial treatment Lawrence brings the confession into the modern age: see Richard D. Beards, "*Sons and Lovers* as Bildungsroman," *College Literature* 1 (1974): 204–17.

32. The rosebush scene has been commented on plentifully. It is the primary focus of discussion by Martz, who argues that the earlier and later sections of the book use an omniscient narrator, while in the middle sections "we cannot wholly trust the narrator's remarks . . . for his commentary represents mainly an extension of Paul's consciousness; . . . the voice of the narrator tends to echo and magnify the confusions that are arising within Paul himself" ("Portrait of Miriam," 351); for the contrary, see Spilka, *Love Ethic,* 45–53.

33. For many critics positing one of these meanings becomes the crux for a reading of the passage, the relationships, the book. For Ben-Ephrain, Paul understands Miriam's sexual longing for him but transforms it into a "spiritual" longing so that he does not need to deal with

it (*The Moon's Dominion*, 100). This is similar to Martz's conclusion that "Miriam offers him the freedom of natural growth within a mature relationship" ("Portrait of Miriam," 353). Diane S. Bonds offers, using a mild Lacanian approach, a similar reading: *Language and the Self in D. H. Lawrence* (Ann Arbor, Mich.: UMI Research Press, 1987), 45–48. For John Stoll, the scene's imagery contrasts "the sexual deadness of Miriam and the life-principle beginning to assert itself in Paul": *D. H. Lawrence's "Sons and Lovers": Self-Encounter and the Unknown Self* (Muncie, Ind.: Ball State University, 1968), 33–34; Spilka's view (*Love Ethic*, 53) and Graham Holderness's, in *D. H. Lawrence: History, Ideology and Fiction* (Dublin: Gill and MacMillan, 1982), 154–55, are similar to Stoll's. Dix thinks that "Paul, for Miriam, is a sex-object" (*D. H. Lawrence and Women*, 84).

34. Bonds points out that the narrative ambivalences support the way Paul uses words to evade "intimacy" (*Language and the Self*, 33). Sagar makes a similar point (*D. H. Lawrence: Life into Art*, 82).

35. Letter to Edward Garnett, *Portable*, 560.

36. That Mrs. Morel's words to herself are really about herself and not about Miriam is a common feature of critical comment: see, for example, Martz, "Portrait of Miriam," 353; Ben-Ephrain, *The Moon's Dominion*, 103. In these readings, the mother is blamed for the failures of the son. Blame for Paul's difficulty in maturing seems to be placed on the mother, yet the book never provides us a clear notion of what "maturity" should be, either the mother's notion or anyone else's.

37. *Letters*, vol. II, no. 539.

38. In the original Foreword to *Sons and Lovers* (rpt. in *Letters of D. H. Lawrence*, ed. Aldous Huxley [New York: Viking, 1932]), also written January 1913, Lawrence writes of the rose as masculine: "These curious pieces called men are like stamens that can turn into exquisite-coloured petals" (101), yet he suggests the androgyny of the perfect, "eternal" Rose which, although called the "Father," should be called the "Mother" (102). At the same time Lawrence celebrates the powerful spiritual symbolism of the rose: "The vision itself, the flutter of petals, the rose, the Father through the son wasting himself in a moment of consciousness, consciousness of his own finitude and gloriousness, a Rose, a Clapping of the Hands, a spark of Joy thrown off from the Fire to die, ruddy in mid-darkness, a Snip of Flame, the Holy Ghost, the Revelation" (102). In accounting for the moral weighting of the rosebush scene, Spilka sees that Paul is "spontaneous" when he comes into contact with "God-stuff" (*Love Ethic*, 51). According to Spilka, Miriam sees flowers with "false reverence"; Paul sees them "with love, like a lover"

(53). Holderness believes, too, that Miriam turns the flowers into "cult-objects" (*D. H. Lawrence: History, Ideology and Fiction*, 154).

39. Sagar points out that in *Paul Morel* Paul, not Miriam, was associated with touching flowers (*D. H. Lawrence: Life into Art*, 97).

40. H. M. Daleski, *The Forked Flame: A Study of D. H. Lawrence* (London: Faber and Faber, 1965), sees Lawrence as a feminine personality struggling with manhood. Since then writers have frequently stressed either Lawrence's or Paul's "sides." For instance, Dix writes to show that the phallic is also feminine (*D. H. Lawrence and Women*, 118–19). Spilka in "For Mark Shorer with Combative Love: The *Sons and Lovers* Manuscript," *D. H. Lawrence: A Centenary Consideration*, ed. Peter Balbert and Phillip Marcus (Ithaca, N.Y.: Cornell University Press, 1985), 29–44, writes that *Sons and Lovers* shows that "the essence of maleness lies not in dominating phallic power but in nurturing tenderness" (40). See also Judith Ruderman, *D. H. Lawrence and the Devouring Mother* (Durham, N.C.: Duke University Press, 1984), 187. Kiberd, *contra* Millet and De Beauvoir, tries to demonstrate that Lawrence was androgynous (*Men and Feminism*).

41. From Robert Brannon, "The Male Sex Role: Our Culture's Blueprint of Manhood, and What It's Done for Us Lately," *The Forty-nine Percent Majority: The Male Sex Role*, ed. Robert Brannon and Deborah David (Reading, Mass.: Addison-Wesley, 1976). See also Michael V. Cicone and Diane N. Ruble, "Beliefs about Males," *Journal of Social Issues: Male Roles and the Male Experience* 34 (1978): 5–16; Joseph H. Pleck, *The Myth of Masculinity* (Cambridge, Mass.: MIT Press, 1981).

A. O. J. Cockshut writes of Lawrence's conception of sex roles: "To speak of the virility of true womanhood, and the womanliness of true manhood [as Edith Ellis did in *Attainment* (1909)] is, for Lawrence, . . . [a] great absurdity. . . . The polarity of the sexes, with its manifold implications about contrasting roles in the family, in work and in society was . . . for Lawrence . . . a sacred mystery": *Man and Woman: A Study of Love and the Novel, 1740–1940* (New York: Oxford University Press, 1978), 152. The much-quoted letters about androgyny (*Letters*, vol II., no. 731, To Arthur McLeod, 2 June 1914, and no. 746, To Thomas Dunlop, 7 July 1914) indicate, at most, that for a few months Lawrence entertained such thoughts. However, a closer examination indicates that while he believes that a man should get to know the great woman-secret and even mingle with it, he never compromises on the point of sexual essentialism.

42. *Portable*, 559–60.

43. Qtd. in Corke, *D. H. Lawrence: The Croydon Years*, 41.

44. Again, in the series of "androgynous" letters, Lawrence writes to Edward Garnett on 22 April 1914 (D. H. Lawrence, *The Letters of D. H. Lawrence*, ed. George J. Zytaruk and James T. Boulton, [Cambridge: Cambridge University Press, 1987], vol. II, no. 718) that he wanted to write of "woman becoming individual, self-responsible, taking her own initiative." He states, however, that he has failed and instead made the women "flippant," "vulgar and jeering." In the same letter he upbraids Garnett for calling his latest writing "Cockney" and common. Lawrence states that he only writes like that "when the deep feeling does not find its way out," that he has a "religious" belief in a "*real* being." This "*real* being" in both the women characters and in himself is contrasted with the common, superficial being that he also shares with the women. This is what Stoll means when he writes that Lawrence saw Gertrude, as well as mothers generally, as a "culture carrier," who destroys "the right of the person to respond freely to his emotions and to fulfill himself humanly" (*D. H. Lawrence's "Sons and Lovers,"* 1). It is only *beneath* the surface that real man-being and real woman-being are to be found. It is precisely this surface being, what he called his "ordinary meal-time me" (qtd. in Holderness, *D. H. Lawrence: History, Ideology and Fiction,* 92), that Lawrence associates with the feminine and rejects in favor of a deeper self, what he called the "demon"—"inhuman, timeless animal, perhaps even diabolical" (Holderness, 92). Anne Smith, "A New Adam and a New Eve—Lawrence and Women: A Biographical Overview," *Lawrence and Women,* ed. Anne Smith (New York: Barnes and Noble, 1978), argues that feminine elements are present in Lawrence's ideal of manliness, and that these "feminine" elements embarrassed him (10–13).

45. Henry Miller, *The World of D. H. Lawrence: A Passionate Appreciation,* ed. Evelyn J. Minz and John J. Teunissen (Santa Barbara, Calif.: Capra Press, 1980), 15, 43. Of course, a group of women workers at the factory in which Lawrence worked in Nottingham did surround him one day and "pants" him, thus giving traumatic confirmation for the types of role shifts and stresses.

46. "Emotional Intimacy among Men," *Journal of Social Issues: Male Roles and the Male Experience* 34 (1978): 108.

47. J. Bardwick and E. Douvan, "Ambivalence: The Socialization of Women," *Women in Sexist Society,* ed. V. Gornick and B. Moran (New York: American Library, 1971) 113.

48. Lewis, "Emotional Intimacy," 114.

49. Hillary Simpson, *D. H. Lawrence and Feminism* (DeKalb: Northern Illinois University Press, 1982), states, "Paul conceives of sexual desire as something impersonal" (34). We need not think that sexual desire

is "personal" to agree that the impersonality with which Paul seeks to overwhelm intimacy is pathological. As Sander points out, "Paul has used Miriam without regard to her needs or desires as a person" (*D. H. Lawrence: The World of the Five Major Novels*, 47). See also Ben-Ephrain, *The Moon's Dominion*, 109ff.; Faith Pullen, "Lawrence's Treatment of Women in *Sons and Lovers*," *Lawrence and Women*, ed. Smith, 71–74; Martz, "Portrait of Miriam," 350. Spilka identifies this as the father's problem ("For Mark Shorer," 39).

50. Smith, "A New Adam," 13.

51. Both Sander in his Marxist reading (*D. H. Lawrence: The World of the Five Major Novels*) and Simpson in her feminist reading (*D. H. Lawrence and Feminism*) criticize Lawrence for placing responsibility for human actions on the individual, rather than on the greater social, economic, and sexual forces that control humans. In fact, Lawrence is guilty as accused. But both writers confuse "individual" with "personal." For Lawrence there are no people, only individuals severed from a single source, each informed by great forces that are not social or economic or political, but are psychological and so, according to the theories of the time, are abstract and eternal. The "personal," on the other hand, is different, in that it implies that people have historically fixed times and places, that they are complexly constructed of many forces greater than themselves and the interactions of these forces that constitute a matrix of the self. Cf. Maurice Merleau-Ponty, *Phenomenology of Perception* (New York: Humanities Press, 1962).

52. Qtd. in Dix, *D. H. Lawrence and Women*, 71.

53. Daniel Schneider, *The Consciousness of D. H. Lawrence: An Intellectual Autobiography* (Lawrence: University Press of Kansas, 1986), 69.

54. Dix, *D. H. Lawrence and Women*, 70.

55. Of course in his Foreword and elsewhere Lawrence himself invoked the Oedipal conflict. The Oedipal theme was critically recognized by Alfred Booth Kuttner in "*Sons and Lovers*: A Freudian Appreciation," *Psychoanalytical Review* 3 (1916): 295–317. Lawrence complained of Kuttner's article, calling it "vicious half-statements of the Freudians": *Letters*, vol. II, no. 1285, To Barbara Low, 16 September 1916. The theme has been thoroughly explored by Daniel A. Weiss (*Oedipus in Nottingham*). The incredible amount of blame that Gertrude has endured in the last twenty years can only be attributed to a general social malaise that gave rise to the illusion of a "surge of pathological motherhood," a phrase from Hans Sebald's *Momism: The Silent Disease of America* (Chicago: Nelson-Hall, 1976) and encountered in cultural works as seemingly diverse as Philip Roth's *Portnoy's Complaint* and Alfred Hitchcock's *Psycho*. See Martz ("Portrait of Miriam"), Smith

("A New Adam"), as well as David J. Kleinbard's "Laing, Lawrence and the Maternal Cannibal," *Psychoanalytical Review* 58 (1971): 4–13. Recently pre-Oedipal problems have been discussed as the cause of Paul's fear of intimacy; see T. H. Adamowski's very interesting "Intimacy at a Distance: Sexuality and Orality in *Sons and Lovers*," *Mosaic* 13, no. 2 (1980): 71–85.

56. Throughout this section I have been basically in agreement with Ben-Ephrain, *The Moon's Dominion*, 109–10. One important dissenting voice is Peter Balbert's, who finds "mature and healthy sexuality" throughout *Sons and Lovers*: "Forging and Feminism: *Sons and Lovers* and the Phallic Imagination," *D. H. Lawrence Review* 11 (1978): 92–113.

57. Both the identification of Baxter and Walter and of masculinity and the working class have been made before. See Weiss, *Oedipus in Nottingham*, 26; Peter Scheckner, *Class, Politics, and the Individual: A Study of the Major Works of D. H. Lawrence* (Rutherford, N.J.: Fairleigh Dickinson University Press, 1985), 30–33; Pullen, "Lawrence's Treatment of Women," 51. Lawrence Lerner, "Blood and Mind: The Father in *Sons and Lovers*," *D. H. Lawrence, "Sons and Lovers": A Casebook*, ed. Gamini Salgado (London: Macmillan, 1969) finds Lawrence's usual dichotomy of "feminine" middle-class men and "masculine" lower-class men broken down in the ambiguous (and moving) portrait of Walter Morel (216).

58. In fact, a few have complained that the passage is more sensual than the heterosexual passages (see Smith, "A New Adam," 38; Pullen, "Lawrence's Treatment of Women," 58–59). However, Spilka points out that in the ten percent of the cuts Garnett made in the manuscript, some were of sensual heterosexual scenes ("For Mark Shorer," 38). It makes sense that a public would find less "prurient" glowing descriptions of male chests whereas it would be shocked by similar descriptions of female chests. This fear of women seems to be society's as a whole.

59. I am referring here to Lionel Tiger, *Men in Groups* (New York: Random House, 1969). For fistic male bonding see *The Quiet Man* (dir. John Ford) or *Red River* (dir. Howard Hawkes).

60. Or, as Weiss believes, Paul must be punished and forgiven by the father and so come to identify with him (*Oedipus in Nottingham*, 26–28).

61. Adamowski finds that Lawrence, and by implication Paul, had fear of both masculinity and femininity ("The Father of All Things," 81). Scheckner sees Paul as "the individual caught between the values of two classes" (*Class, Politics, and the Individual*, 39).

Conclusion:
Masculinity: What Is It?

O God, show me the enemy. Once you find out
who the enemy is, you can kill him. But these
people here they confuse me. Who hurt me? Who
spoil my life? Tell me who to beat back. I work
four years to save my money, I work like a donkey
night and day. My brother was to be educated,
the nice one. And this is how it is ending, in
this room, eating with these people. Tell me who
to kill.

—V. S. Naipaul, *In a Free State*

THE SERIES of snapshots of masculinity and male experience that
have been developed in these six disparate works, situated as they are
intermittently over one thousand years, can give insight into the distinct, yet familiar, tensions that men experienced at the moments each
work represents. Seen as pages from a flip-book, the pictures together
produce a sense of the necessary instabilities of the idea of masculinity, the powers, pleasures, and difficulties associated with masculinity, and the need men have felt to stabilize the idea of masculinity
from age to age. Understanding the patterns and displacements that
emerge in the six pictures of masculinity, we can also perhaps better
appreciate the certain failure of most current efforts to stabilize the
idea of masculinity on a new essentialist foundation under the pressure of upheavals in the social, economic, and political relationships
of men and women; the changes in technology to favor those with
patience, fine motor skills, quick reactions, and good judgment; the
widening of the service-sector economy.

Among the new ideas of masculinity that have emerged, one of the most widely publicized comes from the eminent American poet Robert Bly, who is trying to rehabilitate men scarred by the macho of the fifties and the feminization of the seventies.[1] We should not be surprised that Bly speaks of D. H. Lawrence as an inspiring father of his ideas[2] or that crucial aspects of both Lawrence's and Bly's masculinity evolved with developments from the nineteenth century: the rise of feminism, the interclass warfare of England, the economics of industry and empire, the theology of Muscular Christianity and Arnoldian culture. Bly himself overtly pays tribute to this nineteenth-century ideology by employing a nineteenth-century folktale as the source for his ideas. A brief examination of the development of the idea of primal masculinity invoked by Bly's construction and found even in scholarly works, like that of David Gilmore,[3] may illuminate the contribution of our snapshots to understanding contemporary construction, issues, and problems.

From the survey of our six works we have become aware that a modern concept of primal masculinity—uncivilized, wild, natural—emerged, as did all concepts of masculinity, gradually, obliquely, and over long periods of time. It has evolved from elements that are incongruent and in many cases even antithetical to it. For instance, in *Sir Gawain and the Green Knight*, traces of primal masculinity appear personified as antagonists to Gawain's knightly ideal, such as the folk fertility figure, the wild man, a figure with whom Bly associates his own vision of masculinity.[4] Masculinity in the fourteenth century seemed to fear and reprehend the figure of the wild man because, at least in *Sir Gawain*, that figure incorporates soft, irrational, feminine features antithetical to a hard, heedful, civilizing masculinity. The Green Knight, in his guise as Bercilak, seems to offer an alternative masculine civilization, one of ease and altruism. This stands in striking contrast with aspects of modern masculine constructions that equate sexuality with hardness, knighthood with nature, and men with brawling camaraderie.

As an intervening step between current notions of masculinity and the masculinity of *Sir Gawain*, the seventeenth and eighteenth centuries offer ideas of a noble savage, of whom Adam stands as an example, whose civilizing morals conform to and embody principles of nature. But nature in both Gawain's and the noble savage's worlds diverge widely from modern Freudian concepts of eros and Darwinian concepts of instinct. Changes in masculinity, then, have been informed by changes in the definitions of such categories as nature and desire, at times pressured by other cultural changes, in philosophy, religion, or science, for instance, that have further disrupted these categories.

In addition, social change shapes the categories on which definitions of masculinity stand. In part, the Arthurian knight's rejection of primal masculinity not only justifies the knight's importance as a protector of society, but serves as a definition for an upper class. Arthur's court ridicules the Green Knight as a "churl," an uncivilized bumpkin. If, as a folk figure, the Green Knight embodies an ideal of masculinity shared by "churls," by those of an underclass beyond the peripheries of the court, then the definition of knightly masculinity becomes a way to exclude that underclass and to identify an "overclass." We witness this today as debates over masculinity often diverge on lines of class, in what Lillian Rubin sees as the reproduction of a child's sex role according to a parent's perceived demands of future position and in consonance with class-community values.[5] We witness the power of sex role as a feature of social class in the low ratio of blue-collar males, black and white, seeking higher education—low numbers that reflect fears of education as a feminizing, middle-classifying process for men and as an empowering one for women. In *Gawain,* where natural man is not only implicitly an enemy of the overclass but also considered an ally of other enemies and defined in part by his alliances, natural man is considered womanish. So today class differences often result in similar types of equation and analogy, though the gender-specific traits that tag class status have shifted.

Another important element in the development of modern primal masculinity has been the notion that men have lost their archetypal masculinity, that it has been obscured by the imposition of civilization on the natural. The notions of archetypes and of their concealment appears in our artifact from sixteenth-century England. In the description of his father as an ancient god, Hamlet not only identifies masculinity with a divine archetype, which later gets displaced to heaven, but further allies masculinity with a classical culture that itself had been obscured. The uncovering of works of Greek and Roman civilization during the Renaissance seemed to recover an earlier important masculine attribute as well—reason, the main element in the classical definition of humanity, a definition that excluded women, children, and slaves. Powerful changes in the Renaissance developed from the notion that the slumber and sediment of culture obscured the original and primitive virtues and foundations of civilization and human institutions. By encouraging accounts of the origins of social institutions, the primitive, considered as originating archetype, also grounded political dissidence in the seventeenth century, as witnessed in the ontology-morality connections made by Milton.

In *Paradise Lost,* when Milton writes about the primal scene of Genesis that history has obscured, he overtly allies primitive religion with primitive masculinity. Because of the notion of discovery available to him, Milton could ground ideal social order on an original and archetypal human nature that God created. Yet the idea of virtue being allied to the original and archetypal did not die out when religious accounts became contested. It still had and has powerful consequences when one moves that origin from Eden to the ooze of prehistoric Africa or to the polymorphous, perverse psyche of the developing child. For Milton, however, the primitive male was typified by the Reason that the Renaissance had rediscovered. Men were naturally, primitively, originally thinking animals, and the better they thought, the more masculine they were.

We have also noted how the nineteenth century made its own contribution to the modern formulation of the primal by its development of a compelling metaphor to describe a hidden, powerful, mysterious force driving human behavior—the fire that drives an engine. As in *Hard Times,* a closely pent interior fire keeps the machines of society moving. This force needs to be unrepressed to make one healthy. Thus a powerful, raw, explosive energy is thought to be hidden at the core of human beings. Of course in Dickens this unrepressed fire turns to embers on the hearth, spreading warmth and domesticity—Dickens's masculine ideal.

In its repudiation of middle-class, sentimental notions of a domestic masculinity, then, the early twentieth century inherited all these elements from which to construct its own version of masculinity. In the pressure of its own social and cultural moments, in negotiation with women and other men, in accommodation of its own experiences, pleasures and pains, men have transmuted the wild man, the original man, the repressed man into contemporary primitive man. But, as we can see, much has been changed in the founding notions that this new masculinity invokes to argue its tradition: for the wild man was altruistic, the original man reasonable, and the repressed man domestic, while the primitive man of Lawrence and others became the antithesis of these aspects, in some sense inverting the masculinities of nine centuries and even resonating with the feminine ideas that males had battled in previous centuries. This tortuous growth of contemporary primal masculinity makes clear that while masculinity does exist, it exists as a distinct feature of each historical moment.

The artifacts exhibit not only variations and malleabilities of masculinities but also processes of adaptation and accommodation that suggest some common behaviors and patterns. For instance, the artifacts suggest that even the most heroic, those who serve as models of masculinity for others, only partially fulfill codes of manhood, codes which they find painful. Heroes, and men in general, rarely attain rewards of glory or of hoped-for transcendent self-realization sufficient to compensate their pain. Moreover, none of the men in these works exemplify what for them would have been the unequivocally "masculine"; masculinity seems instead, if intermittently, an unreachable and even dubious ideal. Because these men can neither escape the ideal nor value and act upon experiences and feelings contrary to that ideal, they are doomed to pain. For the same reasons, they are likewise often doomed to see themselves as enemies both of masculinity and of the happy situation they desire. In their attempts to accommodate themselves to their roles, on one hand, and to their intuitions, on the other, they experience longing, frustration, rage. For these men the world is often filled with enemies who are also their closest associates—parents, partners, friends, even themselves.

Second, diverse themes raised in one piece of literature—birth, sex, death, change, growth, the here-and-now—continue to trouble men and the concept of masculinity in subsequent pieces. The resulting attitudes of enduring and arming themselves endured in different forms, whether it was the overt muscular aggression of the athlete or warrior, the holier-than-thou pedantry of the cleric or scholar, or the obdurate passive-aggression of the so-called effete or "feminized." The armor changed, the enemy changed, elements of the stance remained.

Third, in these disparate snapshots, we see that men usually define masculinity in opposition to a femininity that they construct, a masculine/feminine definition that tends toward binarism, regardless of how or why each term shifts in relationship to the other. As strong as this impulse to binarism has been, however, the works also suggest interesting qualifications to the notions that masculinity excludes traits marked as feminine, that it exhibits uniform fears of femininity or that it takes form without negotiations with women. Dickens, for instance, although trapped in the language of gender dualism, sought to blur the characteristics considered appropriate to each gender; he seems to suggest that men and women need to acknowledge shared traits. In the case of Lawrence, certain types of masculinity are themselves defined as feminine. Such cases that suggest overlaps in gender may actually stimulate further binarisms by spurring the formation of masculine ideals to clear the boundaries of definition and enforce role conformity.

While women themselves help construct and restructure masculinities in much of the literature, a feature not focused on in this study, the principle of erasing this power in women can be witnessed within the works themselves. In the case of Mr. Gradgrind, while the conversion of his role comes through negotiations with his daughter, those negotiations cut him off from other men, who deride him and deprive him of public power. In *Sons and Lovers*, Paul's mother oversees the construction of his masculinity, a construction that she hopes will overcome the failures she finds in Paul's father, a construction that she hopes will permit Paul to escape the working class. Unfortunately, such a construction alienates Paul from his father, whom he winds up seeing as the source of true masculinity. So while both books include negotiations with women and even class as parts of the construction of masculinity, each book also sees those negotiations as costly for men and to some extent unhealthy. Each work compromises with the notion of a foundational binarism.

Thus opposing impulses appear to emerge from the few scattered examples here: an impulse to construct and abide by an oppositional ideal of masculinity, an impulse to negotiate with others, to overlap genders, to break away from restrictive male codes. Given, then, the apparent instability of the idea of masculinity and the pain of sustaining the masculine role, why do men continue to stake out a particular set of characteristics as their special province? The answer may well involve aspects of gender formation like those outlined by John Money; even aspects of biology, like those discussed by

Melvin Konner; or larger social needs, as discussed by Marvin Harris, Lionel Tiger, or David Gilmore.[6] But from our examination we can see it involves other characteristics of masculinity as well. The works have implied that masculinity functions as a cultural and subcultural marker, working even within groups to define privileged loci of power, allowing men to hold high positions, exercise autocratic power, possess great wealth and prestige. But the works also imply that from contests over power alternative masculinities arise and that these in turn produce anxiety and stimulate new definitions of masculinity as a way to relieve that anxiety.

Moreover, while the positing of definitions of masculinity often seeks to restrict notions of gender, the quest to stabilize masculinity has itself served as a vehicle for men to explore what it means to be part of a group called "men." That is, the need to define masculinity may arise from a need to explore and claim new parts of men's experience. In that sense, the artifacts gesture at masculinity in Western culture as a category stretched to consider and, in fact, to encompass an ever-increasing range of experiences. While all experiences may be viewed as historical constructs in the sense that certain stimuli are observed and made significant at certain points in a cultural story,[7] the givens of birth, death, sexuality, parents, bodies have become more intimately known and accounted for in each subsequent work. The claims of each succeeding fiction have generally become more particular, more concrete. And while each new masculinity leads to repression of certain characteristics, taken as a whole, masculinity has exposed more and more of men to themselves—paternity, childhood, sex.

How fiction increasingly reveals more of men can be measured by briefly comparing a passage from D. H. Lawrence to one from Philip Roth. In 1920 D. H. Lawrence wrote,

> She closed her hands over the full, rounded body of his loins, as he stooped over her, she seemed to touch the quick of the mystery of darkness that was bodily him. She seemed to faint beneath, and he seemed to faint, stooping over her. It was a perfect passing away for both of them, and at the same time the most intolerable accession into being, the marvellous fullness of immediate gratification, overwhelming, outflooding from the source of the deepest life-source, the darkest, deepest strangest

life-source of the human body at the back and base of the loins. . . . He stood there in his strange, whole body, that had its marvellous fountains, like the bodies of the sons of God who were in the beginning. There were strange fountains of his body, more mysterious and potent than any she had imagined or had known, more satisfying, ah, finally, mystically-physically satisfying.[8]

For Lawrence the male body may be wrapped in a spiritual mystery that today we find excessive, yet that Lawrence claims that body and affirms its beauty is new and important. It is also new the way that Lawrence claims the sweat of sexuality that repelled others. Thus he is able to describe the body and sex with sensual immediacy and detail lacking in previous fictions.

Compare the above with this scene from Philip Roth's *Portnoy's Complaint,* written nearly fifty years later:

I stand at attention between his legs as he coats me from head to toe with a thick lather of soap—and eye with admiration the baggy substantiality of what overhangs the marble bench upon which he is seated. His scrotum is like the long wrinkled face of some old man with an egg tucked into each of his sagging jowls. . . . *Shlong:* the word somehow catches exactly the brutishness, the *meatishness,* that I admire so, the sheer mindless, weighty, and unselfconscious dangle of that living piece of hose through which passes streams of water as thick and strong as rope—while I deliver forth slender threads that my euphemistic mother calls "a sis." . . . "Do you want to make a nice sis?" she asks me—when I want to make a flood: I want like he does to shift the tides of the toilet bowl.[9]

Much of Lawrence's masculinity is still intact, though transformed, in Roth's work. Like Lawrence, Roth thinks of potency ("successful in business, tyrannical at home") as the ideal male attribute.[10] Also like Lawrence, while the world of the mother, a world both loved and hated, is typified by social approbation, the world of the father is typified by the primal, in this case the place of Grendel, the "oozing bog that was the earth," "in some sloppy water time," that he connects with the water-urine-jism that passes through his father's "fire hose."[11]

Yet if the change appears small between Lawrence and Roth, it traverses significant territory. There is both a humble depiction of genitals and of emotional intimacy in this visit to the Turkish baths that is not in Lawrence. Roth's "shlong" is, like the word, meatish, "mindless, weighty, and unselfconscious," a "living piece of hose"; for Lawrence it is a "full, rounded body," "the darkest, deepest strangest life-source." The penis and scrotum that Roth describes directly, the "mindless" body that Roth finds, the relationship with the father that he remembers, the emotions that the scene rouses differ significantly from anything in Lawrence. Like Lawrence, Roth mourns that "if only I could have nourished myself upon the depths of [my father's] vulgarity, instead of that too becoming a source of shame."[12] Yet Roth is able to mourn and love his father's vulgarity aloud. That Roth's "masculinity" too is a fiction, a fiction of the current age, does not detract from what seems a further disrobing, another dimension of male experience recorded.

From our artifacts we have observed that new masculinities are constructed in the dynamics of shifting cultures and societies, shifts that precipitate changes in cultural patterns and concepts on which definitions of masculinity rest, shifts that precipitate changes in men's experiences of themselves and their milieu. Part of the shift in masculinity comes from the definition of new subgroups, their rise as public forces—peasants, workers, women, the middle class. Part comes from the press of new technologies—armor, guns, machines. Part from the exigencies of survival. Thus, for instance, as time becomes a central concern of Gawain's culture, men see themselves as more and more involved in the processes of time; as the gun emerges in Renaissance warfare and the walled city becomes more anomalous, semiotic patterns of masculinity adapt to these new circumstances.

Of course, the central object of this study has been role stress itself as a stimulus to change in masculinity. The variety of roles for most humans create frictions, as do dissonances among behaviors, beliefs, and experiences. Moreover, because societies often offer alternate masculinities and because all masculinities are stretched by the exigencies of change, the processes of accommodating old definitions to new conditions drive men to reexamine their experiences and reinvent their masculinity, renegotiating power and pleasure with the other people and elements of their world, generating new ideas of such cru-

Table 1.

Book	Mode[a]	God	Masculinity	Feminir
Beowulf	Space	*Metod* ("measurer")	Laws, Social Organization, Boundary-building	Instinct, P Passion, Violence
Sir Gawain	Time	Endurer	Social Customs, Morals	Time, Mo tality, Dea
Hamlet	Change/ Stability	Artist	Idealism: Courtier, Artist, Soldier, Rule of Fathers	Growth, Change, t Present, R of Mothe
Paradise Lost	Origins	Father	Ontological Morality, Right Reason	Will, Feeli Imaginati Obedient Childishn
Hard Times	Utility	Love	Fact, Calcula-tion, Abstrac-tion, Utility, Sympathy	Sympathy, Fancy, Pa-tience, To
Sons and Lovers	Social Artifice	Instinct	Instinct, Blood Relations, Sex, Violence	Society, th Personal, Beauty

[a] "Mode" is the subject of supervenient concern in the society depicted in the work.

cial categories as nature and femininity at the same time. The evolu-tion that we have observed in the notion of masculinity indicates that the ideals and behaviors mark simultaneously an attempt to fit cultur-ally, to comprehend a large share of resources, to understand man-hood, to feel comfort in one's environment.

Looking at Table 1, one observes that masculinity claims an impor-tant position in dealing with what emerges as a society's important issues, what I have labelled "mode." At the same time, the construc-tion of a God or transcendental force seems to be both the solution to the problem of mode and the model for masculine behavior. Femininity appears to be the construction of an opposite to the masculine. We can observe some continuities in the changing shape of masculinity, while we can also observe how masculinity and femininity change in relationship to each other, even trading places, as in *Beowulf* and *Sons and Lovers*. To claim that any writer has grasped the essence of manhood would be difficult because of the way masculinity situates itself in any text—caught in the web of cultural forces, of pathways to power, of discomforts and expectations.

Finally, the examples have all, both separately and taken together, questioned the idea of an essential masculinity. But more, one may remark that even were there a mystery of masculinity to unlock, the task would become vitiated by the cultural concerns that the reader's historical masculinity pushed forward. A brief look at the criticism of *Sons and Lovers* illustrates this point. An early phase of criticism of *Sons and Lovers* suggested that Paul wrestled with the typically male problem of the Oedipal complex and the "sex instinct."[13] Later, in the mid-fifties and sixties, critics found that, like most men, Paul was a victim of "momism": Paul "is like a child, with a child's limited outlook. His mother's influence has reduced all other human beings to unreality."[14] If Paul could escape his mother, he could enjoy "freedom of natural growth within a mature relationship."[15] By the eighties, following the object-relationists' psychoanalytical insights into men, unfinished pre-Oedipal business was to blame for Paul's immaturity.[16] By mid-eighties, male critics blamed Paul's father for the insufficiencies of his son's "masculine identity." The book, rather than being an indictment of women and society, as it had earlier appeared, became testimony to the insight that "the essence of maleness lies not in dominating phallic power but in nurturing tenderness."[17] Critics, in other words, had moved from finding a picture of the "brutal instinct" of masculinity to finding a "nurturing tenderness" that constituted maleness. In each revision the critics testified to society's own changing notions of masculinity, traces of which can be found in the works they read. Each reading suppressed certain aspects of the work and polarized and valued "masculine" and "feminine," using these words and words like "individual," "nature," and "instinct" in ways that suggested a belief in a single, transhistorical meaning, that "individual" did not mean something different from what it meant one hundred years or even one hundred days ago.

My own study is contaminated in the same way, and in part I have tried to show that such contamination is impossible to escape. The male reader I have constructed certainly fits my historical moment. Through the act of reading, my male appears as one who consciously experiences the role stresses of masculinity, who is aware of its construction, who feels empowered by the masculine, who believes that there may be some underlying contribution that sex makes to gender, but who is embittered by the constructions in which he feels trapped, who feels pulled apart by the various negotiations he must make.

Am I suggesting that we can or should rid ourselves of the idea of masculinity? Whatever biology contributes to gender, it is undoubtedly true that gender has been and will continue to be a social construct that is not fixed, not even by biology, but that is mutable.[18] Up to a point men have been primary agents in defining a gender based in part on male privilege and the oppression of women. Yet I am not arguing that we need to, should, or can scuttle the words "masculine" and "feminine." It has become the fashion in some scholarly circles to chastise gender-related studies because they often dichotomize the universe in artificial ways and often value women above men.[19] It has even become fashionable to suggest that sex differences do not exist, because a logo-, phallo-, and Eurocentric science has arbitrarily divided up sexuality. This is a far cry from the argument that gender is not biologically determined.

After having denied women the right to fashion their own identity for centuries and at a time when women are trying to reclaim or build power and identity, men seem to be practicing what, according to my examination, is a common activity of men—co-option. They are trying to silence women by telling them that gender does not *really* exist, that we are all just humans. Like Lawrence and the men of his era who co-opted the vocabulary of intimacy, or like the men of Gawain's era who co-opted the vocabulary of birth and nurture, men today may be unwittingly suppressing women, replacing and redefining tasks and attributes assigned to them. In this they may be attempting to avoid both having to share power and having to confront aspects of themselves. Of course, it would also be a mistake to believe that "human" is any less a fiction than "masculine" or "feminine."

Yet, assuming that masculinity is a category worth maintaining, how does one define its usefulness and how does one undo centuries of conscious and unconscious misogynist and self-destructive behavior? It seems important that men come to grips with what it is to be masculine at this time and place, what they feel, what they experience, what they are demanded to perform, so that they can understand the male experience and relieve themselves and others of some of the unnecessary pains of manhood. The following suggestions flow from the essays in this volume:

1. Actions and ideas should not be sanctioned by recourse to gender. Nothing should be considered good or bad because it is "masculine" or "feminine."

2. Masculinity should not be used as a category to coerce conformity.

3. We must learn to accept diverse and divergent masculinities. We should jettison ideas that one can be more or less "masculine."

4. Because masculinity purports to be the ideal behavior of those defined as males, the category of maleness itself needs to be examined thoroughly.

5. Since masculinity has always created opportunities for men to explore their condition as men, ideas of masculinity should, in part, encourage men to probe their masculinities, to stretch beyond them, to ask what their constructions of masculinity have inhibited them from experiencing or have denied about their experience.

Ultimately, it seems important for men to understand their historical experience as men and to try to see what underlies that experience—what common bonds, what common problems—and why. What seems unimportant, even dangerous, however, is for men to try to create some new transcendental form of masculinity or to revive nostalgic past ones. We know with some certitude what the results of that will be. Such an effort can only create another damaging fiction of masculinity.

Notes

1. Robert Bly, *Iron John* (Reading, Mass: Addison-Wesley, 1990).

2. Robert Bly, *Talking All Morning* (Ann Arbor: University of Michigan Press, 1980).

3. David D. Gilmore, *Manhood in the Making: Cultural Concepts of Masculinity* (New Haven, Conn.: Yale University Press, 1990).

4. Bly, *Iron John*, 222–31.

5. Lillian Rubin, *Worlds of Pain: Life in the Working-Class Family* (New York: Basic Books, 1976), 126–27.

6. John Money, *Gay, Straight and In-Between* (New York: Oxford University Press, 1988) gives his latest thoughts on gender formation: see in particular 51–78. See also Melvin Konner, *The Tangled Wing: Biological Constraints on the Human Spirit* (New York: Harper and Row, 1982); Marvin Harris, *Cannibals and Kings: The Origins of Cultures* (New York: Random House, 1977); Lionel Tiger, *Men in Groups* (New York: Vintage, 1970).

7. One can think of Anne Vincent-Buffault's *Histoire des Larmes* (Paris: Editions Rivage, 1986).

8. D. H. Lawrence, *Women in Love* (New York: Viking, 1960), 306.

9. Philip Roth, *Portnoy's Complaint* (New York: Bantam, 1970), 54–55.

10. Ibid., 56.

11. Ibid., 53–54.

12. Ibid., 54–55.

13. Alfred Booth Kuttner, "*Sons and Lovers:* A Freudian Appreciation," *Psychoanalytical Review* 3 (1916): 295–317.

14. Louis L. Martz, "Portrait of Miriam: A Study in the Design of *Sons and Lovers,*" *Imagined Worlds: Essays on Some English Novels and Novelists in Honour of John Butt,* ed. Maynard Mack and Ian Gregor (London: Methuen, 1968), 360. See also Dorothy Van Ghent, "On *Sons and Lovers,*" *The English Novel: Form and Function* (New York: Rinehart, 1953), 245–61; John Stoll, *D. H. Lawrence's "Sons and Lovers": Self-Encounter and the Unknown Self* (Muncie, Ind.: Ball State University, 1968).

15. Martz, "Portrait of Miriam," 353.

16. Strong influence comes from the work of Nancy Chodorow, *The Reproduction of Mothering* (Berkeley: University of California Press, 1978). On Lawrence see, e.g., T. H. Adamowski, "Intimacy at a Distance: Sexuality and Orality in *Sons and Lovers,*" *Mosaic* 13, no. 2 (1980): 71–85; Daniel Dervin, "Play, Creativity and Matricide: The Implications of Lawrence's 'Smashed Doll' Episode," *Mosaic* 14, no. 3 (1981): 81–94.

17. Mark Spilka, "For Mark Shorer with Combative Love: The *Sons and Lovers* Manuscript," *D. H. Lawrence: A Centenary Consideration,* ed. Peter Balbert and Phillip L. Marcus (Ithaca, N.Y.: Cornell University Press, 1985), 40. See also Carol Dix, *D. H. Lawrence and Women* (Totowa, N.J.: Rowman and Littlefield, 1978), 118–19; Declan Kiberd, *Men and Feminism in Modern Literature* (London: Macmillan, 1985), 139.

18. In *Not in Our Genes* (New York: Pantheon Books, 1984), R. C. Lewontin, Steven Rose, and Leon J. Kamin write, "We do assert that we

cannot think of any significant human social behavior that is built into our genes in such a way that it cannot be modified and shaped by social conditioning. Even biological features such as eating, sleeping, and sex are greatly modified by conscious control and social conditioning. . . . Yet at the same time, we deny that human beings are born *tabulae rasae*, which they evidently are not, and that individual human beings are simple mirrors of social circumstances" (267). But as science has shown lately, "Neither organism nor environment is a closed system; each is open to the other" (273).

19. Most recently see Richard Levin, "Feminist Thematics and Shakespearean Tragedy," *PMLA* 103 (1988): 125–38; Jonathan Goldberg, "Shakespearean Inscriptions: The Voicing of Power," *Shakespeare and the Question of Theory*, ed. Patricia Parker and Geoffrey Hartman (London: Methuen, 1985), 116–37. Peter Erickson, among others, has voiced concern over this reaction: see "Rewriting the Renaissance, Rewriting Ourselves," *Shakespeare Quarterly* 38 (1987): 327–37. Lynda Boose, reviewing the Goldberg essay, suggests that the "new historicism" might be another macho evasion: see "The Family in Shakespeare Studies; or—Studies in the Family of Shakespeareans; or—The Politics of Politics," *Renaissance Quarterly* 40 (1987): 707–42.

Index